EVERYBODY WINS!

A LIFE IN
FREE
ENTERPRISE

Gordon Cain in 1996. Photograph by Gittings & Lorfing.

EVERYBODY WINS!

A LIFE IN FREE ENTERPRISE

GORDON CAIN

To Mary & Ken

Gordon Cain

CHEMICAL HERITAGE PRESS

PHILADELPHIA

Printed in the United States of America.

The Chemical Heritage Foundation Series in Innovation and Entrepreneurship
records, analyzes, and makes known the human story of chemical achievement.

For information about CHF publications write
Chemical Heritage Foundation
315 Chestnut Street
Philadelphia, PA 19106-2702, USA
Fax: (215) 925-1954

Library of Congress Cataloging-in-Publication Data
Cain, Gordon, 1912–
    Everybody wins : a life in free enterprise / Gordon Cain.
       p.   cm. — (The Chemical Heritage Foundation series in
innovation and entrepreneurship)
    Includes index.
    ISBN 0-941901-14-9 (hc)
    1. Cain, Gordon, 1912–   . 2. Chemical engineers—United States—
Biography. 3. Chemical industry—United States—Biography. 4. Free
enterprise—United States.   I. Title.   II. Series.
HD9651.95.C34A3   1996
338.7′66′0092—dc21
[B]   96-48448
                                                CIP

TO MY WIFE MARY,
WHO MEANS EVERYTHING TO ME.
WITHOUT HER, NOT MUCH OF THIS
WOULD HAVE HAPPENED,
AND IT WOULD NOT HAVE BEEN
AS MUCH FUN.

CONTENTS

ILLUSTRATIONS

Acknowledgments

To acknowledge all the people who have helped me would take another volume as large as this one. A few are mentioned here, but to the many who have gone unrecognized, I offer my deepest gratitude. The success of each of my endeavors has been directly related to the ability of those around me. All my ideas have been improved by exposing them to my colleagues. Any good ideas of mine are the synthesis of many people's ideas.

I would never have had the nerve to start this book without the help of my good friend Dr. Linda Driskill, Professor of English at Rice University, who undertook the job of teaching a semiliterate engineer how to put words together in an orderly fashion. To the extent that she failed, blame it on the material she had.

When I had done all I could to the manuscript, my friend Robert Bradley, head of the Institute for Energy Research, took over the job of putting it into a shape that a publisher would not reject on sight. For his advice and help I am very grateful.

My associates Minnette Smith and Joan Jordan have spent hours on the word processor—typing, retyping, correcting spelling and grammar. For their hard work and infinite patience I am again very grateful. I am also thankful to my daughter, Peggy Oehmig, who read the manuscript and made corrections and suggestions.

And I am deeply indebted to Arnold Thackray, Frances Kohler, and Mary Ellen Bowden of the Chemical Heritage Foundation for completing the conversion of my rough manuscript into a book.

Finally, the book owes much in a different way to Mary's and my long-term friend and housekeeper Doris Hollins, who has made our lives much more comfortable.

GORDON A. CAIN

PREFACE

BY MICHAEL C. JENSEN
Edsel Bryant Ford Professor of Business Administration
Harvard Business School

GORDON CAIN AND THE STERLING Group played a major role in the restructuring of the U.S. chemical industry during the 1980s. I am pleased to write the preface to this book, in which Gordon Cain details much of that experience first-hand. I would like to start by putting LBOs and restructuring in historical context.

The decade of the 1980s, during which Gordon Cain did his largest and most successful deals, actually began in 1973 with the energy crisis. The twenty-odd years since then have witnessed the first part of a modern industrial revolution. The revolutionary changes in the economic landscape during this period are comparable to those occurring in the industrial revolution of the mid-nineteenth century. The forces driving this modern industrial revolution are dramatic technological change, such as in computers and telecommunications, and political change: the deregulation of American business under Jimmy Carter, changes in the tax code under Ronald Reagan, and the failure of centrally planned, closed, communist, and socialist economies in Eastern and Central Europe and Asia. I expect these changes to continue for several more decades.

As in the nineteenth century, this modern industrial revolution is bringing about large increases in productivity in many industries throughout the world, and this in turn is leading to excess capacity, massive restructuring, downsizing, and exit (divesting a firm of enterprises outside its mainstream). While increases in productivity are the source of increase in aggregate real living standards, the dramatic changes in the last twenty years also impose substantial adjustment costs on labor and on capital, which must move out of industries with excess capacity to find new employment.

Through the great mergers and acquisitions boom of the 1890s, the capital markets played an important role in eliminating U.S. excess capacity in the last industrial revolution. Capital markets also played a major role in the adjustment to the excess capacity generated in this current industrial revolution because the internal control systems of most large corporations have been unable to deal effectively with the required downsizing. The capital markets helped force companies to take their medicine quickly during the 1980s, and LBOs like those sponsored by Gordon Cain and The Sterling Group were an important part of this phenomenon.

In the late 1980s and the early 1990s, however, legal and regulatory changes occurred that have vastly reduced the influence of the capital markets on the renewal of corporate America. As a result we now see the effects of the product markets on those organizations that could not adjust voluntarily and were not forced by the capital markets. Many of these will not survive in anything approaching their former grandeur.

I and some of my colleagues have had the good fortune to study Cain Chemical and Sterling Chemicals closely over the past several years in the process of writing several case studies and a scholarly article on these companies. We and our students have learned much from this process. Cain and The Sterling Group took chemical and fertilizer plants out of larger, more diversified organizations and put them on their own. They implemented visionary management techniques, including increases in debt (to soak up the organization's free cash flow), performance-related compensation, equity holding by managers and employees, and total quality management programs. These changes resulted in large payouts of resources from stable to declining business, increases in efficiency and profits to Cain, Sterling, managers, employees, and debt holders. You, the reader, now have the opportunity to understand more about LBOs through the eyes of one of the important actors of the time. I commend this book to you.

August 31, 1996

*Gordon Cain holding his first grandchild, Gordon Daniel Oehmig,
born May 15, 1983.*

CHAPTER ONE

WHY I WROTE
THIS BOOK

ABOUT TWELVE YEARS AGO, I WAS blessed with my first grandchild. Now there are three. Around the same time, books such as *Barbarians at the Gate** were published that depicted businessmen as amoral creatures driven by greed, and leveraged buyouts (LBOs) and junk bonds as instruments of the devil. These books, written by observers from outside the business community, were full of interesting characters, but they had no heroes.

Conscious that I would be gone from the scene long before my grandchildren reached maturity, and remembering that I had wanted to know more about my own grandfathers, who died when I was young, I speculated about what my grandchildren and their descendants might learn about their ancestor (me) if they went to the library. Certainly they would learn that I was involved in doing LBOs and selling junk bonds. They would also find many editorials, plenty of statements by politicians, and a good supply of books critical of business in the 1980s—and especially of LBOs and junk bonds.

If they stopped there, they might feel guilty at living well from the proceeds of such activities. If they continued their research, however, they might find in the library announcements such as the two that follow here, which were released less than nine months apart.

---

* An account of the leveraged buyout (LBO) of R. J. Reynolds, written by Bryan Burrough and John Helyar.

1

PRESS RELEASE
July 10, 1987

The Sterling Group, Inc. announced today the purchase of seven ethylene based chemical facilities in a leveraged buyout and the formation of Cain Chemical, Inc. to own and operate the facilities.

Acquired from E. I. du Pont de Nemours & Co. was an ethylene plant at Chocolate Bayou, Texas, a polyethylene plant at Beaumont, Texas, a polyethylene plant at Bay City, Texas, and a polyethylene plant at Victoria, Texas.

Acquired from Imperial Chemical Industries PLC was an ethylene-glycol plant at Bayport, Texas.

Acquired from Corpus Christi Petrochemicals, Inc. was an ethylene plant at Corpus Christi, Texas, a pipeline and ethylene storage.

Acquired from PPG Industries, Inc. was a half interest in an ethylene-glycol plant in Beaumont, Texas.

The purchase price of $1.1 billion was financed with bank debt and high-yield (junk) bonds.

The employees of the company will own slightly over 43% of the equity.

PRESS RELEASE
March 28, 1988

The directors of Cain Chemical, Inc. announced today that they have signed an agreement to sell the stock of the company to Occidental Chemical Corporation for $1.2 billion.

The 1,325 employees of the company own approximately 43% of the stock and will receive $536,000,000. About one-third of this will go to 150 managers who bought stock. One-third will go to 75 top managers who received stock through stock options, and a third will go to all the employees through a stock ownership plan, ESOP. The lowest paid employee will receive over $100,000.

Together they tell a story very different from those chronicled elsewhere, one in which everybody wins.

This book is written in part to satisfy my grandchildren's curiosity. It is also written to provide the other side of a complicated story. True though they may be, *Barbarians at the Gate* and the other books failed to say that LBOs resulted in more productive and competitive business organizations, better jobs, and a higher standard of living for many people—although some were hurt in the transition process.

This is not a book on how to do LBOs. A business school professor could do a much better job. (In fact, the Harvard Business School published case studies about two of my transactions, which are reprinted at the end of this volume.) Nor is this book about the personalities and the drama behind LBO transactions. The other authors of LBO books were professional writers who took detailed notes when they started covering the story, knowing that they would write a book. My writing is being done long after the fact, with only a few notes covering matters of substance. I do not mention all the participants in the various meetings: The list would be too long. Nor do I attempt to reproduce dialogue. This is no great loss: Except for a few good one-liners dropped to ease tension, nothing colorful or even memorable was ever said.

Instead, this book is an account of one man's journey from a small town in Louisiana through the halls of high finance, with a few stops to do some LBOs. I have no illusion that my account of doing friendly LBOs will be nearly as interesting as some of the more critical books. However, partly to justify ten years of my life and partly to defend my many friends in the financial community, I felt obliged to write it. The LBO story I describe in Part II of this book is a simple account of how honorable men, advised by competent lawyers and investment bankers who never violated a confidence, carried out transactions in which everybody wins. Buyer, seller, employees, management, and community—all benefited. The principals in all the transactions became and remain good friends. There were a few villains, but only in minor roles. The real villains were the inertia and

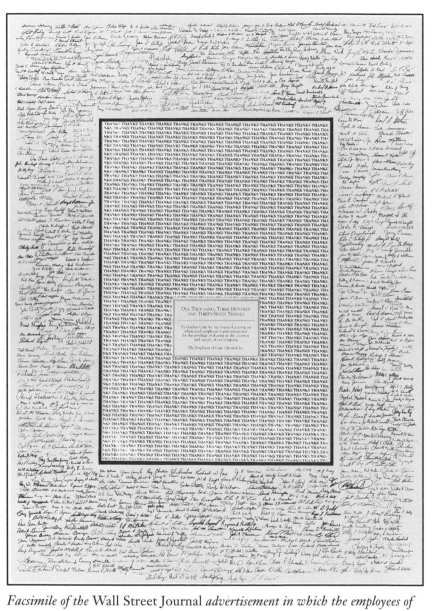

Facsimile of the Wall Street Journal *advertisement in which the employees of Cain Chemical, pleased at the results of the deals described in the March 28 press releases, expressed their thanks 1,337 times (May 5, 1988).*

the bureaucracy of large institutions and the inexorable ticking of the clock that brought deadlines faster than I could cope with them.

As a practitioner of the art of doing friendly LBOs, and one who has done six transactions worth over $200 million each and one worth over a billion dollars, I have known and worked with some of the investment bankers and lawyers mentioned in these critical books. I looked for some familiar note, some situation common to my experience. In the end, I had to conclude that these books were written about a completely different ball game from mine.

No doubt many U.S. businesses took on more debt than was prudent in the 1980s. Was this caused by the greed of LBO organizers, or was it simply a rational response to a tax code that made debt a cheaper source of capital than equity? Certainly the organizers of hostile takeovers expected to make money. Some may have made far more than they deserved. Whether this should be attributed to greed, or to the fact that many companies could be bought for less than their intrinsic value because they were poorly managed, depends on one's point of view. In any event, the so-called barbarians who took over R. J. Reynolds in an LBO were an improvement over the clowns who had been running it.

THE THREE SECTIONS

My first draft was a bare-bones recital of what happened. It might have been of interest to someone doing research on business in the 1980s, but to no one else. It was called a "discovery draft" by my friend Linda Driskill, Professor of English at Rice University, whose criticism and suggestions have done much to shape this book. I owe any interesting details to my wife, Mary, who reminded me of stories that I related to her when I returned from trips to arrange the LBOs.

Further, simply describing several business transactions would not explain to my grandchildren how I came to the world of LBOs. Hence Part I of my book describes that long, circuitous route. I was raised in rural Louisiana by a black nurse, my grandparents, various aunts and uncles, and a great stepmother after my mother died when I was six. My father was a model of integrity and good manners, but heavily burdened with supporting a large family in the middle of the Great Depression. After attending college, I decided to become a chemical engineer instead of a history teacher only because engineers got higher salaries than teachers. Then my career in the only job I could find at the time got off to a bad start. This was fortunate. Had I started with a good company, I would probably have stayed and become a good corporate type. Instead, I developed the detachment from my employer that has kept my blood pressure and stress level low ever since.

Four years in World War II did more to change my life than did four years in the university. The war converted an unsophisticated engineer, who never had been or expected to be a "boss," into a decorated battalion commander and veteran of some of the toughest fighting in the Pacific. Then followed a routine corporate career, interrupted by one unsuccessful effort to start a small business, until boredom led me to leave the corporate world. Unplanned and unlikely activities then led to the LBOs described in Part II.

At some point, an old man's conceit that he has some wisdom to pass on intruded, and I began writing Part III, about how I think businesses should be run. This section clearly owes much to my experience with LBOs. Business organizations in the last decade have made a substantial improvement in efficiency and productivity through greater emphasis on quality. It is now recognized that most organizations are overmanaged, have too much overhead, and are too concerned with control and avoiding mistakes. One result of this new management philosophy is fewer middle managers. Employee stock ownership, profit sharing, and employee involvement have all increased. These changes might have happened in time, but only the naive believe they were not hastened by the threat of hostile takeovers. Even the companies that were not threatened behaved as though they were.

Just as I did not intend to write this book when I started it as a letter to my grandchildren, I did not set out to do an LBO. My initial plan, after spending years in the chemical business, was to buy a small chemical operation and spend my retirement years as a part-time chairman of the board, letting some energetic young managers support me. After making several unsuccessful attempts to buy a small operation, I raised my sights because I sensed something that later became obvious, that is, large deals are easier to do than small ones. The reasons lie in the structure of the organizations with which one must deal. On a big transaction, one deals with decision makers both in the selling and in the financing organizations. On small transactions, one must convince the junior people with whom one must work, then depend on them to convince their bosses, sometimes several echelons removed.

The decision to do a large deal was not as foolish as it sounds. First, years of running troubled companies had given me broad experience. I had faced most business problems, usually without outside help. I knew people in the financial community, and I had some reputation as a good operator of chemical businesses. Second, about this time many large companies decided to sell parts of their businesses that were not in the principal area of their effort. Also for reasons that are still not clear to me, capital became readily available.

The first logical big target for me was a firm that I headed and helped develop from 1964 to 1970: the Conoco chemical business. DuPont had acquired Conoco in 1981 and was operating its chemical business as an autonomous unit, although it was much smaller than other DuPont units. I got the sense that DuPont did not know what to do with this appendage to the oil business and might be willing to sell. While these negotiations were under way, I acquired a small company, Arcadian, that is now a major producer of nitrogen fertilizer. To make a long story short, in less than three months I bought two companies for over $600 million without putting up any of my money. By this time, because of the expense of putting deals together, I had very little money left. Thus started an exciting and rewarding period.

Buying and selling companies was new to me. I would soon find out that one experienced only in producing and selling goods must make certain adjustments when he enters the world of finance. Bankers, accountants, and, to a lesser degree, investment bankers regard symbols as reality. The numbers that result from the application of certain accepted accounting principles can be more important to them than the business from which the numbers came. The numbers recorded as the "book value" of a plant can be more important to financiers than the condition or profitability of the plant.

Another thing that one must learn is that lenders, whether commercial bankers or asset-based lenders, have a different vocabulary from that used by the rest of the business world and are likely to promise more than they can deliver. At different times in the early years of my LBO career, three major financial institutions made what would ordinarily be considered commitments to lend money, only to back out at the last minute. This has not happened since I have become more successful, but the trauma of the early experiences made me scratch these institutions off my list.

TO SUM IT UP

Some day my grandchildren will study history and economics. Unless what they study is more accurate and objective than many current accounts, they will conclude that they are descendants of a latter-day pirate and that free enterprise is a license to steal. In contrast, my story vindicates the free market as an economic system in which anyone who can produce a better product or service cheaper can make money. My story also shows that the best way to ensure good fortune in the marketplace is to give all the employees an economic interest in the success of the operation.

My descendants will read about a life characterized by unpredictability. Part of this came from outside factors, part from my low tolerance for boredom in my work, and part from a stubborn attitude that blocked any thought that failure would be a disaster if it happened. It was a life that fate or chance diverted several times to an unexpected direction. There is more autobiography here than necessary to explain business in the 1980s. However, the autobiography is one way to show newcomers to the business world that there are career paths off the beaten track, and that losing or quitting a job is not always a disaster.

But first let's go back to the beginning, and in the beginning there was a small bug that influenced both my father's and mother's lives and hence mine.

I.
THE
UNEXPECTED
PATH TO
ENTREPRENEURSHIP

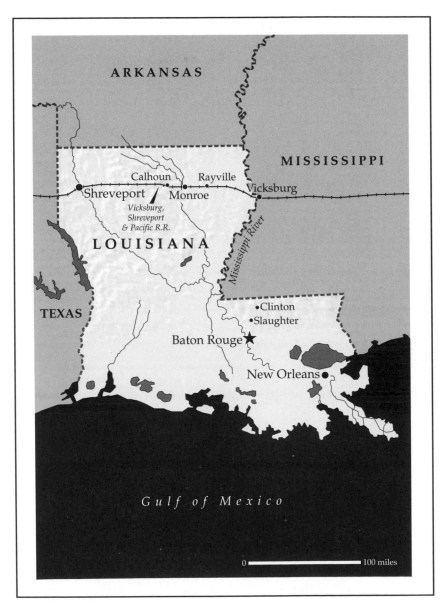

Map of Louisiana showing the places mentioned in this chapter, including the towns where Gordon Cain spent his youth: Slaughter, Calhoun, Rayville, Clinton, and Monroe.

CHAPTER TWO

THE
BEGINNING

K ILLER BEES, ORIGINALLY BROUGHT
into Brazil from Africa to improve honey production, have over the
last few decades migrated from Brazil, through Central America, into
Mexico. Some accounts tell of the bees killing animals, and some
stories even describe the deaths of people from killer bee attacks.
That these bees would cross the Rio Grande into the United States
was inevitable, and, in fact, in the fall of 1990 the first colony of killer
bees was found in Texas. The bees were destroyed, but the border
with Mexico is too long to keep them out forever.

In 1892—about a century earlier—another insect, smaller and with
none of the lethal inclinations of the bees, came across the Rio Grande.
But for one bad habit, this small immigrant might have passed un-
noticed. At this time, except for the cultivation of sugar cane in south
Louisiana and tobacco in the Carolinas, the economy of the region
from the Rio Grande to Virginia depended on cotton. There was no
industry of consequence. The fortunes of the Deep South rose and
fell with the state of the cotton crop and the price of cotton.

THE BOLL WEEVIL

Cotton seed is planted in the spring. A few weeks after the cotton
plant sprouts, it develops a bloom. In the normal course, the bloom

13

is pollinated and falls off, leaving a small nodule about the size of the head of a kitchen match. Left alone through hot Southern summers, this small nodule, called a "square," grows to golf-ball size by late summer. The "boll" bursts open. Cotton hangs from each of the five compartments in the open boll, waiting to be picked.

The small insect that came across the Rio Grande in 1892 was endowed by Nature with the instinct to put its eggs in a safe place where its offspring could develop unharmed. The female chooses to puncture the square that remains after the cotton bloom falls off and to lay her eggs in it. The punctured square, instead of developing into a boll of cotton, becomes a home for a family of young insects called boll weevils. When the square falls to the ground, the young insects mature and remain to repeat the cycle the next year. If there are enough weevils, the cotton crop will be completely destroyed.

The boll weevil moved from the Rio Grande across Texas at the rate of about sixty miles a year. It first appeared in western Louisiana in 1903. By 1904 all the parishes on the western border of the state were infested. The severe winter of 1904–1905 set the migration back about one year.

My paternal grandfather, Stanhope Cain, had a five-hundred-acre farm north of Clinton, Louisiana, in East Feliciana Parish in the southeastern part of the state. The boll weevil first appeared there in 1907 and was in full force by 1908. Cotton production in this parish in 1908 was 7 percent of what it had been before this pest arrived. This drop did not come as a surprise. Just as the movement of the killer bees has been followed through Mexico into this country, so was the migration of the boll weevil.

As early as 1892 various agricultural experts tested the available insecticides, which were mostly arsenic compounds. None had more than a minor effect on boll weevils. In 1903 the governor of Louisiana appointed a commission to study ways to control the pest. The winter of 1904–1905 demonstrated that cold weather helped. As one moved farther north in the Cotton Belt, the effect of the boll weevil decreased. Until some of the new organic insecticides were intro-

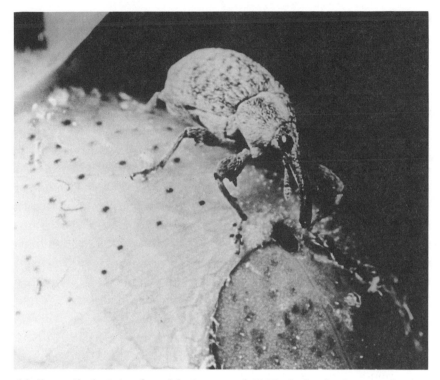

A boll weevil. Arriving from Mexico around 1892, the beetles devastated cotton crops as they migrated north through the Cotton Belt. Adult weevils puncture cotton bolls with their snouts and lay their eggs inside, causing the bolls to fall to the ground instead of developing. Courtesy Clemson University, Department of Entomology, Cooperative Extension Service.

duced after World War II, the only effective control consisted of destroying the cotton plants after picking, followed by plowing to bury the weevil-infested plants.

This cultivation practice and the colder weather permitted the production of cotton in northern Louisiana at the pre–boll-weevil level. In the southern part of the state and in sections where the land was poor, farmers simply stopped cultivating cotton. My paternal grandfather and my mother's family, who had a farm southeast of

Clinton, Louisiana, both converted their cotton fields into pasture and raised cattle.

This change substantially reduced the incomes of my grandparents on both sides. It had an even greater effect on the black families who lived on the farms and grew the cotton. My first clear recollection of these farms goes back to 1917, ten years after the boll weevil hit. Half the houses were empty. The former occupants, the younger part of the group, had moved to Baton Rouge to find work. The remaining half of the people were all past middle age. Their houses were neat and well kept. Each had a garden and a pigpen with one or two pigs, and some had a milk cow. There was a communal corn field to feed the pigs and cows and the few horses and mules that remained. The rest of the farm except for the woodlands had been converted into pasture. The cows were a nondescript lot. The original stock had been milk cows, but they had been bred to Shorthorn bulls to produce something that might be called beef cattle. Angus and Herefords had not yet come on the scene. Here and there a farmer had a Brahman bull, but these were as rare as Episcopalians.

This kind of cattle raising required little effort. There were fences to be mended, hay to be cut, and an annual session of castrating and branding, which was handled by the few able-bodied men left. The rest of the process was left to the cows and Mother Nature. With no mortgage on the farm, the small cash income was enough to pay the taxes and to support the family and the few people left on the place, with little to spare.

MY ANTECEDENTS

Like most families mine has had a few amateur genealogists. None has done a very thorough job. My father's ancestry seems to have been entirely English and Scotch-Irish, which in this case does not mean a mixture of the two but rather refers to Scots who emigrated to northern Ireland and subsequently to the United States. Family names were all Anglo-Saxon, like Chance, Dunn, Maxwell, Gordon, Daugherty, or Doty, with no Latin or European-sounding names. There were no prominent politicians in the family, only an occasional sheriff or clerk of the court. These ancestors moved freely among the better-known Protestant sects—Baptists, Methodists, and Presbyterians—with no Anglicans or Episcopalians.

Stanhope Cain was a cotton farmer until the boll weevil came, but that is not an adequate description. He wrote and read Latin and Greek as did all his close friends. His library, part of which my father inherited, could have kept a Great Books discussion group busy for months. He was affluent enough to send all three of his children to Louisiana State University (LSU). He knew my maternal grandmother slightly, but their farms were too far apart for there to be much visiting between them.

My maternal grandmother, whose maiden name was Azlee Beauchamp (the name is French in origin, but the family has been British since the Norman Conquest), was an only child whose parents died when she was in her early teens. Her guardian, selected by her parents, was a middle-aged widower named Benjamin Franklin Arbuthnot who had a daughter my grandmother's age. When my grandmother finished the Silliman Academy, a girl's school in Clinton, Louisiana, that has long since disappeared, her guardian became her husband. He lived long enough to sire two daughters, my Aunt Emma and my mother. On his death he left my grandmother with two daughters, not quite teenagers, and about seven hundred acres of land southeast of Clinton. This operation had also been converted from cotton to cattle.

My mother's antecedents, like my father's, were largely Scotch-Irish and English, but hers were more colorful. The Arbuthnots are a minor clan from the northeastern part of Scotland, and one of their claims to distinction is that several have been professors of medicine at the University of Edinburgh. In addition, John Arbuthnot, a contemporary of Addison and Steele's, was the inspiration for the cartoon character John Bull. The man who commanded the British fleet that blockaded our coast during the American Revolution was an Admiral Arbuthnot. Another Arbuthnot made the history books when he was hanged by Andrew Jackson, who accused him of inciting the Indians of northern Florida to attack the local white settlers.

MY FATHER

As far as I can determine, my father, my mother, and their siblings were the first of my ancestors to attend college. My father was the oldest of three children, followed by a sister and then a brother. When he was six, his mother died. For reasons known only to my distraught and devastated grandfather, he gave each of his three children to his brothers and sisters to raise. Thereafter, my father saw his father, brother, and sister only during summer vacations. My father had only the kindest things to say about the aunt and uncle who raised him. But I was aware—after I became sensitive to such things—that he only made an annual perfunctory visit to his foster parents even though he was frequently near their home. Their relationship must have been correct but not warm. He did have a desire to see his sister and brother frequently and was obsessed with keeping his family together: Any serious family conversation included my father extracting promises from his boys to keep the family together if anything happened to him.

My father, Gordon Dunn Cain, born in Point Coupe Parish on October 22, 1886, was five feet, eight inches tall—small by today's standards but about average for his generation. He had a slight frame and a full head of hair that he kept to his death. My brothers—Frank, Edward, and I—are all bald, so one can only conclude that our mother came from a long line of bald men. My father was a quiet, calm man. He could get angry, but I never saw him lose his composure.

His foster parents and his father between them produced a man of honor and integrity. In the years I knew him, he never did anything less than the completely honorable thing. Like some of his

*Gordon D. Cain served first as director of an experimental farm run by the
U.S. Department of Agriculture and Louisiana State University in Calhoun,
then as county agricultural agent in Rayville. This copy of a now-lost WPA
painting from about 1934 depicts the elder Cain as county agent, with the
Richland Parish Court House visible in the background above.*

generation, he was almost elaborately polite to women. His belief in
his fellow man led him into investments he should not have made
and into partnerships with people unworthy of his trust. He made
many small investments, all of which looked promising at the time,
but none were successful. His concern for paying bills promptly was
unique in a community of people who lived from one cotton crop to
the next.

My father had planned to go to medical school after his sophomore year in college, but by this time it was evident that the boll
weevil would ruin his father and all other cotton farmers financially
within a few years. There would not be enough money to pay for the
four years of medical school plus keeping his brother and sister in
college. Instead of becoming a doctor, he took his degree in chemistry and spent his first year after graduation teaching chemistry in the
high school in Slidell, Louisiana. Then he became a chemist in a
laboratory of the Agricultural Extension Service, where he did largely
analytical work on fertilizer, soils, and pesticides in connection with
programs designed to increase the yield of various crops.

BATON ROUGE

I have no memory of my first two years in Baton Rouge, where I was
born on May 31, 1912, but I do have a souvenir of the period: a scar
in the brow of my left eye. Shortly after I started walking, I must
have decided that this new means of locomotion was too slow and
mounted a tricycle. A fall on the sidewalk made a wound over my left
eye that took three stitches to close and left an H-shaped scar.

This left eyebrow must be accident prone. In a head-on automobile collision near Houston twenty-five years later, the only damage
I suffered was a cut over my left eye that took three stitches to close.
To round out the series of three, a piece of shrapnel hit me over the
left eye on the fifth night after I landed on Okinawa. An army doctor
sewed it up by the light of a flashlight, and I went on my way with a
bad headache and some aspirin.

IN THE COUNTRY

When I was about two years old, we moved from Baton Rouge into my maternal grandmother's house about twenty miles away, where we lived with my grandmother and my maiden aunt Emma. Mother (Ola Arbuthnot) and Aunt Emma, my mother's older sister, both graduated from Silliman Academy, as did my grandmother. Both also graduated from LSU and were among that institution's first women graduates. Emma stayed in graduate school and received a master's degree in history, but my mother chose to marry my father in 1911 instead of continuing her education.

We were to save money by moving in with Grandmother. Then my father started a dairy, which was the first of several endeavors he made either to make or save money. None of them could be called harebrained, but none were successful. The people who worked on the place did the milking and looked after the cows. My father supervised the operation, which meant getting up before daybreak. He drove five miles to the railroad station to deliver the milk to the "milk train" and then took the train to Baton Rouge, where he worked as a chemist for the Agricultural Extension Service. The schedule was grueling and lasted about two years. I have a vague recollection of a lot of activity around the house in the early mornings.

My grandmother's house was new, but I remember it as being different from the houses of our neighbors. Theirs were vaguely Victorian. Hers was a one-story structure with porches on three sides, one screened. Years later I saw the inspiration for this house: the beach cottages along the Gulf Coast of Mississippi. Because of the heat, we slept on the screened porch most of the time. The grown-ups had an unspoken rule that no one appeared to see the others in the morning until all were dressed.

Until shortly after my father and mother married, my grandmother and Aunt Emma had lived in Clinton, Louisiana. Clinton had a population of about three thousand people and was the parish seat. It had seen its best days early in the twentieth century, but after the boll

*Ola Arbuthnot Cain on
July 3, 1911.*

*Gordon Arbuthnot Cain at
approximately two years
old, at his grandmother's
house in Slaughter, 1915.*

weevil hit that part of the South in 1908, a slow, steady decline set in. The town had an air of shabby gentility and could have been the venue for either a Faulkner or Tennessee Williams work. It was not part of the plantation South, nor was it redneck or hillbilly; rather, it was a synthesis of the two, captured better by Faulkner than any other Southern writer. Clinton had the manners of the Old South, but the red clay soil around it could not provide the means.

In addition to her farmland my grandmother must have been left other assets, because she was able to send both her daughters to LSU. This expense must have depleted her funds, however, leaving the farm as her only source of income. So she moved from Clinton to the farm to manage it. About every other year Emma would take a job teaching in one of the nearby schools to replenish the family treasury.

My grandmother, when we moved into her house, was about sixty years old but already completely gray-haired. She was five feet, two inches tall and weighed about one hundred pounds. In repose she could have been the model for Whistler's Mother, but she was seldom in repose. She had managed her farm successfully, mostly on horseback, for the more than twenty years since her husband's death. She and my Aunt Emma were the only women, except in the movies, I ever saw ride sidesaddle. My mother rode astride. All three wore voluminous riding skirts that we would use, when we were not caught, to make tents to play under.

Aunt Emma was a little shorter than Grandmother but much heavier. She was affectionately described as "dumpy," but not to her face. The antithesis of my mother and grandmother, who were quiet, Aunt Emma was voluble. They were serene; she had wide swings of mood. In another time and place she would have been an active feminist, but in her own era she was a part-time teacher and occasional historian. She had notebooks full of research she had done on the history of the Florida parishes of Louisiana, material for a book that never got written. Books were a part of my childhood—both Grandmother and Aunt Emma were great readers to little boys. Some of my nicest memories are of sitting in their laps while they read to me.

This was also the beginning of the automobile age. My father's first automobile was what then was called a roadster. It had one seat with a luggage trunk in the back, although the trunk had been modified to carry the milk cans he hauled to the train each morning. (It was the ancestor of today's pickup truck.)

Since the single seat provided room for only two adults, and the car was available only on weekends, trips to the store or to the neighbors were made in my grandmother's two-seater surrey. A few years later my grandmother bought her first automobile, a Saxon. Its distinctive feature was a box at the base of the gearshift lever with slots to show where first, second, third, and reverse were.

I have no recollection of any evening social activity, but I do remember a lot of exchanges of visits with ladies on the adjacent farms, much of which involved horseback riding. There were also excursions to a clear, sandy-bottomed creek. The pools were too shallow for swimming, but it was a great place for children on a hot summer day. Although my grandmother, Aunt Emma, and my mother were considered active, athletic women for their time and spent hours on horseback, a bathing suit was not part of their wardrobe. They sat on the bank, and any monitoring of our aquatic activities was done by a black girl without shoes and with her skirt tucked up.

Until I was about thirteen, my brother Frank (Frank Arbuthnot Cain, born December 15, 1914) and I—joined in the course of time by my brother Edward (Edward Maxwell Cain, born May 6, 1918)— spent part of each summer with Grandma and Aunt Emma. These visits stopped when Grandma's health declined and she had to move to Baton Rouge to be close to medical facilities. I owe a lot to these two women. Whatever self-esteem I have started with them. They assumed that I was more mature and intelligent than I was and had me reading books far beyond those recommended for my age.

CLARA

My memories of my early years are influenced by family stories and old photographs, but my memories of Mammy Prudence and Clara are not prompted by snapshots. Mammy Prudence joined my grand-mother when her first child was born, and she stayed until the last daughter left for college. She lived in a house on the farm about a mile away and sometimes visited us. These visits were an occasion. They were announced several days in advance, and we were bathed and dressed before her arrival and cautioned to be on our best be-havior. My mother considered Mammy Prudence's approval of how she was raising her children more important than the opinions of her family or contemporaries. Mammy would arrive on a farm wagon that was drawn up to the back porch so that she could get in without having to climb down from the wagon and up the stairs. After she entered the house, we would scramble to find one of the few chairs that would hold her three hundred pounds. Frank and I were then brought forward for inspection, a brief inquisition, and a hug.

After we decided to move back to Baton Rouge, Mammy Pru-dence visited to discuss with my mother which one of her nieces would go with us to take care of Frank and me. After several confer-ences Clara was chosen. Clara was one of the three or four nieces who had been taking turns looking after the two of us.

It must have taken great courage for Clara, who to this time had not been more than twenty miles from home and who was part of an extended family, to leave for the unknown. If she ever felt apprehen-sive or homesick, we never knew it. She slept in the same room with the youngest child and was a member of our family until her un-timely death ten years later.

BATON ROUGE AGAIN

Of the next two years in Baton Rouge, from ages four to six, I have only a few impressions. We spent the first few months in a boarding house operated by my father's Aunt Ellen Platt, one of his mother's many sisters. The house was near the governor's mansion, and I can remember watching automobiles come and go with the certainty that each carried the governor

We were within walking distance of downtown. The big treat was walking to an ice cream parlor on Third Street with my mother, where the shop was furnished with marble-top tables and chairs made of entwined, round steel rods. I have vague recollections of World War I, of seeing my first soldiers in uniform, of posters with Uncle Sam pointing a finger at me, and of conversations between my parents that I did not understand. Toward the end of this period I went to kindergarten, my only real memory of which is that it was great fun.

My father's work as an analytical chemist was dull and unrewarding, and when he was offered an opportunity to be director of an experimental farm in Calhoun in the hill country of north Louisiana, he took it. This was part of a series of such farms operated jointly by the U.S. Department of Agriculture (USDA) and the state agricultural colleges—in this case, LSU.

CALHOUN: A CHILD'S HEAVEN

My parents, Clara, my brothers Edward (two months old) and Frank (not quite four), and I (age six) arrived in Calhoun in the summer of 1918. We landed in a small boy's heaven.

The headquarters of the farm was a campus of about forty acres. Its purpose was to develop better farming practices for Southern hill farms. Much of the high productivity of U.S. agriculture can be attributed to such farms and to the work of the Agricultural Extension Service, another joint USDA and state agricultural college project.

The policy of the USDA at that time was to encourage what might be called "subsistence agriculture." Farmers were encouraged to have a garden, a small orchard, chickens for eggs and meat, a milk cow, and a few pigs. The cash crop, in this case cotton, was almost an afterthought. Such a rural Eden may sound ideal to a romantic in Washington, but having a one-cow dairy, a dozen hens, and a small orchard is inefficient for producing milk, eggs, and fruit.

Visitors were frequent—agricultural officials from Washington and Baton Rouge and from foreign countries. This kind of farming seemed

The house that the
Cain family occupied
on the USDA farm
in Calhoun, with
Frank and Gordon
visible on the porch.
Visitors would stay
on the top floor.

Clara with Frank
and Gordon at the
barn in Slaughter.

to be of particular interest to Filipinos and Central Americans, some
of whom stayed several weeks. As there was no hotel nearby, all of
these visitors stayed in our house, where the upstairs was kept for
this use. Some of the guests from the tropics were much darker than
the local people. I remember hearing comments from my school-
mates about the Cains having dark-skinned visitors. My parents were
not concerned, and so neither was I.

We had a large, two-story house with more room than I had ever
seen. Besides the residences there were several barns and machinery
sheds, a pavilion for meetings with farmers, and an exhibit hall to
display things of interest to farmers. Two more white families and
six black families lived in houses scattered around the campus. One
of the white families had two girls our age, and the other had rela-
tives our age who visited frequently. None of the black families, however, had young children. Jobs on this farm were greatly prized by
blacks, and once they started work there, only death terminated their
service. Consequently, these families were middle-aged, and their
children were all older or adults themselves.

Calhoun was then and still is an unincorporated village, although
"village" suggests a more organized entity than it really was. At that
time the center of activity was the Vicksburg, Shreveport, and Pacific railroad station. The VS&P ran east and west from Vicksburg,
Mississippi, to Shreveport, Louisiana. The "Pacific" probably was
added to help sell stock.

One "furnishing" merchant had a store north of the tracks and
one south. The term *furnishing* meant that a merchant could furnish
everything a farmer needed, from groceries to overalls to plows, and
do this on credit that extended to the next harvest. As one would
expect, the prices reflected the risk and cost of credit. A third store
on the north side of the tracks sold merchandise for cash only. The
prices were lower, but its customers were limited to the few people
who had cash.

Except for a shipment of apples at Christmas time and an occasional stalk of bananas, none of the stores had fresh meat or produce.

Gordon D. Cain with his sons Frank, Gordon, and Edward, ca. 1919.

Gordon D. Cain with sons Gordon, Frank, and Edward, ca. 1933.

Whatever fresh food we ate came from our garden or orchard or from butchering chickens, hogs, and an occasional calf. (The development of the modern grocery store with its supply system has done much to make our lives more pleasant.)

Two churches, the Baptist and the Methodist, originally provided for Calhoun's religious needs, but about the time we arrived, they merged. We went to Sunday school while our parents were in church. Next to the church was the Masonic Lodge Hall. Almost all the substantial men in communities like this were Masons. I never knew what their secret rituals involved, but together with the church they formed the backbone of the community and a primary source of charity and social work. My impression is that, like the furnishing merchants, the Masons are no longer major factors in the small-town social scene.

Monroe, then a town of about 15,000 people, was sixteen miles to the east over a dirt road. In wet weather the roads over the red clay hills were too slick to be passable. In dry weather the sand in the valleys became parched and loose and became a big sand trap for the uninitiated. An automobile trip to Monroe was an all-day adventure demanding days of planning. Often completion of a trip required help from a local farmer and his team of mules to pull the automobile out of a sand bed or ditch.

Each year the roads were improved. By the time we left Calhoun four years later, we were making frequent automobile trips to Monroe. Today the two are connected by an interstate highway, although the change has not been completely for the good. What was once a close community in which each person knew and cared about his or her neighbor is now a bedroom community for Monroe, with many of the residents strangers to one another.

Calhoun was distinguished from the other villages by its high school. The school and church together provided whatever focus the community had. This feeling was reinforced because the school principal was also the superintendent of the Sunday school. About three-fourths of the dozen teachers were permanent fixtures, wives or widows of local men. The other three or four were from else-where, and each fall the few local bachelors hoped there would be an attractive woman in the group.

There was also speculation each fall about who the Methodist minister would be. The hierarchy of the state Methodist church met each October and assigned pastors to the churches in the district. A policy seemed to be in effect of reshuffling the assignments frequently, because we got a new man every year or so. He always had children in school, and they had the problem of moving to a new school about a month after school started.

Calhoun had one doctor, and until about 1920 he made his calls in a horse-drawn buggy. Evidently he did not trust his new automobile, because I remember that he kept the horse and buggy for several years after he bought his first car. We were one of the few families with a car in 1918, but we also had a horse-drawn buggy that saw almost as much use as the car. There were no school buses. I walked the mile and a half to and from school every day unless bad weather required someone to take me in the car. It is difficult to imagine a better setting for a six-year-old boy.

When I entered the Calhoun school, all eleven grades were in one building. My classmates were children of local farmers and of the few merchants and railroad employees. I entered this school with long blond hair in what was called a Buster Brown haircut. Tradition would have it that I spent my first months fighting my classmates. The truth is that I only remember being chased by high-school girls who wanted to play with my hair. My father stood this for a few weeks and then, without my mother's knowledge, got me a real boy's haircut. My mother shed a few tears that night before accepting one of the rites of passage of her firstborn.

Radio was not yet in widespread use. All important news came by telegraph. The news of the end of World War I came and was spread by the telegraph operator at the railroad station. The sight of Pat Mason, the local station agent, at the door with a yellow envelope in his hand was almost always bad news. Sometime after we arrived, however, we got a telephone. Our telephone and those of the four or five others on the party line were the first in the community.

MY MOTHER

In the fall of 1918 the influenza epidemic started. In the category of disasters in the United States in this century, only wars and the Great Depression were worse. In one winter 550,000 people in the United States died of the flu.

My father, Frank, and I recovered from cases of flu thanks to my mother's care, but then she became ill. The flu was a serious threat by itself, but the real threat was that it might become pneumonia. Without sulfa drugs and antibiotics the mortality rate for pneumonia was high, and Mother did develop pneumonia.

I had a sense that something was wrong. My maternal grandmother and my Aunt Emma were there, back soon after a Christmas visit. Clara, our nurse, was not giving us her usual attention. Our father, who was a quiet, reserved man, usually devoted some of his time before dinner to us but had been too preoccupied to do so for several days.

My most lasting childhood memory is of an evening in January 1919. My father held me and my brother Frank on each knee and told us that our mother, who was seriously ill with influenza and pneumonia, would not live through the night. I was four months short of seven and Frank was four. Our brother Edward was eight months old.

The next morning someone decided that two young boys should be spared the post-death activities and sent us away with the teenage son of a neighbor. Wherever Stewart Calhoun is, he is a candidate for sainthood. He kept two disturbed little boys occupied all morning until midafternoon. We must have done many things, but the memorable event was being allowed to shoot his .22 rifle. To a six-year-old who was only beginning to aspire to a BB gun, this was a giant step toward manhood.

The original plan was for us to spend the day with our friend. At the last minute someone decided that we should attend our mother's funeral. The service was held at the house because the church was filled with other funerals. We were picked up as the procession went from the house to the cemetery. We went in the clothes we had been playing in.

There was a graveside service. The coffin was lowered into the grave. The preacher stood at the end of the grave and preached much too long. Then he dropped dirt in the grave. It made a hollow sound as it hit the coffin. There were words about ashes and dust. Then men from the party took shovels and filled the grave, taking a long time to make a neat mound. The funeral party sat under an awning on folding chairs. There were no chairs for the little boys. We leaned on my aunt's chair, knowing that something terrible had happened without being fully aware just what. Later they stopped the heartless business of having the family sit and watch the grave being filled one shovelful at a time.

Because of his own experience my father was determined to keep his family together after my mother's death. Clara was there to look after the three children. My father asked his Aunt Genie, his mother's widowed sister, to come to live with us and run the house. She was glad to come because she had been living with one of her sons whose wife she did not like.

Aunt Genie must have been in her sixties at the time, but she seemed very old to me. My first impression was that she was a kind, gentle person, completely encased in a corset. When she sat down, she had no lap, only a cylinder of whale bone. She lived with us for more than five years and helped fill our mother's place as well as anyone could.

RUTH

The next seven months passed quickly. Then early one August morning Aunt Genie and Clara took my brothers and me to my father's room and put us in bed with my father and my new stepmother, Ruth. Ruth Finklea had grown up near Calhoun and had gone away to college. My father met her when she came home in June for summer vacation after teaching in southern Louisiana. It was love at first sight, and they were married less than three months later. Ruth decided that getting started on the job of looking after three little boys was more important than a honeymoon. They spent their wedding night at our house, and she met her new sons early the next morning.

Now there were three women in our household—anyone's recipe for discord—but somehow friction was averted. Ruth was much wiser than most twenty-three-year-olds. Clara looked after Edward, who was at that time a little over a year old. Aunt Genie took care of Frank and me, including monitoring my school work. When I was ten years old, she decided that I was a religious illiterate and assigned to me a chapter in the New Testament to read each week and discuss with her on Sunday.

A NEW FAMILY

With the coming of winter, another flu epidemic struck, and I was one of the victims. My recovery was so slow that my family was concerned that I might have tuberculosis of the lungs. Family conferences were held to decide what should be done with this puny child. One possibility was to send me to Arizona, where the dry air was supposed to be good for weak lungs. Ruth suggested that while they were waiting to decide what to do with me, and to get me away from the other children so I would not infect them, I should go to live with her parents, her sister, and her sister's husband.

Grandma and Grandpa Finklea lived in a new house about two miles north of Calhoun on a lightly traveled public road. Grandpa Finklea had little education, but he read newspapers, farm publications, and things related to the Masons, of which he was an active member. He knew enough mathematics to help me with my

Ruth Finklea Cain in 1919.

Gordon's sisters Pola, Billie Jean, and Ruth with their mother, Ruth, second from right.

third-grade arithmetic. He was unusual in that he was the only man
of his standing in the community who actually worked on his own
farm, 120 acres that he maintained with the help of one man. The
two worked about 50 percent more land than usual for farmers in the
area and had better-than-average yields per acre. The helper, Mr.
Chamblis, was a bachelor of about fifty who lived alone in Grandpa's
old house. He was a complete recluse with no visible friends. He ate
dinner with the family on Christmas, but at no other time. Whenever Grandma sent lunch to Grandpa in the field, she would also
send enough for Mr. Chamblis; otherwise, he did his own cooking
and housekeeping.

Grandma Finklea was in her early fifties but was already in my
eyes an old woman. She was a good cook and housekeeper and looked
after me very well. Although all her neighbors had servants in their
homes, she refused to do so. Her one concession was to have someone do the washing and ironing each week. She was proud of the
children she had raised, but to her nothing had a bright side. If you
asked her how she was, she would tell you in great detail of her physical
ailments, the high price of groceries, and where the younger generation was going—and would then predict the imminent collapse of
civilization.

Ruth's older sister, my Aunt Mae Carleton, and her husband, Uncle
Charlie, also lived across the road in a new house. These new houses
were evidence that cotton prices had been high in the early 1920s.
Aunt Mae was a big, handsome, outgoing woman, the antithesis of
her mother. She liked to cook, and although she had a servant, she
did most of the cooking. She did not have children but wished that
she had. Because I was more comfortable there, I spent much of my
time on their side of the road. They had about six hundred acres of
land, all devoted to cotton except that required to raise corn to feed
the mules and the people.

Uncle Charlie, like Grandpa Finklea, was not cut from ordinary
cloth. He cultivated a reputation for laziness—for him to get caught
doing physical labor was a great humiliation. In time I learned that

he spent hours in the morning repairing farm equipment. He was careful to finish and get in his rocker on the front porch or in his truck to ride around the farm before any outsiders appeared.

A few years later his deception was exposed. Cotton prices went so low that cotton farming was hardly a break-even exercise. Rather than skimp and go into debt, Charlie started a dairy and within a few years had a large, profitable operation. When the neighbors were barely getting by financially, Charlie and Mae were buying new cars every year and remodeling their house. Dairy farming is the most demanding of all farming, with the need to milk cows at the same time each day. After a short while in this enterprise Charlie lost his reputation for laziness.

RABBIT HUNTING

An important part of Charlie and Mae's household was a pack of aging foxhounds. These dogs were relics of a time when the local husbands had been freer of wifely restraint. There had been a fox hunt every week in the spring, fall, and winter, weather permitting. These hunts were not the pink-coat, jumping-horse affairs of England or Virginia. Rather, they were occasions when men could go away and be men, or at least talk about being men.

Until a few years before, these hunts had taken place nearly every week except in the summertime; then some of the hunters began to pay more attention to the bourbon bottle than to the dogs and stories. Enough wives barred their husbands from fox hunting that there were now only one or two hunts a year. These hunts were partly a memorial to better times and partly a weak statement by some of the husbands that they were not completely under their wives' thumbs.

Uncle Charlie took me on two or three of these hunts. After supper (dinner was something you ate at midday), the group gathered at the appointed spot in the woods where the foxes were likely to be. The dogs were turned loose, a fire started, and the bourbon bottle opened. The older men sat around the fire, the young men went with the dogs to give them encouragement they did not need, and any youngsters sat quietly in the background for fear of irritating some elder and being barred from the hunt. The stories would start— never dirty stories. This was a Puritan community, and sex, which they thought happened only in the dark, was never mentioned. The dirtiest word I ever heard in these sessions was "horse manure." The stories were about previous hunts and particularly about the unusual talents of one of the speaker's dogs. Occasionally, the stories stopped when someone heard a bark and said, "That's my Old Blue." Another would remark, "That's my Mike, but he's chasing a rabbit." Finally, the dogs would jump a fox, and the chorus of barking would start.

The countryside was covered with patches of woods from ten to forty acres each, separated by several hundred yards of open fields. The fox would start in one wooded area and make a dash to another with the dogs in full cry behind him. Then the fox would hide in a dense briar patch until he was rested and dash to another set of woods. When the fox had enough exercise for the evening, he would go into a hole in the ground. Pandemonium would ensue, with the dogs barking and trying to get into the hole and the young men yelling and trying to get the dogs away from the hole so that the fox could live and run again. Meantime, back at the fire, on hearing the dogs and knowing what had happened, the eldest hunter would rise, stretch, and announce the end of the hunt by saying, "Well, boys, it's time to piss on the fire and call the dogs."

Because he hunted so little, Charlie had quit raising dogs. As a result his pack was getting old and slow but not so old that they did not need exercise. My first chore was to take the dogs, go out with two or three black boys my age, and let the dogs run rabbits. We never caught any, but we must have helped a lot of rabbits develop their leg muscles.

Soon the chore became my full-time occupation. My day would start after an early breakfast. There was no thought that a boy, even a puny one, should lie in bed and make his grandmother fix two breakfasts. I ate breakfast with Grandpa Finklea before daylight. After breakfast I would leave with my lunch—a hard-boiled egg and a baked sweet potato inside my shirt—the dogs, and the boys. I suspect that at first Uncle Charlie bribed these boys to come with me. Except for an occasional interlude to go fishing, this is how I spent the year and a half with Ruth's family, with whom I became closer than if they were blood kin.

Good things must end, and the time came for me to go back to school. During my sabbatical as a rabbit hunter I had the same books as my classmates and studied on rainy days. The reading and spelling I could do alone. Uncle Charlie and Grandpa Finklea helped me with third-grade arithmetic. I went back to school with no problem except that they had learned about the parts of speech. There was no mention of nouns or verbs in the books I had studied.

Writing this sets me to thinking about my black hunting comrades. I cannot remember having any of my friends tell me they could not go hunting because they had to go to school. There was a two-room building a few miles away that was called the black school, but I have no recollection of ever seeing it used. If my memories are correct, my friends must have gone into the world with at least two handicaps, being black and being uneducated.

I, on the other hand, was lucky. I cannot remember having a bad teacher from kindergarten to high school. Most were mature, married women who had taught their subject for years. It was before many other careers were open to women, so teaching got the best. They were trained before the great modern heresy that learning should be made easy. They knew that just as learning to kick a football or to swim competitively requires work, so does learning to write or compute.

Less than a year after my father and Ruth were married, but long enough not to cause any gossip except a few passing comments like "they certainly didn't wait long to get started," my sister Ruth was born. She was followed at almost exactly two-year intervals by my sisters Pola Mae and Billie Jean. It has never occurred to them or me or my brothers that we are anything less than full brothers and sisters. Nor have I had any different feeling for Ruth, who took my mother's place, than I would have had for my own mother. The parents and surrogate parents I had in these early years were all loving, kind people. I was very fortunate.

RAYVILLE

For reasons that I have never understood, my father decided to take a new job in Rayville, Louisiana, as what is called the county agricultural agent (except that in Louisiana counties are called parishes). His job, still part of the Agricultural Extension Service, was to help the farmers of Richland Parish to farm better.

Louisiana is shaped like a boot. Southern Louisiana was settled in the seventeenth and eighteenth century by the French, first from Canada and then from France. The Florida parishes, which form the toe of the boot, and northern Louisiana were settled by the overflow, largely Scotch-Irish and English Protestants, from the states east of there. The early French and Anglo settlements were built along the waterways so that the settlers could more easily transport their cotton to market.

Rayville was different from most of the other Louisiana towns in that it was relatively new. In eastern Richland Parish, along Bayou Macon, and to the west, along the Boeuf River, there were old farms of five hundred to three thousand acres worked by black tenant farmers. Until about 1900 the center of the parish and the site of Rayville were covered by a virgin hardwood forest owned by a few large lumber companies. As they cut the timber, they sold the land at low prices to farmers who cleared the remaining stumps and small trees. After clearing, the rich land was planted in cotton, and the yields were high.

The farmers who bought this land were mostly from the hill country, where the combination of poor land and the boll weevil had made cotton farming uneconomical. These farmers were like Grandpa

Finklea. They only farmed one hundred to two hundred acres and did most of the work themselves.

I kept no diary and have no orderly memory of the next years; however, I do have a clear memory of some things.

On my first day in the fifth grade in Rayville, I made the discovery that some girls are different from other girls. A few seats ahead of me was Annie Lee, who had everything a fifth-grade boy could want. I admired her from a distance until with a broken heart I had to accept that I could not compete with the older boys who had discovered her.

About a year after we moved, the wife of one of Aunt Genie's sons became ill, and Aunt Genie left us to run his house. Shortly thereafter, Clara announced that she had met a man she wanted to marry. My parents met the man, did not like him, and tried unsuccessfully to discourage Clara. She married him and moved out of the house but continued to work for us. In a few months, after a long weekend, word came that Clara had died. It was hard to believe that a healthy, twenty-four-year-old woman with no symptoms had died so suddenly. My parents insisted on an investigation, but the local coroner found no sign of foul play.

In a short time we went from a household of three women to one— Ruth. There were six children, starting with me, just past twelve, to Billie Jean, not quite one. Up to this time we had been spared the usual childhood diseases, but our luck ran out. Over a period of two years mumps, measles, and chickenpox would first hit me and then go down the line to the youngest. As many as three of us would be in bed at once. With either no help or temporary, untrained help, Ruth could barely recover from one set of ailments before another hit. During part of this time I was the only person around to do the cooking. As a result I became and still am a good cook.

Along the way my father decided that with the volume of milk that six kids consumed, we should have a cow—which later became two cows. At first he milked them, but he taught me to milk in case he was delayed at the office. The delays became more frequent until soon I had regular morning and evening jobs milking. There is no more demanding job. Cows must be milked at the same time every day, rain or shine. I continued to perform this chore until I went away to school, and then Frank relieved me.

BACK TO CALHOUN

There must have been a bad cotton crop in 1924 or 1925 because Richland Parish could not pay their part of my father's salary, so he had no job. However, to encourage him to stay in Rayville, they offered him a job as deputy clerk of the court at about two-thirds his former salary. To save money, he decided to move the family into Grandma Finklea's vacant house in Calhoun. He stayed in Rayville thirty-five miles away and visited us on weekends.

We moved back to Calhoun, and I enrolled as a sophomore in the high school. No one was recruiting five-foot, nine-inch, one-hundred-pound forwards, but I went out for the basketball team anyway. Because of a shortage of bodies the coach kept me on the squad, but just barely. For our first game away from home we were to leave the school early one Saturday morning. I arrived at the appointed time to find that the bus had left without me. No one noticed the absence of a third-string forward.

I returned home as close to tears as a thirteen-year-old would let himself be. My father and Ruth were sympathetic, and after an hour or two they came and said that they were taking me to Monroe. We attended a matinee performance by a touring company of a New York musical, *No, No, Nanette*. Instead of sitting on the bench at a basketball game, I saw my first Broadway show. I also got a new perspective on my father, who I had thought was impervious to the problems of small boys. He had taken time he could have spent with the rest of the family and money that was needed many places to ease my pain.

After a year the financial situation of Richland Parish improved, my father's job was restored, and the family moved back to Rayville.

When I talked to the Rayville school officials, I found that because of the courses I had taken in Calhoun and the courses available in Rayville, I could not finish high school in two more years, whereas I could finish in two years in Calhoun. Arrangements were made for me to stay with the Mason family. Pat Mason was an Irishman and the railroad station master who for years had delivered yellow envelopes bearing news of deaths, births, and weddings to the community.

The Masons had a son in my class who was two years older. With him I got a job cleaning the school building, which we did early each morning or late in the afternoon. For the first time I had spending money of my own. I also became part of an older group who had already started to smoke and drink anything they could get their hands on. That I did not become addicted to tobacco and alcohol I owe to my father. He told me that I was free to drink, smoke, or do anything else as long as the decision to do it was my considered decision and not a decision made in response to peer pressure. I was a nonsmoking teetotaler in a group whose pressure on me to change only made me stand firmer.

BACK TO RAYVILLE

At the end of the year the school situation in Rayville had changed, and I was able to graduate there. In Rayville basketball was a minor sport; the focus was on football. Again no coach was looking for an end, now weighing a hefty 110 pounds, but I tried anyway. The coach was soft-hearted; he kept me on the bench and put me in the last part of games that were either clearly won or hopelessly lost.

In May 1928, about a week before my sixteenth birthday, I graduated from Rayville High School. This was a year early because I had gone through the sixth, seventh, and eighth grades in two years.

The quality of our lives during my boyhood was determined largely by the kind of help we had. As long as Clara was alive, life at home went smoothly. For about five years after her death a procession of

Gordon Cain as left end on the Rayville football team. From Palmetto, *the high school annual for 1928.*

The chemistry building at LSU. Courtesy LSU Library.

women was hired, none of whom stayed very long. My memories of these years are of impromptu meals, sick babies, and a badly over-worked Ruth keeping house, tending to sick children, and worrying about paying bills.

About the time I went to college, however, Penny came. Penny was an unmarried black man of about forty. He had worked for and been trained as a cook by an affluent bachelor in a nearby town. He took over the kitchen and housekeeping, leaving Ruth free to return to teaching arithmetic in the local junior high school. He stayed until the start of World War II, when he went to the West Coast to work building ships. Penny was replaced by Rosa, a wonderful woman who stayed until both my father and Ruth died. Rosa still lives in a house they gave her for life. I made a small repayment to Rosa in the 1960s, when I got her son C.W. a job at Petro-Tex. C.W.

had children, all of whom have gone to college and now have professional jobs.

From these years I feel that my greatest debt is to my stepmother, Ruth. She was a wonderful wife and made my father very happy. He easily could have been a disappointed and frustrated man: He had expected to go to medical school and become a doctor, but the boll weevil had punctured this hope. With his intelligence, personality, and character he should have been much more successful professionally than he was. His few ventures into business were all unsuccessful. I suspect that having six offspring to feed and educate inhibited him from taking chances he might otherwise have taken.

Without diminishing in any way my father's status as head of the family, Ruth became the backbone. She handled the money, and as soon as the last child entered school, she resumed teaching. Her pay as a teacher provided the funds to let the six of us attend universities, and she did all this with grace and good humor.

WORKING ON THE RAILROAD

It was always assumed that I would go to LSU after graduating from high school. To help with the cost, I had planted about an acre and a half of cotton, from which I expected to harvest a bale. Whatever I earned from this would be part of my school money. The family financial situation must have been difficult at the time, because the mention of my going to LSU was always a little tentative, and I was mentally prepared to be disappointed.

Then fate intervened. The lady who worked as a clerk in the local Missouri Pacific office stepped in front of a switch engine and was killed. The station agent, who was a friend of my father's, offered me the job as her replacement. Two months later, at the time I was to go to LSU, I had a job that paid $135 a month (about $1,500 in 1995 dollars). The decision to let me work for a year and save money was easy. It was not until three years after I graduated from LSU that my salary reached this high level again.

By the usual standards my job of checking freight in and out, reading car numbers, and preparing bills of lading was dull work, but to a
sixteen-year-old who had never been more than a hundred miles from
the lower Mississippi, it was exciting to be sending things to faraway
places.

About a month after I would have gone to school had I not had
this job, I was given a lesson in railroad labor union contracts. A
smiling man showed up one morning with a piece of paper that said
he was "bumping" me from my job. Under the terms of the union
contract any member who lost his job could bump anyone with less
seniority.

There were 110 regular jobs in our unit. My replacement was 111
in seniority, and I was 112. Enough people were away ill or on vacation to let him work almost full time and me about half time. For a
year I spent periods of one week to one month in towns between the
Louisiana–Arkansas border and Alexandria, Louisiana, with each job
terminated by the appearance of the same man. Instead of having a
year's pay to use for school, I had about half that amount. However,
I had time to produce another bale of cotton.

My knowledge of unions was formed partly by reading Jack London and partly by the newspaper accounts of the International Workers of the World, the "Wobblies." I knew that the railroad employees
belonged to unions and that some of the local craftsmen had union
cards so that they could work in the big cities when things were slack
at home. Union membership was like atheism: You knew there were
such people, and you regarded them as well-meaning but misguided.

I knew that all the regular clerks belonged to the union, but because I considered myself temporary, I resisted suggestions that I
join—and each time I was told that I would not be able to say no
when the head man came on his annual trip from union headquarters. Finally, the day of the visit arrived, and I was told to be in a
certain conference room in Monroe at a particular time. I showed up
fully expecting to be browbeaten into joining the union. Instead, I
met a very nice man who asked about me, my family, and my plans.
When he learned that I planned to go to college, he wanted to know

where and what I planned to take. At the end he wished me well without even mentioning the union. My attitude toward unions today is more favorable than it would have been without this experience.

LSU

When I left for Baton Rouge to enter LSU, there were a half dozen other prospective freshmen on the train. Then, any graduate of a Louisiana high school could enroll in the university without restriction. It was a shock to my serious nature to learn that about half this group did not expect to stay beyond the first semester. They were going for the football games and parties, and they fully expected to fail enough courses to be kicked out at the end of that time.

My freshman year I lived in the barracks in an ROTC company that was at least half Cajun. It was my first experience with another culture, and I developed a great affection for my French friends. Hazing was still the custom, and beating with an officer's Sam Browne belt was the usual form. The upperclassmen in one's own ROTC company were perfunctory about their beating, but occasionally a sadist from some other unit would become enthusiastic and create some very sore behinds.

Although the science laboratories and the library facilities at my high school had been very poor, I had no trouble with science and math. My freshman year was the first year that all freshmen were given English tests; those who failed were required to take remedial courses. I did not fail, but I was embarrassed that the essay I wrote was below the caliber of the best ones, which were published in the university newspaper.

Two years of ROTC were required, and they were a dull two years, spent mostly in close-order infantry drill. The second two years included tactics and military history, which I found fascinating. Our instructor was Major Troy Middleton, who in World War II was the corps commander at the Battle of the Bulge. He was a great teacher and awakened in me a lasting interest in military strategy.

Between my junior and senior years I went to an ROTC camp in

Edgewood Arsenal, Maryland. The trip had a side benefit: One of my chemistry professors wanted someone to drive his car from Baton Rouge to Baltimore, which I did with a friend. We had plenty of time and toured the southeastern part of the country, spending a few days in Washington, D.C. It was the summer of 1932, and the city was besieged with veterans from all over the country who were there trying to pressure Congress into increasing their benefits. A few weeks later General MacArthur and the army broke up the camps and drove the veterans out of town.

My major, chemical engineering, was demanding, but very good teachers made it easier. My social life was limited by a shortage of funds and the lack of an automobile. After my freshman year, however, I developed a modest source of income coaching freshmen in mathematics. Some of my clients were athletes; some were of Italian origin from the strawberry-growing region of southeastern Louisiana, sons of the only prosperous farmers in the state. Some of these farmers were determined to keep their sons in LSU and were willing to pay me to help. Between the engineering professors' demands and time spent coaching freshmen in math, I had no time for the liberal arts courses I would have liked to take. In all, my four years at LSU were filled with study, work, and some play, but they were not fun-filled years.

CHAPTER THREE

CHOICE
AND
CHANCE

LAUNCHING A CAREER

IN A SENSE MY BUSINESS CAREER started in June 1933, when I received a B.S. from Louisiana State University in chemical engineering. The sixty-plus years since then have been interesting, rewarding, and at times exciting. Except for the death of my mother when I was six and the death of my first wife, Lucia, nothing really bad has ever happened to me.

My decision to become a chemical engineer was based on an incorrect premise and a logic that could only come from a bright sixteen-year-old. I was permitted to skip a grade. At the time I thought that meant I was smart. Now I realize that very early I mastered the art of passing tests and impressing teachers with only a minimum amount of learning. Skipping grades might have kept me challenged in school, but it meant that my social life was with boys and girls who were two years older. I was never president of the class or captain of a team, which gave me the idea that I had no leadership qualities, no skill with people. Therefore, I reasoned that my career should be in a field that did not require these qualities—science or some application of science such as engineering. The idea of studying history because I loved history was unthinkable. The only job for history majors was teaching, and teachers' salaries were being cut.

I went to the library, as I still do when I have a problem. My research showed that of all the technically related professions chemical

49

engineers received the highest starting salaries. I decided to become a chemical engineer without having more than a vague idea of what one did.

FIRST JOB

My professional career started at a low point. In the spring of 1933 the newly elected president, Franklin Roosevelt, closed all the banks for about a week. The strong banks reopened after one or two weeks; some never reopened. Our hometown bank was closed for a month or so, but LSU let students sign for cafeteria meal tickets. These became the medium of exchange at the university and surrounding businesses, and I finished my last two months in college on credit. That spring not a single corporate recruiter visited the engineering school. Not a single graduate had a professional engineering job.

No writer can give you a true picture of life during the Great Depression. The unemployment rate was about 25 percent, with no government welfare program. At least half my classmates gave up any effort to find professional jobs. My father had a job, but it was always possible he might lose it (and he did for about a year). To be sure that we would always have something to eat, he bought a small farm, where we had milk cows, pigs, chickens, and a large vegetable garden. My summers were spent not on the beach or in a boys' camp but working in the garden or cotton field. We were all busy milking cows or helping preserve fruit and vegetables for the winter.

I went to LSU by working, borrowing money, and getting money from my family that they could not afford to give me. With two of my brothers in college as well, I could not take any more money from my family. My only employment opportunity was a fellowship to do graduate work in chemical engineering and to be a teaching assistant. The pay covered a little less than living expenses and left no time to earn money outside. I needed a paying job and spent the summer looking for one—without success.

A week before time to return to the university I learned of a man, Charlie Gill, who had graduated a few years before me in chemical engineering. He had a job but wanted to go to graduate school. I wanted a job badly. We met in his boss's office; called Charles E. Coates, the dean and head of the engineering school (the Audubon Sugar School, an institution that provided most of the technology and technologists for the sugar industry worldwide); and made a deal. We traded my fellowship for his job. My replacement in graduate school, who in time became a friend, did his thesis on odorizing natural gas, which has no odor of its own. Shortly after he graduated, natural gas leaked undetected into the basement of a school in East Texas. It exploded, killing many children. Charlie, who was then the country's only expert on odorizing natural gas, parlayed his skill into a multimillion-dollar fortune over about fifteen years. Whenever I speculate about whether I could have done likewise had I gone to graduate school, I must accept that I was not sophisticated enough at the time to do what he did.

Had the dean been away, out of sorts, or not disposed to being pushed into a decision over the telephone, I probably would be a retired professor of chemical engineering. Had I gone to graduate school, I probably would have stayed in the academic world. (I like to teach. Much of my function as a manager has been teaching.) At the end of our telephone conversation Dean Coates remarked, probably idly, that if ever I wanted to come to graduate school there would be a place for me. The thought that I could go to graduate school if I became too unhappy with my situation helped me to endure some of the irritations of my first job.

This job was with a utility company—the Louisiana Power and Light Company—in a large gas-fired electrical generating plant. The plant was located out in the country about thirty miles from Monroe, Louisiana, the nearest town. Because this rural area did not offer its employees adequate housing, the company had built a small village for them around the plant. It included a twenty-room hotel for bachelor employees and visiting officials. In the hotel with me were five or six young single men and an equal number of older divorced or widowed employees.

The operation was run by a former merchant marine captain who was very proud of having been a U.S. Navy officer during World War I. He managed the plant and handled the people as though he was still commanding a ship. We punched a time clock on starting and leaving work. Punching in one minute after the appointed time was a major offense, the reason for which one was required to explain personally to the top man. He usually levied a penalty of half a day of extra work. My title included the word *engineer*, but it was difficult to feel very professional in this juvenile camp atmosphere.

The work was not any more inspiring than the atmosphere. We treated boiler feed water, calibrated and maintained instruments, and made efficiency calculations. The pay of $125 a month sounds very low now, but it was twice what some of my classmates were getting riding bicycles around an oil refinery to pick up samples. It was also ten dollars a month less than I had made five years before, working for the railroad. As bad as the job was, I was able to pay my debts from college, buy a used car, and accumulate enough stake to give me the nerve to move on.

All this was complicated by the development of my first serious romance. Through high school and college I had dates with many different girls, but except for a few short infatuations there was nothing serious. Winifred was a blond with a slight trace of freckles. She was pretty, intelligent, and comfortable. She lived in a town about fifteen miles away, where her father was a banker. Our paths first crossed at interschool functions and then at summer 4-H Club camps. She went to Sophie Newcomb in New Orleans, and I went to LSU in Baton Rouge. A few times each school year I would accumulate enough extra cash to go to New Orleans to have a date with her.

Winifred graduated and could not find a job teaching art, so she stayed home for a year. I graduated and found a job I did not like. We talked of marriage, but always in the future tense. At that time no serious couple considered marriage without a job and enough money to make a down payment on a house. I was several years away from such affluence. Living together without marrying was not something we considered. At the end of the first year Winifred got a job teaching in West Texas. Our romance continued by mail for several years until I went to Cuba and she married the boy next door.

Had my first employer been a good company, I would probably have become a career employee and retired at sixty-five with a watch I did not need. In this job, however, I developed a detachment from employers that was atypical of those times. My philosophy, which did not change in my time in the corporate world, was fourfold: to do the best possible job; not to worry about promotion and pay; to have a good life off the job; and to move on if the job was not satisfying.

Moving on was not easy. Few jobs were available, and all my fellow employees believed that they would get fired if it became known that they were looking for another job. In spite of this I wrote friends, professors, and acquaintances and even answered blind ads for engineers to go overseas.

After two discouraging years I hit pay dirt. I received a telephone call from one of my classmates telling me that he was working for the Freeport Sulphur Company in Freeport, Texas, and that if I showed up there, he was sure I could have a job. The same week the sales manager of an instrument company told me that he had a job for me subject to my going to the headquarters in Connecticut for a physical exam. Two job prospects (one 500 miles southwest, the other 1,500 miles northeast), neither one hundred percent certain, were enough for me to quit my job at the power plant and drive to Freeport, where I went to work in May 1935. I was prepared to drive the 2,000 miles to Connecticut if the Texas job did not pan out.

FREEPORT SULPHUR COMPANY

Freeport lies on the Gulf Coast about sixty miles south of Houston. It was established by the Freeport Sulphur Company in 1912, when they started mining sulfur at Bryan Mound, a salt dome a few miles away. Under much of the Gulf Coast lies a bed of salt. Pressure from underlying formations has caused it to flow upward in places, resulting in plugs of salts—the salt domes—which are scattered throughout the area. The tops of some of these domes reach the surface, as at Avery Island, Louisiana, where salt is mined commercially. Others are submerged from a few feet to several thousand feet below the surface.

The top of a salt dome is overlaid with a "cap rock," which is just what the words imply. This cap of rock is shaped like an inverted bowl over the top of the salt and frequently traps oil or natural gas, making the domes good "prospects" for oil and gas drillers.

The cap rock is composed of either limestone (calcium carbonate) or anhydrite (calcium sulfate). In a few places the hydrocarbons trapped under the cap rock have reduced part of the calcium sulfate to elemental sulfur. Many unsuccessful attempts were made to mine this sulfur until about 1900, when the German émigré chemist and inventor Herman Frasch pumped hot water into a sulfur formation in a salt dome near what is now Sulfur, Louisiana. The hot water melted the sulfur, which was lifted out of the formation with air. The molten sulfur was next pumped into large vats, where it solidified, then was shipped to customers, mainly sulfuric acid plants. The resultant acid was used primarily to make phosphate fertilizer.

When I joined Freeport Sulphur, except for some sulfur mining around the volcanoes of Sicily (a monopoly operation before the Frasch process), the Frasch mines were the world's principal source of sulfur. Freeport had one large competitor, Texas Gulf Sulphur Company, and two small ones, Jefferson Lake Sulphur Company and Duval Texas Sulphur Company. Freeport is now Freeport McMoran. Texas Gulf is now part of PCS Phosphate, Jefferson Lake has disappeared from the scene, and Duval is now part of Pennzoil Company.

Freeport was a "company" town but did not have the juvenile camp atmosphere of my previous home. I moved into a boarding house with two other engineers. A few months later the three of us rented a house, hired a cook, and established our own bachelor quarters, known as the Chemist Club. Although transfers and marriages brought changes to the membership, the Chemist Club survived long after I left the scene.

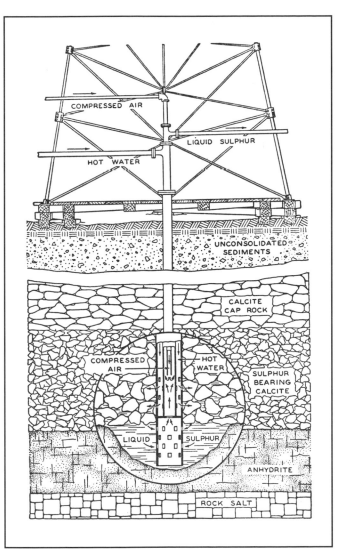

Diagram of the sulfur mining process that Herman Frasch pioneered in 1900. Courtesy PCS Phosphate Company, Inc.

AN EARLY HOSTILE TAKEOVER

Freeport was a good company to work for because of the character of the people who ran it. The three top men, all under thirty-five, had been in their jobs only a few years. One of the three, Langborne Williams, was a tall, bald Virginian with the accent and courtly manners of his home state; a few years before joining Freeport, he had been a new employee of a New York investment bank. His family owned a modest amount of Freeport Sulphur stock and was unhappy with the performance of the company.

Long before the hostile takeovers of the 1980s, at a time when proxy fights to take over companies were rare, Langborne decided to take over Freeport. He enlisted the help of two young associates in the investment bank, Jock Whitney and Ty Claiborne. Jock was very rich, but the three bragged later that they won the proxy fight without using Jock's money to buy stock. Instead, they rode buses all over the country visiting stockholders and soliciting proxies, and they won.

Although not one of the three had any management experience, Jock had become the part-time chairman of the board, Langborne the president and chief executive officer (CEO), and Ty an executive vice president—and they were doing a good job. The idea that a person with limited resources could take over a large company must have slipped into my subconscious at this time.

EARLY ENVIRONMENTALISTS

The principal engineering job in mining sulfur is to produce a very large volume of hot water that will not form scale in the boilers or corrode the equipment. After the hot water has melted the sulfur, it must be brought out of the sulfur formation to the surface. At this point the water is saturated with salt, hydrogen sulfide, and various sulfur compounds, which have a strong odor and are very corrosive. Until about the time I arrived, this foul brew was being released on the marshes of the surrounding area.

Partly to recover the heat in the hot water and partly because there were hunters and fishermen in the management of Freeport who were concerned about the effect of this water on the fish and wild-life, we started a project to reuse the waste water. Somewhere in the U.S. patent office are patents issued to me and others for ways to reuse this water and other subjects relating to sulfur.*

Life off the job was pleasant. The Chemist Club bought a sail-boat, and we had a long, almost deserted beach for the summertime. The duck and goose hunting in the Gulf Coast salt marshes in the fall was the best in the country. After about a year I was occasionally sent to help a customer solve some problem involving the use of sulfur. Many of these customers were easy-to-forget fertilizer plants. One that I do remember was a small company in Hollywood, California, that made the chemicals used to develop film. In return for my help they took me to the first showing of *Gone with the Wind* after the opening night. The audience was full of people trying to look and behave like opening-night celebrities.

CUBA

As part of a diversification program Freeport bought the Cuban-American Manganese Company. This manganese mining operation was located in eastern Cuba, about fifteen miles north of Santiago. Manganese is one of the metals used as an alloy in steel and is essential in producing some important types of steel. At that time the United States was dependent on imported manganese from Russia and South Africa, and there was some pressure to develop sources closer to our borders.

Most useful minerals occur in nature mixed with undesirable material. To have commercial value, the mineral must be separated from the other materials, which are sometimes called gangue. One way to

---

* No. 2,161,245—lowering viscosity of sulfur; No. 2,310,173—sulfur burner; No. 2,616,782 production of sodium cyanide; and No. 2,947,689 saline water heating system.

make this separation is by a process known as *flotation*. The ore is
first ground into fine particles and then is mixed in water with oil
and a chemical that makes the oil wet the desired mineral and not
the gangue. This phenomenon is the same that you see when a drop
of water or oil stands as a round ball on one surface and spreads out
and wets another. If you stir the mixture of ore, water, oil, and wetting agent and pump air bubbles in the bottom, the air bubbles will
attach to the desired material and bring it to the top where it can be
scraped off. Although this process sounds simple, its effective execution is much more complicated. There are many variables, such as
sensitivity to the acidity or alkalinity of the water or to the type of
wetting agent used.

This particular ore body was quite variable. The ore mined near
the surface sometimes required a different set of chemicals and conditions than the ore found a few feet lower. The mill would frequently
run out of a particular type of ore before the engineers found the
optimal conditions to recover the manganese.

Someone reached the obvious conclusion that a small pilot flotation plant should be installed. A few days before a particular type of
ore was to be run in the mill, it would be run in the pilot plant to
determine the best conditions for operation of the mill. My job was
to operate this pilot plant.

R. C. (Bob) Hills, my boss at the time and later CEO of Freeport,
and I sailed from New Orleans to Havana on a Grace Line cruise
ship, one of the luxury liners at the time. I had no idea then that
almost exactly four years later I would sail out of New Orleans on a
similar ship, but this time as an army officer.

We spent a few days in Havana seeing the sights. Havana was a
big, sleepy metropolis whose claim to fame was that Ernest Hemingway visited periodically. Batista had been pushed out of power
with some help from the U.S. government about a year before. One
of the sights we saw in Havana was the cell that Paco Prieto, our
guide and the mining company's representative in Havana, had occupied in the Morro Castle during the Batista regime.

It took two days to drive from Havana to the mine at Cristo, about fifteen miles north of Santiago de Cuba. If Havana was sleepy, Santiago was comatose. It was off the tourist track. The American consul and the managers of the manganese mine were the only Americans around. Soon after arriving, I joined the Santiago Golf Club and a beach club where the gentry of the area gathered on Sundays after Mass. Before long I made many friends among the Santiago people.

At the mine headquarters, the mill, and the club in which the bachelor engineers lived, I was introduced to a completely different society—expatriate miners. Many mines are located in undeveloped parts of the world where the locals do not have the technical and management skills to operate them. There is a high probability that a young mining engineer just out of a university can find a job only in some remote region, or he might choose such a job because the pay and the responsibility are greater. The custom is to take these jobs on a three-year contract, with the conventional wisdom being that anyone who takes his second contract is spoiled for life in a United States operation and destined to spend his career as an expatriate. All the professional expatriates I met were highly competent but very protective of their particular area of activity. All of them could be called "characters."

Counting me, there were ten men in the management of the mining company. Among them they had worked in every uncivilized place in the world. The top four were married and lived in Cristo. That left six bachelors living in the club. Three of us were under thirty, and the other three were old bachelors who had been out on many three-year contracts and were very possessive of their particular fields. I learned this when, after operating the pilot plant and determining the best way to process the ore, I made a recommendation to the mill superintendent. He then operated the mill in a less efficient way to prove me wrong. The impasse continued for several weeks until I developed a solution. I quit making recommendations. I simply sent to him the data from which the answer was obvious, but as long as I did not suggest what he should do, he operated in the proper way.

The other two young single men at the club knew many people in Santiago. About once a month we would have a party to which they would invite six or eight girls and a few young men. The party came with a chaperone, a duenna. The rumba had just become popular in the States, and with some effort I had learned it in anticipation of my trip to Cuba. The effort was wasted. Nice girls in Cuba did not do the rumba, with its suggestive hip movements. They did a sedate version called the danson. If any female hips moved too much, the duenna would frown and tap her fan on the table, and the action would stop.

There was one girl at these parties who I thought was special, and I asked her to go with me to a party at the American consul's home. When I arrived at the house, I met the duenna, a maiden aunt of some age past sixty, whose face had not smiled in years. She said nothing unless spoken to in Spanish and drank an endless number of Coca-Colas. I gave up the idea of having solo dates when I learned that in that part of the world it was considered a step short of engagement.

With the pilot plant and the mill operating well, there was no reason for me to stay longer in Cuba. I went back to the States, this time not on a glamorous cruise ship but on the overnight ferry from Havana to Key West, with a one-day stopover to let me see some of Hemingway's haunts.

NEVADA

After almost a year of fairly routine work, another opportunity for an interesting junket arose. Freeport had taken an option on a molybdenum prospect in Nevada under terms that gave us six months to explore it. At the end of that time we had to buy it or walk away and forfeit a large down payment.

The prospect was in the far north end of Death Valley and was called Alum Gulch because the springs there flowed with a concentrated solution of aluminum sulfate, or alum. It was a dead-end canyon with 1,300-foot walls. Large parts of the canyon's vertical face were covered with high-purity molybdenite, the mineral from which molybdenum is obtained. The coating of molybdenite was thin, and the rock a few inches deeper was barren. It was hoped that this surface coating had been leached from a large body of ore deeper in the mountain. Our job was to find this bonanza.

The Freeport party consisted of three mining engineers or geologists, one of whom was the boss, and me. Our plan was to hire diamond drill contractors to drill holes and take samples from the top of the cliffs and then have a crew of miners drive tunnels in the side of the cliffs in the direction we thought the ore would be. My job was to analyze the samples.

My arrival on the scene was by a train from Houston to Los Angeles, a train to Las Vegas, and a bus north to the small town of Goldfield. It was the fourth or fifth time I had made the Houston–Los Angeles trip. Each time it was like my idea of a voyage on an ocean liner. Shut up in a confined space for sixty hours with the same forty or fifty people, you find a few congenial souls with whom you exchange Christmas cards for years.

Until Boulder Dam was built in the early 1930s, Las Vegas had been little more than a railroad station and two bars. During the building of the dam it became a boom town with hundreds of construction workers and the usual hangers-on. At the time I arrived, the dam was finished but much of the construction camp remained. I had no idea that all this would in a few years become the Las Vegas we now know.

Goldfield was about halfway between Las Vegas and Reno on what was the main highway, but not many cars passed through. In the early 1900s Goldfield was the scene of the last big gold rush in this country. Someone discovered a very high-grade gold deposit, and a town of thirty thousand people grew up around it. They had street cars and a stock exchange, but no sign of either was left.

Goldfield has a special place in the history of labor relations. In December of 1907 Teddy Roosevelt used federal troops to break a strike in Goldfield, one of the few times this was ever done. The strike was not over a prosaic issue like wages but was precipitated by an order from the mine owners that required all miners to bathe and change clothes after finishing each shift. This order represented a major reduction in pay because each miner had been accustomed to filling his pockets and boots with high-grade gold ore when he left work each day.

When I arrived, there were only sixty people in the town, many of whom I remember very well. Foremost were a young doctor and his wife and baby. I rented a room at their house for the times I stayed in "town" rather than at Alum Gulch. Later, we discovered that he was the nephew of our family doctor in Louisiana and that we had played together when he visited his uncle.

The center of activity was the local assay office. Although no signs of mining activity could be seen for miles around, hidden in the hills were a dozen or more one- or two-man gold or mercury mines. Someone had found a small tungsten deposit, and many people were roaming the mountains with ultraviolet headlights looking for scheelite, a tungsten mineral that glows under ultraviolet light. My relation with the assayer was cemented when I taught him how to analyze for tungsten, which let him double his business.

Goldfield had two bars. One bar owner claimed to have a Ph.D. in geology and to be a veteran of the Klondike gold rush. He had become his own best customer. Before closing time he was always asleep on a sofa, and the customers served themselves and put their money in the cash register. Reflecting the frontier honesty, no one cheated when he poured his own drinks. The other bar was owned by an old Frenchman who had been there since the boom days. He claimed that Jack Dempsey had been a bus boy in his saloon and that he had started Dempsey as a prize fighter. The story could have been true. Autographed pictures of Dempsey to the Frenchman hung on every wall. Goldfield sported no stores. For shopping we drove the twenty-five miles to Tonopah.

The blacksmith shop with the smith's bachelor quarters above was almost as active as the assay office because the miners needed to have equipment repaired almost as often as they needed assays. The shop was across the street from the railroad station. The railroad had been gone for years, but the station agent was now the Western Union telegraph operator, and he sold tickets for the two buses a day that came through each way.

To complete the picture, a small cafe was operated by two women who lived in a bungalow behind it. One was distinctly masculine and the other feminine. In another place people might have speculated about their relationship, but the unusual was the norm here, and no one took notice. The Elks' hall was unused except once a year, for a dance. Fortunately, I attended one. It was surprising how many attractive, well-dressed men and women appeared out of the barren countryside.

The trip from Goldfield to Alum Gulch was about two hours by truck. The first leg was to a spot on the map called Lida, which consisted of only one house. From there you took off cross-country over a road we had to build and maintain. It took us into Death Valley, from where we then drove about ten miles up the valley to the camp.

The mining engineers who preceded me had built three camp buildings, partly out of new material and partly from the remains of previous camps. One was a kitchen and dining room with quarters for the cook, Kitty, and her retarded son. The other two were bunkhouses, one for the engineers and one for the mining crew.

A casting director looking for someone to play the part of a tough, heart-of-gold mining camp cook would have found Kitty perfect. She was short, full-bodied, of indeterminate age, and much gentler than one would have expected considering her background. Other than to mention various camps in which she had worked, she said little about her past.

I found on arrival that the assayer who was analyzing the samples for molybdenum was not getting consistent results. When I tried, neither did I. My first chore was to spend a week in Reno at a Bureau of Mines laboratory where together we developed a reliable analytical technique. A week in the Mapes Hotel in Reno, where most of the guests were women waiting for a divorce, was a change from Freeport, Texas, where there were two men for every eligible woman.

The work at the camp was divided between the diamond drillers at the top, who had their own separate camp, and the miners at the bottom of the canyon. To get from the bottom to the top meant either a 1,300-foot climb or a three-hour truck ride through Lida. Many days I made the trip up the cliff twice. We saw little of the diamond drillers except in the daytime. We saw the miners at work, at meals, and at a Saturday night poker game. We learned when we were hiring the miners that you do not hire them one by one. None would agree to work in a crew of strangers. The proper procedure was to hire a foreman and let him hire the crew.

One incident from the Saturday-night poker games—still vivid in my memory (and useful whenever I am pressed to tell a funny story)—underlined this unity forcefully. The three engineers, the miner foreman, and I played poker each Saturday night, with an agreement that we stop at ten o'clock so that we could work the next day, Sunday. None of the miners would play, although we invited them. They all sat behind the foreman's chair to give him support against the outsiders.

At the stopping time there was usually a round of stories, none of them very clean. This night the foreman told a particularly dirty story, then he told a second story that I still remember:

> A farmer walking along the road carrying a broken rake met a neighbor.
> Neighbor: Who broke your rake?
> Farmer: The hired man.
> Neighbor: Is that the same hired man that got your daughter pregnant?
> Farmer: Yep.
> Neighbor: Awkward, ain't he!

Possibly because we were all tired or possibly because the story was so much milder than the foreman's other bawdy stories, none of the four of us laughed at the joke. After a long moment of silence the foreman slammed his hand on the table and said, "Write out my check!" None of us thought he was serious at first, but then we attempted to dissuade him, with no success. Writing the check took a while because the time records had to be checked, and we did not hurry, thinking he would cool down. After the foreman received his check, each of the miners came up one by one and said, "Write out my check."

They had come in what had once been a small school bus. When they loaded and tried to leave, the bus would not start. They worked on it for about an hour without success; then one of the engineers who was a good mechanic fixed the problem, thinking this evidence that we were good guys would persuade them to stay. It did not, and at about two in the morning they rattled down the canyon and out of our lives.

In the morning we were faced with no miners, our option getting closer to expiration, and the embarrassing job of reporting to headquarters that the job was shut down because we all had odd senses of humor. Luckily, in a week we were able to find a new foreman who brought a new crew and continued the work. Yet in the end all of the effort was wasted, because when the option expired, we had found nothing to indicate there was a major body of ore there.

Going back to Freeport, Texas, and the routine work of mining sulfur was bearable only because I had good bosses who did their best to find me interesting assignments. One of these bosses was Walter "Doc" Grey, the senior technical person in the New York headquarters. I remember Doc fondly. Whenever I took a business trip with him, we spent our spare time in museums and our evenings at the opera, symphony, or ballet. My companions on other business trips always found the loudest nightclubs.

MERCK AND COMPANY

After spending much of the previous two years in the western mountains of the United States and in a remote part of Cuba, the prospect of living near New York encouraged me to listen to the director of engineering at Merck and Company, whom I sat next to at lunch at an American Institute of Chemical Engineers meeting in New Orleans in early 1941. He offered me a job in New Jersey. Merck was a family-owned company before World War I, with branches of both the company and the family in the United States and Germany. During the war the company was divided. By 1941 the U.S. branch had become a large public company; though its chairman was George Merck, he was the last of the family to be involved in the business.

Merck was the leader in this country in developing sulfa drugs and synthetic vitamins. The war in Europe had created a big demand for sulfa drugs, and the Food and Drug Administration had recently approved the fortification of flour and bread with vitamins, creating a big demand for synthetic vitamins. Merck needed engineers to design and build plants in which to make these products. The opportunity to do so much engineering was attractive, and I moved to New Jersey.

At Merck I found a congenial atmosphere with supportive bosses and competent associates. I was part of a small group responsible for designing and building these plants. In a year or so I did more chemical engineering than many of my peers do in a lifetime. My last job was to design an extraction column for the recovery of penicillin from the small amounts being grown in laboratory flasks. It was the first step in taking the production of penicillin—recently discovered by Sir Alexander Fleming in England—from the laboratory to full-scale manufacture. Dr. Norman Heatley, one of Fleming's associates, had come from England to start the commercial development of penicillin at Merck. He was a quiet, shy bachelor who lived in the same apartment house where I did, and we became good friends. At this point Merck was growing penicillin in big glass flasks and extracting it in laboratory equipment. As the number of flasks and the amount to be extracted grew, the process required a larger piece of extraction equipment, which I built for them. It consisted of a four-inch piece of Pyrex glass pipe packed with ceramic packing. From this they were able to produce about a dose of penicillin an hour.

If not for World War II, I would now be a retired vice president of engineering at Merck.

CHAPTER FOUR

IN
THE ARMY

FROM ENGINEER TO MANAGER

IRISHMEN ARE REPUTED TO HAVE hangovers after St. Patrick's Day. I had one on St. Patrick's Day in 1942—the second one in my life. The first was during my freshman year in college, when I deliberately got drunk one night at a stag party in the woods simply to see what it was like to drink too much. Being in possession of all of my physical but none of my mental faculties was so frightening that I was determined never to do it again—and never did. The second hangover was an accident. My colleagues in the Merck engineering department threw a party to bid me farewell on my journey from Merck to the army.

I was one of the few people in the Merck group to go into military service; the others were needed much more in their professional capacities. Because I was the only one likely to enter the service, my associates were very enthusiastic in their send-off. Obviously, I cooperated, because someone had to take me home, and I woke up the next morning with a terrible headache.

I had attended a university with an ROTC program and had a reserve commission. I had been interested in military affairs, and in school I did well in military tactics. On tactical exercises my units always distinguished themselves as the best. Since graduation I had attended two two-week reserve officers' summer camps, one in Fort Benning, Georgia, where I came away with a high regard for the

Infantry School. It is one of the best teaching institutions in the world. Part of its job is to train infantry platoon leaders who only need to learn one command—"follow me!"—borrowed from the French infantry's "suivez moi!"

By this time I had been promoted in the reserve to captain. Although Merck could have kept me out of the army, I wanted to get in. The war was the biggest thing likely to happen during my lifetime, and I did not want to miss it. My orders to report were delayed several times by Merck until I finished a few jobs that were in progress.

My first days in the army were a letdown. At a post near Baltimore I was part of a pool of fifty or sixty officers, all engineers. We were assembled there so that other officers from various army sections could interview us to see if we were suitable for their particular jobs. The interviewers were other engineers who were in charge of manufacturing operations such as munitions plants; they were looking for design engineers and manufacturing supervisors. Most of the interviewers seemed less competent than I was and certainly less competent than the people I worked with at Merck. For this reason and partly because I wanted to join the "real" army, I made myself as unattractive as possible. Because many other officers wanted these assignments, I had no trouble avoiding being taken.

The job interviews did not take all our time. We trained a great deal on the rifle and pistol range and listened to lectures on military subjects. I remember one particular lecture by a young, unimposing-looking, regular-army captain. He talked about leadership, but not about the cheerleader kind of leadership. He talked about the importance of integrity, fairness, and clarity of purpose and the ability to instill confidence in others. For the first time I realized that leadership skills might be learned rather than innate.

I received orders to report to the port of debarkation in New Orleans. My final destination was supposed to be secret, but in typical army fashion the orders listed among those slated to get copies the commanding general of the Panama Canal Zone. It did not take a lot of imagination to guess where I was headed.

I had enough time to drive to New Orleans. My brother Frank had just finished medical school, had become a navy doctor, and was stationed in New Orleans. By chance, my father was also there when I arrived, having a hernia operation in the Ochsner Clinic. I had to stay in New Orleans two or three days, which allowed me to see both of them.

Shortly thereafter I boarded a Grace Line ship with a name that started with *Santa* (the same type as the one I had taken to Cuba almost four years before). It had been a combined passenger and cargo ship, sailing from New Orleans through the Panama Canal and down the west coast of South America. At this point it was a troop ship, but the only military people on board were either regular-army personnel stationed in Panama who had been on leave in the States, or army wives returning to Panama after trips to the States. It was the only military ship I sailed on during the war that was comfortable and uncrowded. Aside from the fact that everybody on board was in uniform, a cruise ship atmosphere prevailed, although this was somewhat moderated by reports of ships that had been sunk at the mouth of the Mississippi River and of German submarines operating in the Caribbean. The trip to Panama was uneventful, however, except that I met a number of army nurses.

PANAMA

My arrival was more auspicious than I had expected. I was met by a full colonel, brought off the ship ahead of everyone else, and taken to the headquarters at Quarry Heights, where I was given orders to return to the States immediately and report to the Corps of Engineers in Washington. Evidently, someone at the officers' pool where I had been interviewed had changed his mind and wanted me assigned to his unit. This meant that I would go back and be an engineer for the rest of the war and not a soldier. I was unhappy about it.

In the headquarters was a group of three or four sergeants whose job it was to get me back to the States as quickly as possible. This task was not simple because there was no regular passenger service. Arrangements had to be made for me to take the next available Air Force flight back through Central America. Meanwhile, one sergeant, who was on the fringe of things and who recognized that I was unhappy about the prospect of returning, pointed out to his associates a recent order stating that the headquarters that issued the orders sending me back to the States did not have authority to order people out of the combat zone. Then he found another army order that defined the Canal Zone as a combat zone, although no shot had been fired in anger there since the early 1900s; therefore my orders were invalid. A sergeant typed an endorsement to my orders saying that because of army regulation XYZ and because the area was a combat zone, they were unable to comply with the orders to send me back. One sergeant had the colonel sign the letter, and I breathed a great sigh of relief.

From there I went to an officers' pool, an old post called Corozal, where I found that my immediate job was to get tailor-made khakis. No officer was considered respectable in Panama wearing GI khakis. Some of my Panamanian khakis lasted through the war and long after.

While I was in the officers' pool awaiting assignment, I stopped by headquarters each day to see my friends the sergeants, so that they could tell me what assignments were likely to come up. I pointed out the ones I did not want, mostly supply jobs of one kind or another. Then I was told of an assignment that nobody else wanted, and the sergeant was sure that I would not want it either. The job was commanding an old, regular-army, heavy-mortar company. He was surprised when I told him that was exactly what I wanted, and within a day orders were issued making me commanding officer of First Separate Heavy Mortar Company.

This company was a relic of World War I. Many of the men were on their fourth or fifth enlistment; the youngest were on their second. It had been a mule-pack outfit, but they were in the process of losing their mules and getting jeeps. The mules were being shipped to a mountain division that was being formed in Colorado. Part of my job would be to train these ex-mule skinners to drive and maintain jeeps. I arrived at the new company, met my predecessor (who was promoted to major), and was assigned to the headquarters. My predecessor was a West Pointer and regular army, and he was helpful when I had problems with the headquarters.

This was the first time I had ever been responsible for directing the efforts of more than one or two people. In short, it was my first job as a manager. My own life and the lives of several hundred men depended on how well I learned this new skill. I had to be not only competent in my new job but also able to give my men confidence in my ability. Their effectiveness would diminish if they were concerned that their commander might screw up and get them killed.

I read every army manual that pertained to my job. Before we went into the jungle, I studied the map of the area until I knew every feature of the terrain. I could not come to a fork in the road or trail and show any sign of uncertainty. The two lieutenants assigned to the company were greener than I was and of no help. The noncommissioned officers were all old-timers and very competent in peacetime army activities.

I soon found that underneath this veneer of competence the men did not have the basic skills to fight effectively. They had been in Panama for years, surrounded by jungle. They were likely at any time to be sent to the jungles of the South Pacific. But they had no experience operating in the jungle. Their training had been in eastern Panama, terrain more like southwest Texas. In addition, their ability to do their primary job of supporting the infantry with mortar fire was barely passable.

Our basic weapon was the 4.2-inch mortar. The infantry had smaller 60- and 85-millimeter mortars that were smooth bore and relatively inaccurate. Our mortar was originally developed by the Chemical Warfare Service to fire white phosphorus and chemical-agent shells, but it had been converted into an effective weapon for the close support of infantry. It fired a 44-pound projectile with a maximum range of 2.5 miles and the accuracy of a 105-millimeter howitzer. It could fire twelve rounds a minute, which meant that a four-gun battery could drop a ton of explosives a minute in a given area.

The infantry mortar is a smooth-bore tube with the bottom end resting on a base plate and the tube held at an angle of more than forty-five degrees to the horizontal by an adjustable support at the top. The range is changed by adjusting the angle of elevation. Small changes in direction can be made in the adjustable support. Major changes require shifting the base plate and support. In all mortars the shell is dropped down the tube and hits a firing pin at the bottom, which ignites the propellant, and then the shell is launched in its trajectory.

The 4.2-inch mortar differs from smooth-bore mortars in that it is rifled. This is accomplished by a copper ring in the base of the shell held between two steel plates. When the propellant goes off, the steel plates squeeze the copper ring and expand it to engage the rifling in the tube, which creates a tight seal between the shell and the barrel and makes the propellant more efficient. The rifles impart a rotational motion to the shell that stabilizes it in flight for greater accuracy.

I found that the tactics for using the 4.2-inch mortar were the same as for the infantry mortar and did not take advantage of its great accuracy and range. I borrowed a field artillery manual and adapted artillery techniques to the mortar. This process required map reading and simple plane geometry, skills that taxed my regular-army soldiers. A few months after my arrival we were assigned our first draftees. They were young, eager, and bright. They learned quickly. The burden of operating the new fire-control system fell to them.

My career as a commander might have been aborted at the start but for luck. The first sergeant, Sergeant Heywood, was on his eighth three-year enlistment. All his service had been in this unit; he was proud of it and determined that no civilian would come in and mess it up. He took me under his wing and made a good officer of me without letting the soldiers see what he was doing. He and the other senior sergeants seemed to enter a quiet conspiracy to teach me my job.

There was a moment during the first day when my ability to command this unit, and very likely my military career, hung in the balance. I was outside the barracks, separated from the first sergeant, when a soldier walked by me and failed to salute. I turned around and could see a smirk on his face, almost as if he were saying, "I tested the guy, and he isn't tough." I knew that something had to be done, and it had to be the right thing. I was very much interested in the job of being an officer, and I wanted to be a good one, but I had no concern about the formalities of military life. Saluting seemed to me a minor matter, an exchange of greetings between military people, not material for a federal case. However, this incident was obviously not an oversight but a test of the new commanding officer.

Without the temperament or the experience to do a good job of chewing the man out, I instinctively did the right thing. I called the first sergeant and gently chided him for the state of the military courtesy of his unit. He was very proud of having a well-disciplined, highly trained outfit, and suggesting that he was running something less than a first-rate operation was all I needed to do. He found the offender and gave him more hell than I could ever have done; from then on I had no further problems with any of the men. I realized that I did not need to be good at all parts of my job. I only needed to be able to find people who could do well the things I could not.

We were part of the Panama Mobile Force, which consisted of an infantry regiment, an artillery battalion, and auxiliary troops like us, who were to be available to face any invaders of the Canal Zone. By this time it was evident that the navy was able to keep the Japanese fleet away from the canal, and we were in no great danger. Our most exciting time was when we made plans to land on Guadeloupe and Martinique. Two French warships had escaped from France to these islands. Concern that the Vichy government would turn these ships over to the Germans precipitated plans for a combined army–navy operation to capture the ships. Our main interest, however, was in the thousands of beautiful French girls we expected to be waiting to be liberated. This great operation was aborted by some diplomat who negotiated an arrangement with the French to immobilize the ships so they would not be of use to the Germans.

We were beginning to hear stories about fighting in the jungles of the South Pacific, where our fate was likely to be. So we started jungle training. I began taking my company into the jungle to gain experience operating there and found that our army was badly equipped for this environment. We had leather shoes that were completely unsuitable for the marshes we encountered. We slept in pup tents on the ground where crawling things were more dangerous than any enemy. The pup tents were designed years ago, when soldiers were smaller; now the average man's head or feet protruded. The GI mosquito netting was ineffective. The rations we had were completely unsuitable for field operations. The army had been on the edge of the jungle all this time, yet had done little to prepare for forays into it. We were equipped to fight in the hills of the southern United States and nowhere else.

About this time I heard that two geologists, reserve officers who had experience prospecting in the jungle, had started a program to develop suitable jungle equipment. I do not know who in the military hierarchy was astute enough to encourage them, but someone was. These two were responsible for developing hammocks, canvas boots, and mosquito netting for use in the field as well as several other things that made operation in the jungle much more effective. Part of our job was to go through a newly established jungle-training school—first to be trained, and second to train others how to use heavy weapons in this type of environment.

I was also given a second job—designing and installing a smoke screen around the Pacific locks of the Panama Canal. The first installation consisted of a number of smudge pots, the kind used to heat orchards. They were placed around the locks, and the soldiers manning antiaircraft batteries in those locations were responsible for maintaining and lighting them. My job was to decide where to place the pots and to outline the program for lighting and keeping them maintained.

In 1942 the Canal Zone was one of the vestiges of the U.S. colonial era. In the late 1800s Ferdinand de Lesseps, the French engineer who built the Suez Canal, tried to build a canal in the same area as the present Panama Canal. He was defeated by yellow fever and malaria. These diseases were subsequently brought under control by controlling the population of mosquitoes that transmitted them.

Then President Teddy Roosevelt decided to build an American canal where the French had failed. There was a small problem. The territory that is now Panama was then part of Colombia, and the Colombians did not want Teddy's canal, at least not at the price he was offering. Roosevelt solved this problem by promoting a revolution that resulted in what is now Panama seceding from Colombia and becoming the Republic of Panama. In addition to permission to build the canal, the United States retained a strip of land five miles wide on each side of the canal. The sovereign republic of Panama was divided by a ten-mile-wide strip over which it had no control.

The canal is on the narrowest part of the isthmus that connects North and South America, but from an engineering point of view it is not located in the best place. A canal could have been built at sea level through Nicaragua. However, the Nicaraguans were more difficult to deal with than President Roosevelt's sponsored revolutionaries in Panama, so he chose the Panama route.

This route lay over high ground, and excavating down to sea level would have been a formidable task. Instead, the engineers of the time chose to build a canal eighty-five feet above sea level with locks at each end through which ships could be raised and lowered. The smoke screen I helped establish around the canal was partly to prevent damage to the locks, but, more important, to prevent the body of water held eighty-five feet above sea level from draining out. Refilling the canal would have taken three years. At some point we realized that the most critical place in the canal system was Madden Dam, where the surplus water from the canal overflowed. We installed a smoke screen around it as well.

The management of the canal and the civil administration of the Canal Zone were under the governor, who was a senior officer of the Army Corps of Engineers. The operation was managed by a group of U.S. citizens, many of whom had been born in the Zone. The workers were all Panamanians, but no Panamanians were in the upper levels of supervision. The Panamanians prized jobs on the canal, partly for the higher pay but more for the privilege of using the commissary, which included large general stores operated by the canal administration that sold at prices well below the average. There was segregation, but the terms "gold" and "silver" were used instead of white and black. This terminology came into use at a time when the white supervisors were paid in gold coins and the Panamanian laborers paid in silver. There was no outward evidence that the Panamanians resented us. This three-hundred-pound gorilla, the United States, had been with them so long they appeared to accept whatever it chose to do.

My two jobs kept me busy most of the time, but the atmosphere of the Canal Zone had become relaxed. We worked hard during the week but were careful not to be too tired for the weekend, the highlight of which was a dance at the Fort Clayton Officers Club. There were, considering the time and circumstances, many women around: attractive Panamanians, nurses from Gorgas Hospital and the other army installations, and a few American civilian women who were working in the Canal Zone. I spent some time with a nurse at Gorgas, but no great romance developed.

Being the commander of 150 men who had been living in Panama from three to twenty years led to experiences very different from those I had had as a chemical engineer. Within a day or two of my assignment as commander I had a telephone call from an assistant provost marshal who told me it was customary for all new commanders to be taken on a special patrol (he gave it a designation that I cannot in good taste use here). We spent from 10:00 P.M. until 2:00

A.M. touring the dives of Panama so that I could see how my men spent their recreational hours. These establishments ranged from rather nice beer gardens to places I never would have entered without an armed guard such as the one I had.

One good result of this special patrol was that I developed excellent contacts with the military police (MP). This relationship was helpful when—as happened at least once or twice a month thereafter—I would get a call from someone in the MP office telling me that one of my men was either in or very likely to get in trouble, and I should send someone down to pick him up, which I always did. The MPs had a very relaxed attitude. If someone would take the offender off their hands and keep him quiet, they would not prefer charges except in completely outrageous cases. Their attitude of being guardians of the men was much more constructive than the policeman approach of the MPs in the States.

Another of my duties was to censor the mail sent home by my men. The first time I did it, I felt self-conscious about intruding into the privacy of these people. However, after I had done it for a short time, it became the most interesting part of my day. Reading these letters was like watching half a television soap opera. I could follow one side of the romances, financial problems, and family problems of a group of men—it was *As the World Turns* every day.

Although at the time I was only thirty and single, I had to listen to the family problems of my men. I remember one man coming to me with a letter from his wife that said, "Dear Leon, I have gone to Norfolk with the Garret Snuff salesman. You can stop my allotment." I thought his problem was his wife's behavior with the Garret Snuff salesman, but he regarded that a minor matter. His real concern was how to stop his allotment to her. After a great deal of study of army regulations we found that there was no way to stop it as long as she was his wife. So poor Leon had to continue to support his wife with the Garret Snuff salesman in Norfolk. It was my first failure as a marital counselor.

From time to time officers who had been with the British in the

retreat down the Malaysian peninsula or who had been on New
Guinea or Guadalcanal would be sent to Panama to add their experience to our training. We were obviously ill-equipped and poorly
trained for jungle warfare and increased our training time.

The threat from the Japanese navy diminished after the battle of
Midway. Once German submarines were run out of the Caribbean,
the canal was in no great danger. In keeping with this relaxed spirit I
bought a car and joined a local golf club. The knowledge that we
might leave Panama any time for more active areas kept us on a hard
training schedule, but not one that interfered with my Sunday golf
game.

The end to this tropical interlude came in March 1943. On short
notice we were ordered to Camp Rucker, Alabama; the company was
to be used as a cadre for two new battalions. We—about 150 men
and three officers including me—loaded on a troop ship en route
from the South Pacific through the canal to the East Coast.

A few weeks before we sailed, the first sergeant—who had been
my mentor and had helped me become a good officer—and I shared
a difficult experience. He contracted an obscure disease. A few days
later a letter came from headquarters pointing out that this particular disease was classified as a venereal disease and that under army
regulations no one with a venereal disease could be a noncommissioned officer (NCO). There were no loopholes. After trying unsuccessfully to get the doctors to change their diagnosis, I had to take
away the sergeant's stripes that he had spent twenty-five years earning. I consoled myself with the thought that he was a good man and
would soon get his stripes back. However, by the end of the war he
was only back to a "buck" sergeant, two levels below his former rank.
The sergeant's spirit had been diminished, and competition for promotions from the bright young men coming from civilian life was
tough. We left Panama with a new first sergeant. He was competent,
but the roles were reversed. I was teaching him his new job instead
of being the trainee.

On the troop ship we got our first taste of the war, and many of us

Gordon Cain in uniform, March 1944—his "first job as a manager."

never fully recovered from the experience. On board were the remnants of the troops that had retaken New Guinea. They were from a midwestern National Guard unit that had been called into service before the attack on Pearl Harbor and sent to Australia soon after the war started. They started the ground offensive in New Guinea that finally ended on Okinawa. We did not have air superiority over New Guinea, so our troops were subject to repeated air attacks. There was no front line in the usual sense. They had to find and destroy enemy strong points one by one. After they had cleared the south side of the island, they fought their way across a ten-thousand-foot mountain pass to the north side and cleared that. They were constantly under threat from ambush and air attack. Malaria, dysentery, and a fungus infection of the feet and groin that we called "jungle rot" were part of everyday life. Their clothes, shoes, and sleeping gear were unsuitable for the tropical jungle. They ate whatever their mess sergeants could concoct from the limited supplies. Never in my subsequent military experience did I meet survivors of as severe an ordeal as these men had, except the survivors of the Bataan march.

Of the original unit the able-bodied men were given rest and relaxation in Australia and were already back in action. The severely wounded were in hospitals in Australia or the States. The group on the troop ship was in between. About two thirds of the three hundred were ambulatory but had physical injuries that made them unfit for further service. They were going back to be discharged. The remaining hundred or more men were suffering from what in World War I was called "shell shock," now known as "combat fatigue." These men showed no outward symptoms except apathy and withdrawal. From a number of attempts to talk to these men, I concluded that they were not suffering from the memory of a single horrible experience. Rather they were suffering from the effects of being wet, dirty, and bug-bitten while having their lives at risk for long periods, and they were also trying to live with the knowledge that they had somehow failed their comrades. About fifteen were completely out of touch with reality. When they were on deck in the daytime, they had to be accompanied by two men for fear they would jump overboard. At night they were confined in bunks with heavy wire mesh across the side to keep them in. These men were outwardly stronger than I but had been pushed beyond the breaking point. It was hard not to speculate about what it would take to make the same thing happen to me.

Other units, a total of about five hundred men, were being returned to the States. Before we left port, we had developed a plan that assigned from one to four of our men to look after each of the combat-fatigue victims if we ran into a German submarine. I had regular nightmares about our being hit by a torpedo and trying to get the men out of the caged bunks into a lifeboat.

THE ARMY IN THE STATES

We had an uneventful trip to Staten Island, where we were loaded on day coaches and transported to Alabama. Since our troop movement was not a priority, we wandered around the East Coast for three days before we landed at Camp Sibert in Anniston, Alabama. Spending three nights on a day coach was uncomfortable, but the big problem was keeping everyone on board as we passed through or near some of the men's hometowns. We lost only one man, who got off the train in Philadelphia to make a telephone call and showed up two weeks later. We were to be at Sibert for a few weeks while our barracks were being completed at Camp Rucker, about 150 miles away. Everyone went on leave except me.

My nominal commander at Sibert was a full colonel who was in charge of many units like mine. He joined the army in World War I too late to see action. He had been active in the National Guard since and had become a full colonel. Some higher authority had decided wisely that he should not command troops in combat but would be useful in a housekeeping job. In the course of my time in the army in the States, I met other officers like the colonel.

Possibly because of frustration, but more likely because of natural inclination, the colonel was more interested in form than substance.

He spent his day conducting inspections with a focus on the irrelevant. He dropped thousands of coins on cots to see if the sheets were taut. Finding a tie tucked between the wrong shirt buttons could make his day. The colonel decided that as a potential commander of a larger unit I lacked the proper skills as an inspector and kept me there to teach me. For two weeks I followed him on his rounds.

The colonel was correct. I was not good as an inspector. My men in Panama may not have had high SAT scores, but they had great skill in dealing with the brass, especially inspectors from higher headquarters. We had many inspections, but the old pros of my unit always got top reports. No one ever found anything wrong in our kitchen, my supply sergeant was never short (he borrowed from a friend), and our company books always met the letter of the regulations. I did not know how to find things wrong in a mess hall because I had never seen anything wrong. My concern was how fast and accurately we could fire the mortars, how well and safely we could survive in the field, and how we could give the infantry the support they needed.

It was an irritating two weeks, but in time I was grateful to the colonel. Shortly, I would have mess sergeants who had a few weeks before been running greasy-spoon restaurants and supply sergeants who did not have friends from whom they could borrow. I soon learned that a little sloppiness in the kitchen can cause a lot of dysentery. In his fussy way the colonel made me a better officer.

An unexpected dividend of the stop at Sibert was seeing my brother Edward. He had been drafted, had gone to officer's training school, and was now a second lieutenant teaching marksmanship at Sibert. We were able to have dinner together a few times. He subsequently went overseas as an infantry platoon leader, fought, and was decorated in France and Germany. My brother Frank was a doctor in the navy beach battalion that supported the landing in southern France.

After two weeks the men returned from leave, and we went to Camp Rucker. There the First Separate Heavy Mortar Company was disbanded, and thus ended the first phase of my military career.

I had gained the respect and confidence of these professional soldiers. With this experience came the confidence that I could do the next task of converting a thousand men straight from civilian life into an effective combat unit.

CAMP RUCKER

Camp Rucker was one of the many camps established by the army to train troops for World War II. In April 1943 when we arrived, it was a year old, but parts were still unfinished, giving it the air of a temporary camp rather than a permanent post. It was in southeastern Alabama near the town of Enterprise, which along with the surrounding towns bore very well the burden of the thousands of troops that had been set in their midst. With the help of the local people, the few married officers and NCOs who brought their wives somehow found places for them to stay nearby. Among the unsung heroines of the war were the wives who lived outside the camps in one-room apartments, sharing baths and kitchens with other wives.

The low, rolling countryside with its sandy hills had been farmed, but it was poor farmland, and the owners must have been glad to sell to the army. The land that was unusable for farming had been used to grow pulpwood. It had a cover of scrub pine and oaks about head high with scattered large pine trees and a few small streams.

The 150 men who left Panama with me numbered only 120 when we arrived at Rucker. Some had gone to various special army schools— auto mechanics, cooks, bakers, and so forth. We were split in two: One half was the cadre for the Eighty-seventh Heavy Mortar Battalion, and the other for the Eighty-eighth. I was assigned as executive officer, second in command, of the Eighty-eighth.

The sixty men we had should have been enough to start a battalion, except that more than half—all men with three or more years' service—had no skills nor the ability to develop any skills except those of a private soldier. We requisitioned officers and NCOs with the skills we needed. Over the summer they drifted in. Most of these men had spent a year in training assignments and were happy to join a unit. The specialists—mess sergeants, cooks, bakers, and mechanics—came from various army schools. Six recent graduates of Virginia Military Institute were assigned, all of whom became excellent officers.

By August we had formed the nucleus of a battalion and were prepared for the next job. The commanding officer, Colonel Lewis, was a West Pointer who had spent his eight years as an officer in staff jobs. He was not comfortable with this civilian army, where he was as likely to be slapped on the back as saluted. He left the direct supervision of the unit to me.

On Labor Day in 1943 I watched about a thousand draftees get off trains at Camp Rucker. In about six months we would be fighting somewhere. Their survival and mine depended on how well they were trained individually and as units. My job was to make this collection of individuals into an effective unit and to bring back whole as many as possible. I was determined that none of these men would die because they were poorly trained.

Waterloo may have been won on the playing fields of Eton, but World War II was won in the training camps and factories in this country. There was no place in this kind of job for someone interested only in the big picture. Success comes from endless attention to detail. Weapons, vehicles, and equipment must always be in working order. Men must be in top physical condition. Kitchens must always be sanitary. Officers and NCOs must have the toughness to make these things happen even when everyone is dead tired. I did not know at the time that some of this training would make the difference between my being a survivor or not. Somehow we were able to maintain an intensity of purpose, and before the end of 1943 we had an effective, well-trained unit.

There are two parts to such a training job. One is to teach all the necessary skills such as marksmanship, vehicle maintenance, map reading, and many others. The other is to give the men the physical and mental toughness to carry out these tasks when they are tired, hungry, too hot, or too cold. This can be done only by putting the men through long, hard field exercises. In addition to their training value these exercises also serve to eliminate officers and NCOs who cannot function under pressure. We also had the equally time-consuming and much less rewarding job of dealing with the army and its bureaucracy. Part of the job, the many inspections, was necessary to ensure that we were competent.

Somehow I was assigned as president of the special court-martial for the entire camp. In the army system there were three levels of courts-martial: summary, special, and general. A summary court consists of one officer who can assess sentences of up to one month, a special court consists of five to seven officers who can assess sentences of up to six months, and a general court tries major cases.

Our cases fell into two categories: AWOL cases, where the man was gone a week or more, and incidents involving soldiers and the camp followers who were outside all military posts. The latter sometimes came down from headquarters with a note from the post commander telling me what punishment we should assess. The post commander, a colonel, was typical of many such old reserve or National Guard officers—not bad enough to kick out and not good enough to command troops. There were many like him in these housekeeping jobs. I threw his notes away without telling the other officers on the court about them. When my promotion to major came through six months later than it should have, I learned that the colonel had held it up because of my failure to follow his instructions on the court.

The cases that delayed my promotion involved crimes such as a soldier beating up a card dealer or tearing up a pornography studio. There was no doubt about guilt but a lot of uncertainty about what provoked the act. As long as a generous settlement of damages was made, I saw no point in locking a soldier up for six months when he could be training for his real job.

Social life at Camp Rucker was limited. The few local women and secretaries at the headquarters were outnumbered by the thousands of men on the post. Saturday-night dances at the Officers Club usually saw a ratio of at least five stags for each woman. The few dates I had were all with women who were engaged to someone who had been at Rucker earlier and had gone overseas.

Shortly after Christmas I went into the hospital with pneumonia. When I got out, we went on maneuvers in Tennessee. These maneuvers were the final training exercise before going overseas. The winter was exceptionally cold that year, with temperatures below freezing most of the time. We learned how to survive in the field in the cold, a skill of no great value when we went to the South Pacific a few months later.

One thing we did learn on maneuvers was how to move the entire unit. We had 160 vehicles, a mixture of jeeps and two-and-a-half-ton trucks. Stretched out along the road, they made a convoy five miles long. I had a recurrent nightmare that I was leading the convoy, made a wrong turn, and had to turn around. Dreams like that made map reading a required skill. Before maneuvers ended, we were ordered to San Francisco, our last stop in the States before being shipped to the Pacific.

We spent two weeks back at Rucker preparing to go overseas. Although the official task was to prepare our equipment, there was also a substantial amount of personal preparation. There were wills to be written, even though few had enough estate to cause concern. There was a strong need to have some tie to a woman back home, which may explain my infatuation with a girl in Nashville; it lasted until the first letter, which was written at about a fourth-grade level. There were at least a half dozen weddings among the forty officers of the battalion. On one Sunday I was a best man at noon and gave a bride away in the evening.

Luckily, I was assigned to go to San Francisco a few days ahead of the unit to make preparations for the move overseas. At this point we only knew that we were sailing from San Francisco. Our possible destinations were Hawaii, Australia, or one of the recently taken islands like New Guinea.

Wartime train travel for civilians must have been hell. They were given only the accommodations that the military did not need and frequently were bumped out of whatever space they had to make way for someone in uniform. The trip from Alabama to San Francisco took four full days, all in the same Pullman car with many of the same passengers for the entire trip. Long before the end of the trip we all knew each other. The passengers in our car played bridge, drank together, and exchanged paperback books and life stories.

Among them were two very attractive women, Betty and Frances. Betty was a buyer of women's clothes for a West Coast chain. Frances was an editor for a New York fashion magazine. They knew each other and were sharing the berth above mine. When I could not persuade either that she would be more comfortable in my lower berth with me, I gave them my berth and took theirs.

Men going overseas were either determined to marry and sire a child or, like me, did not want to chance leaving a widow and fatherless child but needed strongly to have a tie to a responsive woman. On the long train trip Betty, Frances, and I became good friends, and they became my girls back home. I wrote both of them regularly through the war, letters that became more romantic the longer I was away. Probably as a contribution to the war effort each responded with increasing warmth. Toward the end of the war I faced returning to two pen pals I hardly knew but with whom I had corresponded warmly for two years. Fortunately, they were separated by three thousand miles.

Just before my return after the war I received a letter from Betty's mother saying that her daughter had been killed in a traffic accident a few weeks before. I could only hope that I had written nothing in the letter from me she opened that would cause her any distress.

Frances and I saw each other frequently after my return to New York. A romance of sorts developed. It tapered off when she told me that I was too laid back to ever amount to much. She wanted someone more ambitious as a permanent part of her busy world.

On my arrival in San Francisco I was assigned to Fort Mason, which is on the bay overlooking Alcatraz, almost in downtown San Francisco. For the first two days I commuted by boat from Fort Mason to the port, where I made all the arrangements for the trip. Everyone in the port knew that our secret destination was Hawaii. There I learned that the unit had been delayed for ten days and that I had nothing to do but check in by telephone each morning.

My sister Pola lived in San Francisco at the time. At twenty she had married the boy next door, who had become a naval aviator. She finished her college studies while he was in training. He went overseas and was killed in the Battle of Midway. She then went to San Francisco to meet his ship and get his things, but she found a job and stayed for the rest of the war. Between her friends and other girls that I knew there, my social schedule was full.

Finally, word that the battalion would arrive the next day ended my fun, and I went back to work. We sailed on a ship so new that the paint was still wet in places. The crew was equally new. We had mildly rough sea outside San Francisco, and most of the ship's crew became seasick.

HAWAII

We arrived in Honolulu and were sent to a tent camp on the southwestern part of the island, just inland from a beautiful beach. There was no room for training. We were limited to classrooms, marching on the roads, and swimming. Honolulu was about thirty minutes away, but there was a curfew that required all military people to be out of the city by dark. The curfew meant that things that usually were covered by darkness now happened in broad daylight. One afternoon, driving on a Honolulu street, we passed a long line of military men outside a house. My driver told me that he had been in such a line a few days before. He gave me an account of a visit to a house of ill repute that was almost exactly the same as one in a paperback titled *The Revolt of Mamie Stover* that I read after the war.

Hawaii is a mixture of all the races and nationalities of the Pacific with little race consciousness. Except for the curfew, everyone moved with complete freedom. The people of Japanese origin were treated and behaved as everyone else. In contrast, all those of Japanese origin on the West Coast had their property seized and were put in an internment camp for the duration. Neither of the two great liberals, FDR or Earl Warren, then governor of California, ever explained why a few citizens of Japanese descent in California were such a grave danger that they had to be locked up, while the many more people of Japanese descent in Hawaii posed no problem. As far as I know, there was never a suggestion of disloyalty among these Hawaiians.

Although the attack on Pearl Harbor had occurred eighteen months before, it was still in everyone's consciousness. All who had been there could, and frequently did, tell you in detail exactly where they were and what they did that morning. The picture that comes through is one of complete surprise: mass confusion with little control and many individual acts of bravery. Recalling my time in Panama, I realized that the Japanese would have been equally successful had they attacked the Panama Canal or even San Francisco.

Race relations briefly appeared to enter into one incident that occurred during our stay in Hawaii. We were camped next to a black unit (the armed forces were still segregated then) that operated amphibious trucks. They were a confident, well-trained unit. We ran into each other several times subsequently, when they brought ammunition for us. Harmony between the two units was broken one night. I was awakened in the middle of the night by a report that a race war was about to erupt between the two. This was a surprise because there had been no sign of a problem until then. My officers and the black officers quickly got things under control.

The next morning an investigation determined that there was not a race problem, but a homosexual triangle. One of the black soldiers and one of my soldiers were fighting over the affections of another of my soldiers, a company clerk. Putting gays in the military may work in units where everyone has a separate sleeping facility, but in combat units in the field, where there is no privacy, it is an invitation to disaster.

The incident also illustrated a larger problem: that of getting rid of officers and enlisted men who were unsuitable for combat units. Solving that problem occupied a part of every commanding officer's time. It was not practical to let each commander reject anyone he regarded as unsuitable: There would not have been enough men to fight the war. How these problems were handled depended on each commander's ingenuity. There were frequent requests for men to go to special schools. Misfits were pushed into these special assignments until the army caught on and limited these assignments to men who had high fitness ratings. One solved this problem by giving the men one wanted to get rid of higher ratings than they deserved.

An imaginative medical officer could be a big help. Just before we sailed from San Francisco, our medical officer helped me by sending three or four unwanted men to the hospital with diagnoses that would require tests that would last until after we sailed. One of these was a soldier who had done a good job and, in fact, had become one of the first new men to be promoted. Just before sailing, he came to me and said that he was a homosexual and was afraid that he would get in trouble if he went overseas.

The army was never comfortable with homosexuals. Officially, homosexual acts were criminal offenses, but there were very few courts-martial. Most commanders did what I did with these men and other "undesirables"—pushed them out through the medical system. This was not completely satisfactory: For one thing, in some cases I had the feeling that I was easing out men who would have claimed to be anything, even lepers, to avoid going overseas.

Soon after our arrival in Hawaii, our commanding officer, Colonel Lewis, was transferred to General Buckner's staff, which allowed him to be promoted to full colonel, and I was made battalion commander. This promotion came just in time for me to preside over the temporary dismemberment of the unit. One company was detached and sent with the force landing on Saipan, while another was sent to Guam and another to Peleliu. The fourth company and part of the headquarters were assigned to the navy and given the job of installing mortars on LCIs (landing craft infantries) to be used to support landings.

I was transferred to Schofield Barracks and assigned to the headquarters of the Seventh Infantry Division, recently arrived from the Aleutians; they had retaken the islands Attu and Kiska, which the enemy had taken and occupied early in the war. The Seventh retook Attu in a short, bloody fight, much of it at close quarters. The Japanese abandoned Kiska after Attu fell.

They were among the few troops in Hawaii who had seen action, and they bore this distinction with pride and some arrogance. I was assigned to share quarters with three officers from the division staff, all lieutenant colonels. They were the division medical officer, the division supply officer (G-4), and the judge advocate (law officer). All were reserve or National Guard, and all were very good officers. I was the youngest and a mere major, so the household chores—for example, replenishing the liquor supply—fell to me.

I was assigned to the G-3 (operations) section, and as an extra hand and a new boy, I was given most of the odd jobs. As at Rucker I was appointed president of the general court-martial. My experience was completely different this time. General A. V. Arnold, the division commander, never tried to influence the court and never commented on any of our actions.

This was my first experience working with highly competent senior officers. Up to this point, I had been in charge of a small separate unit that was either part of a much larger unit commanded by a two- or three-star general who paid little attention to us or to me, or under a post commander of only minimum competence. Authoritarian organizations have a special problem. In carrying out a mission, obedience to the will of the commander is necessary for success, but a wise commander leaves his subordinates some leeway to exercise judgment if the situation takes an unexpected turn. Although subjugation to the commander's will is necessary in the execution phase, it is not necessary or even desirable in the planning phase. To reach

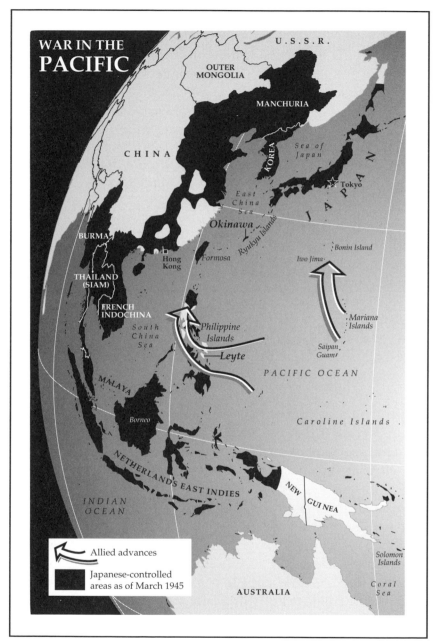

The Pacific theater in 1944–45.

the optimum plan, a commander can benefit from getting the unrestrained views of many subordinates with different skills. I had already learned in Panama that some semiliterate sergeants could teach me a lot. Of all the lessons I took from my military experience, this one is the most valuable.

In the course of my military career I worked closely with about a dozen generals with two or more stars. Few of these men had any capacity to elicit from their staffs completely frank views on any subject. Staff sessions were exercises in trying to anticipate what the commander wanted. General Arnold was one of the exceptions. He had a first-rate staff, and he was able to keep good people because he listened to and respected them.

Our immediate job was to make plans to land on a South Pacific island, the name of which I have long since forgotten. I do remember the thoroughness of the planning for the exercise. Everything was covered in detail, from the exact minute each wave of troops would hit the beach to the body bags for the fatalities. There was even a supply of condoms in case the inhabitants were friendly. We had loaded aboard ship when word came that our mission had been canceled and we were to be diverted to help General MacArthur return to the Philippines.

LEYTE

Our ship, the *Appalachian*, was an amphibious command ship that carried the admiral in charge of the ships carrying troops and supplies. General Arnold and his staff were also on board. It was much less crowded than the troop ships. I shared a cabin with one of the ship's officers, a merchant marine veteran. For a modest tuition he taught me to play cribbage and a navy game, acey-deucey. He also gave me a full appraisal of the merits of the women in the various ports he had visited in his civilian life.

The plans to attack the Philippines were delayed, so we steamed slowly around the South Pacific, stopping at various points. One was

Eniwetok in the Marshall Islands, which boasted the longest bar in the world. It was a stopping point for ships going to the South Pacific and a place for rest and relaxation for troops in the area. One day, while pushing my way through the crowd at the bar, I pushed into one of the mining engineers I had known in Cuba, now a naval officer on one of our escort destroyers. Eventually, our ship anchored in the harbor of Hollandia (now Djajapura), a port on the north coast of New Guinea. There I visited some of the country over which the combat-fatigued men I had seen on the ship from Panama had fought.

The most memorable part of the trip was crossing the equator. The ship's crew had made many crossings, and the long voyage gave them plenty of time to plan the initiation of the neophytes into Neptune's kingdom. They did a thorough, imaginative job. We were hosed with salt water, paddled with wet brooms, and forced to crawl through a canvas tunnel containing about a foot of water with floating garbage. Just when I decided that I had had enough of this foolishness, I saw the assistant division commander, a one-star general, getting the same treatment. The finale was to kneel before King Neptune, a sailor with a huge potbelly, who wore only shorts and a crown. Each neophyte was to kneel, rise and bow, and be touched on the shoulder with the king's scepter. As I bowed, someone pushed my face into the king's Vaseline-coated belly. So in wet underwear, with a sore behind and a face full of Vaseline, I became one of Neptune's subjects.

Among my companions on the trip were a marine officer with whom I had played in Baton Rouge when I was five and an army medical officer who had been sent from Washington to do autopsies on men from both sides who had been killed by flame throwers. Presumably if we understood how they worked, we could make them more efficient. We also had on board a team to establish a civilian government on the South Pacific island on which we were originally to land. The head of the team had no experience on this particular island and did not know the language or the people. His professional experience had all been as a school superintendent on the Philippine island of Leyte. Accidentally, the army got one assignment right.

The Leyte landing was uneventful. Under navy gunfire all the enemy troops except snipers had withdrawn from the beaches. The fighting started about half a mile inland. On the second day I went ashore with the forward part of the headquarters. There was no organized fighting on the beach, just a few snipers to keep everyone on edge. We had no time to build latrines. During the night a major on the staff, a man with whom I had become friends, went away from the camp to relieve himself. A nervous guard heard a noise in the dark and shot and killed the major. It could have been me.

On the fifth or sixth night, when we were about a mile inland, we received word that all navy ships had left the harbor, and soon we saw flashes of gunfire in the distance. Radio intercepts indicated that a naval battle was under way but gave no details. Later we learned about the battle of Leyte Gulf and realized that had we lost this battle, our units would have been stranded on an island with limited supplies and an equal number of well-supplied enemy troops.

Two weeks into the operation some general decided that we should make an amphibious landing on the west coast of the island. The plan required someone to take a patrol to that side of the island and reconnoiter the beaches. As the new man on the staff I got the job. I set out in a jeep with a driver and two war correspondents, Al from a Kansas City paper and Quigg from a wire service, who decided to come along. With us on a small truck were twelve men from the division reconnaissance platoon, who were all well trained for this kind of job.

We went south to an east–west road and then west to a bridge that had been destroyed by bombing. Our engineers were building a new bridge that was almost finished. They put temporary timbers over the unfinished part to get us across. Later I learned that some of these men, while working in the water, became infested with liver flukes, minute worms that penetrate the skin and follow the bloodstream to the liver, which they slowly destroy.

Up to this point we were in friendly territory. Now we faced fifteen miles through unknown country. Intelligence reports said that there were only 250 enemy troops on this part of the island. Usually

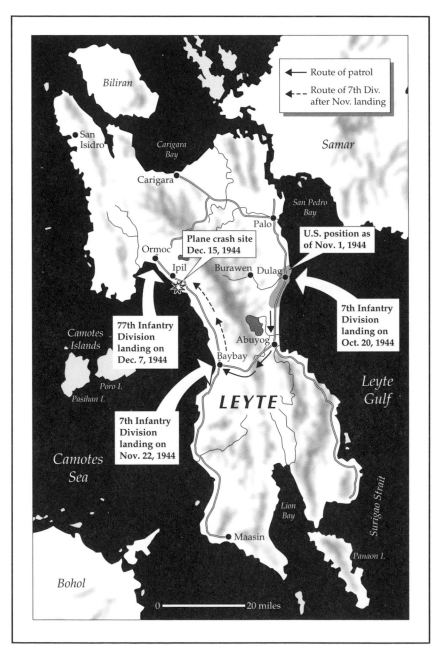

Locations of the Seventh Infantry Division and of Gordon Cain during the
invasion of Leyte in the Philippines.

they were in patrols of four or five men who roamed the country to keep the natives under control. The friendly Philippine guerrillas said that there were no patrols on our road, so we set out at full speed to get to our destination before word of our presence spread.

About halfway we started meeting large guerrilla groups, which gave us some comfort about our safety, but each chief insisted that we toast our alliance with a drink called "tuba," the fermented sap of the coconut palm. The taste was horrible, the odor worse.

We arrived in Baybay to be met by the mayor and a delegation of prominent citizens, who had arranged places for all of us to stay. That night the town had electricity for a few hours. They showed me a diesel generator operating on coconut oil. They were using the supply of coconut oil for the next week for this occasion.

In a few weeks the Seventh Division made an unopposed landing at Baybay and started north along the coast. They met serious opposition a mile out of town. Shortly afterward the Seventy-seventh Division made an opposed landing in Ormoc about thirty miles up the coast from Baybay. They were to drive over the north end of the mountains and join the Eleventh Airborne. The Seventh Division was to clear the west coast.

Because the two divisions were getting close enough together to affect each other, I was sent to the Seventy-seventh Division as a liaison officer. Ten miles of enemy territory lay between us, so I traveled in an artillery spotter plane, a military version of the Piper Cub that I had learned to fly before the war. On my return a few weeks later there was still a five-mile gap between the forces. I took another spotter plane. We were barely to our cruising altitude over the ocean when the engine stopped. We had two choices: Ditch in the water and hope that there was a boat on shore to pick us up, or try to make a dead-stick landing on the beach, not knowing whether it was friendly or enemy territory. We chose the latter. Parallel to the beach was a series of reefs exposed by the low tide. We did not quite clear the first one. The wheels hit the reef, and we made a perfect three-point landing—on two wheels and the nose of the plane. We were sitting in a plane with the nose down almost vertical in the water about four hundred yards off a beach, and we did not know if the land was occupied by friend or foe. It took a few minutes for the pilot and me to recover from the shock and climb out of the plane. As we did, we saw an amphibious truck coming out of the woods toward us. Our concern disappeared when we saw that it was driven by a smiling black soldier, the best-looking soldier I had ever seen.

As the newcomer to the G-3 section I frequently got the night shift. One of the night-shift jobs was to write a summary of what had happened during the day. At the same time I saw what each of my counterparts in the other three divisions had written. Then we saw General MacArthur's press releases, which bore little relation to the war we were seeing.

OKINAWA

Before the conquest of Leyte was completely over, the elements of my battalion started arriving from various parts of the Pacific, and I became a battalion commander again. After a short rest we started preparing to land on Okinawa. Four infantry divisions, two army and two marine, were to land abreast, drive across the island, and then turn south. One of my companies was in support of each division. The company commanders took their orders from the division. My job was to show the infantry officers how to use the mortars and to keep them supplied with ammunition. The last was a major job because the battalion could fire twelve tons of shells a minute.

On the fifth night after landing we came under fire by a single artillery piece that was firing about a shell a minute. I had a Brunton compass on the edge of my foxhole. I would line it up with the flash from the muzzle of the gun, clamp the needle and duck down in my foxhole, read the compass, and give the results to the corps artillery by radio. With a reading from another observer they could locate the gun by triangulation and take it out with 155-millimeter howitzers. I had about fifteen seconds between the time of the muzzle

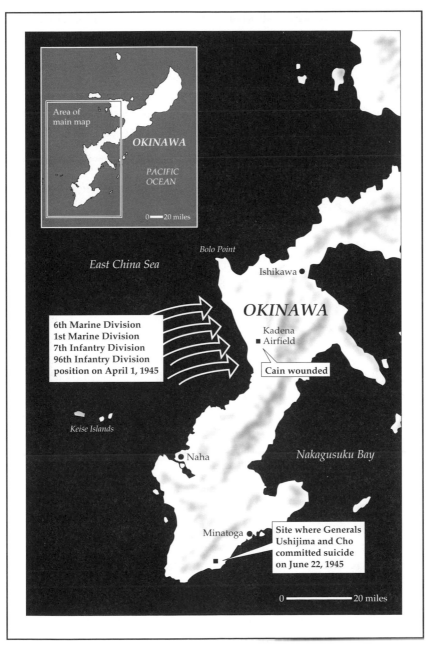

Placement of the U.S. Army divisions during the invasion of Okinawa.

flash and the time the shell hit to take this reading. On what turned out to be my last reading, I got my head down too slowly and a piece of shrapnel hit me over the left eye. This was the last round that was fired. Either the corps' artillery knocked the gun out or the crew decided to quit work for the night. After the initial shock I realized that I was not seriously wounded, and when the situation quieted down, one of my men led me to an army aid station nearby. There a doctor sewed up my wound by the light of a flashlight. He gave me a pocketful of aspirins, and I went on my way.

On Leyte there were periods when I was in danger of being killed, but there were days when I knew that I was relatively safe. From the time our ships came in range of the kamikaze bombers until the end of the Okinawa operation about three months later, the possibility of getting killed was a real and constant companion; even worse was getting only one bath during the whole time in Okinawa. I recalled my earlier discovery that the combat-fatigued soldiers I had met on the ship from Panama were not suffering from a single horrible experience but from the wear of rising each morning with the knowledge that this could be the day you earned a Purple Heart posthumously. I became convinced that fear has a significant physiological element, some gland that determines how we respond. Some mornings I would get up reluctantly and spend the day convinced that this would be my last day. Other mornings I would get up feeling bulletproof.

One day a sniper's bullet cut the inner seam of my pants. An inch to either side and it would have cut a femoral artery. Four inches higher and it would have destroyed my prospects for having children. Another time I was within fifty yards of and headed to talk to an officer commanding a battery of mortars when an artillery shell landed near him and riddled his chest with shrapnel. He was still alive when I got there. We put him on a stretcher and took him to a nearby aid station, where I learned firsthand about military triage.

At times the number of casualties coming into a military medical facility exceeds its capacity. Casualties are divided into three categories: those with minor wounds that can wait, those with serious but treatable wounds, and those with serious wounds that are either hopeless or will take time and facilities better spent on the second-category wounds. My lieutenant fell into the third class, and I held his hand while he died. In so doing, I left the medics with time to save several less severely wounded soldiers.

About halfway through the campaign we had just taken one of the major ridges on the island. Infantrymen were spread along the crest preparing for the push down the hill the next day. I was looking for a place for my forward observers, who would direct the mortar fire to support the infantry. The view from the ridge was partially blocked by a nose of land that stuck out about a hundred yards.

A rough pathway ran through a maze of boulders and scrub trees from the ridge to the point I wanted to reach. Logically, with a battalion of infantry looking down, there should be no enemy along the trail. Even so, I drew and cocked my .45 automatic and started. I had barely begun when about ten yards away on the trail an enemy soldier stood up with his rifle. A big shot of adrenaline must have gone through my body. As I watched his rifle move around to line up on me, I can remember thinking as I did on the pistol range, "Squeeze, don't jerk the trigger. You will get only one chance."

A few days later our headquarters, where I slept, was far enough behind the action that we gave up sleeping in foxholes and slept in slit trenches, grave-like holes about two feet deep. That night I was in a slit trench with the sergeant-major—the highest ranking NCO in the battalion—about twenty feet away, when an artillery shell hit nearby. After the shrapnel stopped falling, I called to ask how my neighbor was and heard only loud moans. Since I would not be able to sleep with this noise, I crawled out and found that the shell had landed about three feet from the sergeant's trench. The explosion had thrown dirt all over and wounded him. The best description of his wound was that he had had his butt shot off. We got him on a stretcher face down, into a truck, and back to a hospital and a trip home.

I was awarded a Bronze Star, the army's lowest medal, for this incident, and another one because my battalion had done well on the operation. These together with a Purple Heart for my head wound and campaign ribbons made an impressive display.

In the foxhole at night I pondered the question of why men participate in wars where nothing of theirs is being threatened. Certainly it is not for political slogans like "making the world safe for democracy." There are several reasons. One is to maintain one's self-esteem. Every man pictures himself a hero, a cowboy fighting Indians or a knight in shining armor rescuing maidens in distress. None of us wants to give up this picture of ourselves. Concern for the regard of our peers is another factor, as is unit esprit de corps. In World War II, however, the thing that drove all of us was a burning desire to get it over with so that we could return home.

We had our share of combat-fatigue cases like those on the troop ship from New Guinea. Only a few folded under pressure. They managed to perform during the operation, but as soon as it was over they went on sick report with vague problems. Word would come in a few days from a nearby hospital that they were being sent home with combat fatigue.

Finally, we took the end of the island and found the headquarters of the Japanese general in a cave overlooking a three-hundred-foot drop to the waves below. A ledge about thirty feet wide stood between the cave and the precipice. The previous night Lieutenant General Mitsuru Ushijima had knelt on the ledge and prayed, then had drawn his saber and tried to commit suicide by cutting open his stomach. He did not have the strength to do the job, so his chief of staff, Lieutenant General Isamu Cho, helped him. Cho then went through the same ritual, but he had to finish the job himself. The general's servants, as they had been instructed, pushed both bodies over the cliff into the ocean.

This story was told by one of the servants, part of an unusual group of prisoners, unusual in that they were some of the few prisoners we took and because they were not typical Japanese. The Japanese called

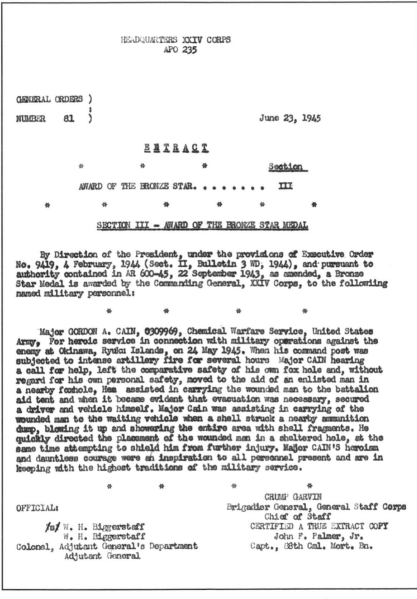

GENERAL ORDERS)
                 :
NUMBER   81   )   June 23, 1945

E X T R A C T

*   *   *   Section

AWARD OF THE BRONZE STAR.   III

*   *   *   *   *   *

SECTION III - AWARD OF THE BRONZE STAR MEDAL

By Direction of the President, under the provisions of Executive Order
No. 9419, 4 February, 1944 (Sect. II, Bulletin 3 WD, 1944), and pursuant to
authority contained in AR 600-45, 22 September 1943, as amended, a Bronze
Star Medal is awarded by the Commanding General, XXIV Corps, to the following
named military personnel:

*   *   *   *

Major GORDON A. CAIN, 0309969, Chemical Warfare Service, United States
Army, For heroic service in connection with military operations against the
enemy at Okinawa, Ryuku Islands, on 24 May 1945. When his command post was
subjected to intense artillery fire for several hours Major CAIN hearing
a call for help, left the comparative safety of his own fox hole and, without
regard for his own personal safety, moved to the aid of an enlisted man in
a nearby foxhole, Hea assisted in carrying the wounded man to the battalion
aid tent and when it became evident that evacuation was necessary, secured
a driver and vehicle himself. Major Cain was assisting in carrying of the
wounded man to the waiting vehicle when a shell struck a nearby ammunition
dump, blowing it up and showering the entire area with shell fragments. He
quickly directed the placement of the wounded man in a sheltered hole, at the
same time attempting to shield him from further injury. Major CAIN'S heroism
and dauntless courage were an inspiration to all personnel present and are in
keeping with the highest traditions of the military service.

*   *   *   *

OFFICIAL:

/s/ W. H. Biggerstaff
W. H. Biggerstaff
Colonel, Adjutant General's Department
Adjutant General

CRUMP GARVIN
Brigadier General, General Staff Corps
Chief of Staff
CERTIFIED A TRUE EXTRACT COPY
John F. Palmer, Jr.
Capt., 88th Cml. Mort. Bn.

*The citation awarding Gordon Cain the Bronze Star Medal for rescuing a
wounded sergeant on May 24, 1945.*

them "hairy" Ainus. Their place in Japanese society was about the same as the untouchables in India. These were not soldiers; they were servants and laborers in the headquarters and were not allowed to carry arms.

We landed with eight hundred men and forty officers. We suffered just under one hundred (12 percent) enlisted and twenty-four (60 percent) officer casualties. Two generals were killed, General Buckner who commanded the operation and General Easley who had been commandant of cadets at Texas A&M. Rank may have its privileges, but it also has some burdens. To fill the gap in the officer ranks, I promoted ten sergeants to second lieutenants and kept them in the battalion despite army regulations prohibiting this.

A day or two after taking the Ainus, I ran into a medical officer I had known in Panama who, feeling sorry for me, invited me to attend a party the next day at his hospital. There would be nurses and steaks. It was too good to be true, and it was not to be. When I returned to the battalion, I found everyone very busy. We had orders to load onto LSTs (landing ship-tanks) with our 160 vehicles and return to Leyte to prepare to land on Japan. We camped on Leyte within a few hundred yards of the spot we had left three months before.

We heard about the dropping of the atomic bomb without any appreciation of the damage it had caused. Shortly thereafter we loaded aboard ship to land on Kyushu, the southernmost of the three big islands of Japan. We expected to be met by a million men who would be fighting on and for their homeland. I did not look forward to this job: I had the feeling that I had used up all my luck on Okinawa.

The operation was delayed, and we were permitted to go back ashore. Our battalion radio operators regularly monitored all radio transmissions they could pick up. They provided a source of news from the outside world and also a source of dirty jokes that spread through the radio network as rapidly as the news. After the first feature of a double-feature movie—which I remember only because the finale was a scene of a well-built woman walking away from the cam-

The cave on Hill 89, Okinawa, where Lieutenant General Mitsuru Ushijima and his chief of staff, Lieutenant General Isamu Cho, committed suicide. From the National Archives and Records Administration.

era that made me think, "This is really what I am fighting for"—the radio operator handed me a bulletin he had picked up: "The Emperor of Japan has asked the King of Sweden to try to negotiate an armistice with the Allies."

I thought I knew enough about Japanese psychology to believe that this was the beginning of the end, but I could not be sure. I read the bulletin to the audience, emphasizing that this could be a false report to keep from arousing hope. There was no second feature. After a few minutes of speculation about the authenticity of the report, everyone, including the projector operator, wandered alone into the darkness. We each had to come to terms with what the end of the war meant to us and to think about those who did not survive and about their families. The question of why them instead of me kept creeping into my thoughts.

Soon thereafter the war was over. Many think that we should not have dropped the atomic bomb. None of these are from the group that was scheduled to land on Kyushu.

COMING HOME

Because all the available ships were needed to transport the occupation force to Japan, none of us could expect to get home for several months. To pass the time, we set up an educational program. We had enough talent to have classes in math at several different levels, English grammar and composition, business law, and other subjects.

In due time we returned to the States and to civilian life. If the war had no other effect, it cured me of any ambition to be an engineer. It also left me with great admiration for the organizational ability of the military. For an operation like the invasion of Okinawa, a quarter of a million men and all their equipment were assembled from various parts of the world. The men landed on the beach exactly on schedule, preceded by air strikes and naval gunfire. They were followed by all the support units necessary to supply, feed, cure, and if necessary, bury them. It was an impressive organizational feat. My admiration was tempered by the knowledge that this same army went into World War II with no satisfactory field rations and with uniforms suitable only for the southern part of the temperate zone— and had resisted the use of any infantry weapon except the old bolt-action Springfield rifle.

Change comes hard to big organizations. It is noteworthy that the solution to these problems came not from within the army but from outsiders. The rations problem was solved by Professor, later General, Georges Frederic Doriot of the Harvard Business School. He developed the "C" and "K" rations, prepackaged meals that a soldier could carry and prepare himself. These have now been replaced with something called meals ready to eat. As bad as our rations were, they were better than the alternative, which was no food. The jungle equipment problem was solved by two reserve officers who were geologists and who developed the hammocks to sleep in, rugged mosquito nets, and rubber-bottomed, canvas-topped boots. And the army was pushed to give up a 1903 model bolt-action rifle by a civilian employee of the Springfield Arsenal. As in many large organizations, the chiefs spent their time developing better solutions to yesterday's problems.

My military experience gave me an exaggerated idea of the effectiveness of authoritarian hierarchical organizations. At the same time I learned how much one can lose by inhibiting communication from one's associates. Eventually, I came to understand that military leadership involves different issues from those of management in civilian life. In the military you are getting people to do things they really do not want to do and might get killed doing. In the civilian setting you generally are asking people to do things that it is in their interest for them to do.

CHAPTER FIVE

POSTWAR

"HANG LOOSE AND
DON'T SWEAT THE SMALL STUFF"

O N MY RETURN FROM THE PACIFIC I started looking for a broader career than engineering, confident that the management skills that had been effective for me as an army officer would also work in business. This management philosophy meant having each person in the organization understand exactly what his or her job was and how it should be performed as well as the structure of the hierarchy surrounding each job. It took awhile for me to learn that although war and business may be equated rhetorically, they are very different in fact.

I went back to civilian life expecting to find a great demand for my newfound skill as a manager. No one seemed very interested. I was offered only two jobs. One offer was from Merck to return to my old job as an engineer at a salary only modestly above what it had been four years before. The other was to work for the Freeport Sulphur Company, for which I had worked in the 1930s. I chose the latter. At that point Freeport had a very profitable business mining and selling sulfur. They generated a large cash flow and wanted to put this money to work in other businesses. My job was to help them find and acquire these businesses, which turned out to be an interesting but unproductive assignment.

At that time Freeport's sulfur business was very profitable and had little competition. There were only two major producers, the other being Texas Gulf, and by-product sulfur was not yet a factor in the market. The other businesses I could find suffered in comparison to the sulfur business, so much so that Freeport could never decide to buy one of them.

GERMANY

For six months in 1946 Freeport lent me to the U.S. Department of Commerce to be part of a group studying German chemical development. Our mission was to find any German technology that might be useful to U.S. industry. The British had a comparable effort, and we worked with them. There was also a French effort, but they generally kept to themselves.

The people in the group were senior engineers and research scientists from manufacturing and engineering companies and an occasional academic. Our headquarters was in the Hoechst building in Griesheim, a town a few miles southwest of Frankfurt, near Darmstadt. When we were not traveling, we lived in Bad Homburg, a spa a few miles away. We wore officers uniforms with no insignia but a patch on the shoulder that said "Scientific Consultant." War correspondents wore the same uniform with a different shoulder patch. We traveled in army vehicles, sometimes with a driver, but often we drove ourselves. We ate in officers messes, and when we traveled, we stayed overnight in the bachelor officers quarters.

It was less than a year after the end of the war, and Germany was in terrible condition. Some streets in Frankfurt were still impassable because of the rubble from bombing. The only work for many people was clearing the debris, which they were doing very rapidly. Only a few factories were running, and there was barely enough food. The people bore these burdens stoically and with some grace. No matter how much you reminded yourself about Hitler, it was still difficult to live and work among people you knew were hungry.

Cigarettes may be a bad word now, but then they were like gold. We were permitted to buy two cartons of cigarettes a week at the

Frankfurt, a city devastated by war. Its cathedral and the surrounding bridges were demolished by Allied bombing during the battle for the city in March 1945. Courtesy U.S. Army Military History Institute.

army-run stores, which we always did, even though I never smoked. Money was unimportant, but cigarettes could buy anything. One of my friends gave me a substantial sum of money to deliver to an old friend in Berlin. With some effort I found her in a partially destroyed apartment building and gave her the money and one carton of cigarettes. She paid no attention to the money but was overjoyed with the cigarettes.

By this time the soldiers who had won the war had gone home. Our military people in Germany, except for a few high-ranking officers, were either people who came in late and were reluctantly serving their allotted time or those who wanted to stay in because they were better off there than they would have been in civilian life. Many were no great credit to their homeland.

I had two missions: One was to examine all chemical processes that related to sulfur, and the other was to investigate the process of making acetylene from methane. I worked alone on the sulfur project, although some other scientific consultants who were between assignments or had a passing interest in the subject would sometimes go with me. I worked with Dr. A. S. "Nick" Carter of DuPont on the methane-acetylene process.

All my legitimate sulfur targets were in the Ruhr, where I found processes to make sulfuric acid and ammonium sulfate from gypsum that do not have any present commercial value. I also found a process for converting hydrogen sulfide to sulfur, the Claus process, that is now being used all over the world.

Nick Carter and I found two locations where methane was being converted to acetylene, one in the Chemische Werke Hüls plant in Marl, using an electric arc, and one in the BASF plant in Ludwigshafen, using partial combustion. Some of the senior people in Hüls had been part of a joint Standard Oil of New Jersey–IG Farben Industrie AG research project and had worked in Baton Rouge, where I had gone to the university. We found many mutual friends, and I started friendships at Hüls that have continued. Unfortunately, their process had no value outside wartime Germany. Hüls was in the British zone, and when we stayed with the British officers, we found that they were living no better than the Germans. The victors had fared no better than the losers.

The other methane-acetylene project involved the firm of BASF (formerly Badische Anilin und Soda Fabrik), located in Ludwigshafen in the French zone. Somehow the French were living far better than the British. In the American and British zones it was clear who was in charge. The French did not behave as victors. I had the feeling that they were aware that next time the Germans might be in charge. Although we received complete cooperation from the German technical people elsewhere, in the French zone we had to dig out information on our own. Several times we had to ask the French authorities to threaten to put Dr. Hans Sachsse, the inventor of the process, in jail to get him to cooperate. His methane-acetylene process would have commercial application in three plants in the United States

All the IG Farben records had been assembled in Griesheim. I frequently needed to review these records to verify some point that had arisen in one of the plants. In Hitler's day most German business letters signed off not with "yours truly" or something of the sort, but with "Heil, Hitler." It was no surprise to find letters from Germans to well-known American business and technical people signed "Heil, Hitler." It was a surprise, however, to find that some of these Americans replied with the same words. There was material to ruin many U.S. executives' careers in these files.

Sulfur or sulfur compounds are used in most industrial processes. This fact gave me an excuse to visit many parts of Germany that I might not otherwise have seen, such as the Black Forest, Lake Constance, and Baden-Baden, where they held the first postwar horse race. I thought that this was a little ostentatious for a country with hungry people until I discovered that the well-dressed men and the ladies in picture hats were French.

An interesting sidelight was provided by the few weeks I was involved with the Russians. Under the Potsdam Agreement, German industry was to be returned to its 1938 capacity. This idea was a variation of one that was current early in the war, that is, that Germany should be reduced to a pastoral country. If German industries had been reduced to their prewar level of production, the country would not have been a major factor in the postwar world.

To carry out the provisions of the Potsdam Agreement, several quadripartite teams were set up. These teams consisted of a Russian, an Englishman, a Frenchman, and an American. I was the American on the first team set up to examine the German fertilizer and sulfuric acid industry and determine its current (i.e., 1946) capacity. If this capacity exceeded the 1938 capacity, then the excess was to be destroyed. The plants we were to visit had all been damaged, which gave us a great deal of latitude in setting capacities. If we had set them high, then much of the German fertilizer and sulfuric acid industry would have been destroyed, and Germany would have had great difficulty ever redeveloping much industrial capacity.

Because what we decided was obviously important to the future of

Europe, I thought we should have a policy. I asked our military government personnel what the policy was and found that on this important matter that could determine the future of Germany there was none. I was predisposed to set the capacity of these plants low so that Germany could easily restore its industrial capacity. By the fall of 1946 it was apparent, at least to people outside the military government, that it was desirable to have a strong Germany between us and Russia.

Our quadripartite team met for the first time amiably and agreed to meet the next morning. At the end of the meeting I made the suggestion that the Russians have their drivers in uniform so that the military policemen in our zone could identify and treat them properly. My Russian counterpart agreed. The next morning when we met to start our journey, a completely new set of Russians showed up, and they were offended that we were not willing to have a Russian civilian driver. We spent the rest of the morning telling them that we really did not care what kind of driver they sent; it was merely a suggestion to make things go smoother. We agreed to meet again the next morning. A third set of Russians arrived, and we continued the same discussion; but by this time, it had expanded into various other inconsequential matters, making it clear that the Russians did not want this mission to start. After about two weeks I gave up. I learned later that another team had started out on such a trip, made a few stops, and then aborted the exercise. By then the Potsdam Agreement—a bad idea in the first place—was a dead issue, and everyone had lost interest in trying to implement it.

Toward the end of my stay I found reasons to go to Zurich, Paris, and London. Just as in Germany, the French in Paris were living better than the British in London.

STANDARD PERLITE

At the end of three years with Freeport I had filled the files with good reports outlining many prospective new businesses for them. Most of these involved utilizing the light hydrocarbons that were abundant in southern Texas but not being used. Many of these outlines were subsequently followed by Dow Chemical Company, Monsanto Chemical Company, Union Carbide and Carbon Corporation, and others in establishing the Gulf Coast petrochemical industry. By this time it was obvious that Freeport would not follow up on any of my ideas. At that time the sulfur business was very profitable and relatively free of serious problems. These new businesses all appeared to have problems and low profitability, at least in comparison with sulfur. Freeport continued to study investment opportunities until long after I left and eventually invested in the oil business.

One day I was talking to the president of Freeport, Langborne Williams, telling him I was tired of writing reports that led nowhere. I wanted to do something else. While we were talking, he got a call from Jock Whitney, then chairman of Freeport and one of the pioneers in the venture capital business in this country. Jock told him that J. H. Whitney & Co. had made an investment in a troubled enterprise on the West Coast and wanted someone to help determine what should be done about it. Sight unseen, I accepted the job and went to Pasadena, California, to join the Standard Perlite Company.

The enterprise was based on a newly developed process to produce expanded perlite. Perlite is a volcanic glass that contains some combined water. If it is heated at the proper rate, the glass softens and the water expands to blow the perlite into a steam-filled globule that is very light and strong for the weight. Perlite was to be mixed with waste newspaper and made into a lightweight building board that had very good insulating properties. In Southern California both the demand for building board and the price had been high because the increased building after the war made it scarce. By the time I arrived, enough additional capacity to produce building board had been added that the price of board had gone down, making this particular method of manufacture no longer competitive.

After a few months' study it became obvious that I had to tell J. H. Whitney & Co. that they had made their first bad investment.

Their reaction was to shoot the messenger. But for luck a horde of consultants would have descended on the scene to make studies and write reports. Months and many dollars later my conclusions would have been confirmed, but I probably would have been gone.

Someone at J. H. Whitney asked Lindley Morton to visit my project and give them an opinion of my recommendations. Lindley was a director of Freeport and highly respected by Jock Whitney. He had graduated from Yale about the start of World War I, had been a naval aviator, and had gone to work for a cement company after the war. After a few years he took over several bankrupt cement companies. He never told me how he did this except to say that he had very little money at the time. Shortly before World War II he sold the companies for enough to make him independently wealthy, then moved to Pasadena.

Lindley became interested in my problems. Twice a week he would come to my office, review the work, and make suggestions. Then he would take me to play tennis and have dinner with his wife, Ruth. Thereafter, I started my reports and recommendations to J. H. Whitney with "Lindley says" and had no more problems.

My job was to salvage something from the project. We made a satisfactory fireproof building board by substituting asbestos fiber for waste newspaper and sold the results to U.S. Plywood. This recovered some of J. H. Whitney's money. There were parts of Standard Perlite left that I thought could be made into a viable business. My bosses did not agree. More to prove that I was right than out of any desire to be an entrepreneur, I made a deal to take over the experimental kiln that we had developed to make expanded perlite for use in lightweight plaster and concrete.

Nothing in my background suggested that I would be an entrepreneur. All my family were farmers, teachers, and professionals— not even a merchant in the lot. I never had a paper route as a boy. I did not work my way through college selling encyclopedias. I tutored other students in mathematics.

In my first entrepreneurial foray I was successful in producing and selling a product, but the capacity of the kiln was too small to be profitable. I could have raised money to build a larger kiln, but to do it would have cost a large fraction of the equity in the company. It became apparent that the return I was likely to get would not be worth the effort. After three years of this I took my losses and went back to look for a job in the corporate world. I carried with me the feeling that I had failed and a determination to do something on my own at the first opportunity.

PETRO-TEX

Bob Hills, the president of Freeport with whom I had gone to Cuba before the war, gave me a temporary consulting job because he knew I was broke. I could have stayed there and repeated my earlier experience. Instead, I took a job with the FMC Corporation doing the same thing I would have done with Freeport, that is, look for businesses to acquire. I decided that FMC was more likely to act than Freeport had been, and I was right. FMC, originally the Food Machinery and Chemical Corporation, was the creation of Paul Davies, who took a small orchard sprayer manufacturer started by his father-in-law and through acquisition built it into a major conglomerate.

An incidental benefit of this job search was that one company where I applied put me through a three-day set of psychological tests. Before this company offered me a job, I took the one with FMC. Several years later I became acquainted with the president of the company that had done the tests, and he gave me the results. After the psychobabble was filtered out, there were two interesting points, one a big surprise. The first was the conclusion that I did not want the job. I thought I wanted the job when I first applied, but the more time I spent in interviews with the company, the less I liked it. The surprise was the conclusion that I could be a good salesman. I was not convinced that the conclusion was correct, but it did encourage me to try selling the first chance I got.

In a sense my next job, which took me into a completely new field, petrochemicals, dates back to the early 1800s. In 1828 Michael Faraday, an Englishman and one of the fathers of modern chemistry, produced the first petrochemical, ethyl alcohol, from ethylene. The process was of no commercial importance for a hundred years because ethyl alcohol could be produced cheaply by fermentation. In the late 1800s the Union Carbide Company was formed to produce calcium carbide, then used to make acetylene for automobile headlights. With the number of automobiles increasing and the demand for acetylene growing, Union Carbide hired a young chemist, George O. Curme, Jr., to look for other ways to produce acetylene. Curme developed a process in which gas oil was passed through an electric arc, resulting in the production of equal quantities of acetylene and ethylene. Curme's search for uses of this ethylene, which began in 1913, started the petrochemical industry, now a worldwide multibillion-dollar business.

His first commercial product was ethyl alcohol, which he produced using the same process Faraday had used almost a hundred years before. His second, which could hardly be called commercial, was dichloroethylsulfide for the production of mustard gas in World War I. A more useful product developed by Curme was ethylene glycol, now used in automobiles as antifreeze.

The electric arc process for producing acetylene and ethylene used large amounts of power and was expensive. Union Carbide looked for other ways to make ethylene and in 1920 established an operation near Charleston where ethane and propane were available from the newly discovered gas fields nearby. Carbide started cracking this ethane and propane in high-temperature furnaces that produced ethylene and propylene. From these hydrocarbons were produced ethyl alcohol, ethylene glycol, acetone, and other chemicals. Because there were more hydrocarbons available than required for the chemical business, Carbide started putting some of these gases in cylinders and selling it as a replacement for manufactured gas. Thus began the bottled gas business.

By the late 1920s the major oil companies—Shell Oil Company

and Standard Oil of New Jersey (now Exxon)—realized the potential value of the ethylene and propylene in their refinery gas streams. Shell started production of butyl alcohol, isopropyl alcohol, and methyl ethyl ketone, all solvents. Standard Oil started a joint research project in Baton Rouge with IG Farben, Germany's largest chemical company. Much of this work was directed toward producing liquid fuel by hydrogenating coal, but some focused on the production of synthetic rubber.

Our entry into World War II resulted in two major chemical supply problems: First was the need to produce large quantities of high-octane aviation gasoline, and second was the need to replace the supply of natural rubber that had been cut off by the Japanese invasion of Southeast Asia. The gasoline problem was solved by the combined efforts of the oil companies.

The Rubber Reserve Company, U.S. government-owned under the direction of Jesse Jones, was set up to produce synthetic rubber. The four major rubber companies—Goodyear Tire & Rubber Company, Firestone Tire & Rubber Company, B. F. Goodrich Company, and United States Rubber Company—were given the job of developing the process and operating the plants to produce the rubber. They started with the technology that Standard Oil had developed in Baton Rouge jointly with the Germans.

The raw materials required were butadiene and styrene. Technology for producing styrene was available from Dow Chemical, which was already in commercial production. There was no commercial production of butadiene, but by combining all the available technology, butadiene plants were built. In a short period a synthetic rubber industry was established. The plants were owned by the government and operated by oil, rubber, and chemical companies. The operation continued under government ownership and direction for about ten years after the war.

A few months after beginning work for FMC, I accidentally met Jan Ostemeyer, an FMC director, at breakfast in Schrafft's in the old Chrysler building in New York City. Jan, a retired president of Shell

Chemical Corporation, was an energetic, audacious man. That same morning an article appeared in the *Wall Street Journal* reporting that Congress had passed a law to permit the sale of the synthetic rubber plants built during World War II and had set up a special commission to implement the law.

Together we decided that FMC should put in a bid on one of these plants. The result was that we entered into six months of negotiations with the commission in Washington for the purchase of a butadiene plant located in Houston that had been operated by the Sinclair Oil Company. We chose this plant because we thought that Sinclair would not be a serious competitor. In time we were the successful bidder.

This initial experience with such negotiations proved to be excellent training for the leveraged buyouts I was involved in later. The sale of the synthetic rubber plants was directed by three very able men, appointed from civilian life by President Eisenhower; these men used their formidable skills to make the best possible deal for the taxpayers. Nowhere since have I faced such tough negotiators.

Paul Davies, head of FMC and my boss several levels removed, was a very aggressive acquirer of companies. His long-time friend Gardner Symonds was the head of Tennessee Gas Transmission Company, now Tenneco Chemicals. Toward the end of my negotiations they decided that the enterprise would be a joint venture between FMC and Tenneco. We set up a company, called the Petro-Tex Chemical Company, to run the new plant we were buying. A few days before closing the deal we met in the Mayflower Hotel in Washington and negotiated the particulars of the joint venture.

These negotiations were all between Davies and Symonds, and at the time I made a note that neither of them understood what the other was saying. This note proved perceptive because within six months these two men who had been friends since college days had an argument about some aspect of the joint venture and said things for which neither forgave the other. They became bitter enemies and never spoke to one another again. Consequently, Petro-Tex ran

*The butadiene plant near Houston that became the nucleus of Petro-Tex.
The plant was purchased jointly from the Sinclair Oil Company by FMC
and Tenneco. Courtesy FMC Corporation.*

for many years as a joint venture between two owners who were not
on speaking terms.

For the first few months the Petro-Tex headquarters was in the
Tenneco building. One day I visited their executive offices with my
counterpart from Tenneco, "Tiny" Mertz. At one of the desks was a
beautiful Latin woman, a Dolores del Rio type. Tiny could see that I
was impressed. The next day he invited me to have coffee with him,
and without telling me, he invited the woman, Lucia La Madrid.

Nothing was ever the same. After years of running at the first sign
a woman was getting serious, I was thinking about marriage on the
first date. We were married a few months later. Overnight, a forty-
four-year-old bachelor with all the bad habits accumulated from years
of living alone became a reasonably good husband. We had a very
happy marriage but unfortunately no children.

I thought I would be the head of Petro-Tex, but the two owners decided to bring in an outsider. I represented FMC; Tenneco put a man in; and a third man, Joe Mares, formerly of Monsanto, was hired to be what was then called managing director but now would be called the CEO. Joe never was a full-time employee; he was only to be a referee in case of differences that never happened. This odd arrangement continued for the nine years I was with Petro-Tex, though Joe was replaced along the way. Except for the interlude at Standard Perlite, my postwar experience had all been in staff jobs, writing reports and giving advice. Now I was implementing what I had learned in the army: getting others to do things for me. Marketing was part of my responsibility, and for the first six months I was the only salesperson. The psychologists who tested me were right; I could sell.

Because I was now married and happy at home, I was not bothered by the odd administrative arrangement of Petro-Tex. I was effectively running the operation, although I was never officially its head. By this time I had recovered financially from my perlite venture, and I started an investment program that gave me the resources to leave the corporate world fifteen years later.

HARVARD

During this postwar period two things happened that influenced my approach to life and especially to business. In the early 1950s, while the Korean War was at its height, I was at the end of a slow-moving line at an airport when two young men joined me. The older one, a veteran of World War II, was seeing his younger brother off on his way to join one of the services. As the line started to move and the two had to part, the older gave the younger a self-conscious hug and words of advice that I still remember. He said, "Remember, Joe, hang loose and don't sweat the small stuff." Stress had never been a significant problem for me, and it is less so now that I "don't sweat the small stuff."

Then in 1959 I attended the Harvard Advanced Management

Program. This thirteen-week program given by the Harvard Business School (HBS) was intended for executives in mid career whose companies thought they were destined for bigger things but needed broadening.

The basic premise of the HBS is that wisdom cannot be taught. The school function is not to teach but to create special learning conditions using analysis and discussion of real cases from business. The first and universal reaction on reading a case is that the person in charge was incompetent and should be fired. Only after getting past the superficialities and trying to determine what really happened and why does the learning process start.

I can remember many times listening to a classmate talk endlessly about what I thought was a completely irrelevant aspect of the case. Just when I was about to say, "Sit down, you dummy," he would make a point I had completely overlooked.

The prevailing view of the time was that a manager's job was to solve problems, and the HBS was doing an excellent job of teaching problem solving. Now I realize that a good manager does not have problems. A good manager anticipates the changes that are likely to cause problems. I hope the HBS has recognized this and changed the focus of their teaching.

The most important part of this experience was spending time away from the press of business and having an opportunity to think. Shortly after leaving the HBS, a bastion of economic logic, I made a trip to India during which I was forced to accept that technology, economics, and logic are no match for politics.

The sale of the U.S. government synthetic rubber plants in 1955 led to the development of a private synthetic rubber industry in the United States. No other country had a comparable industry. Consequently, many industrialized countries became interested in having their own synthetic rubber plants. I spent part of the first few years after Petro-Tex was formed in Europe talking to English, German, French, and Italian companies about joint ventures to produce butadiene, the principal raw material for synthetic rubber. Nothing happened except that I ate a lot of good food and made many friends.

INDIA

In 1958 the Indian government decided it wanted a synthetic rubber industry and invited Goodyear and Firestone each to send a team to India to make proposals. The Goodyear team consisted of a company representative, a man from Bechtel Engineering and Construction Company, some consultants from Stanford Research Institute, and me, posing as a raw materials expert. We spent a month in India in 1958 and another month the next year. Lucia went with me on the second trip.

We thought we were the experts who would tell the Indians how and where to build their plants. We arrived to find that they had already decided for political reasons where to build the plants and what processes and raw materials to use. Each decision was not only wrong, but badly wrong. We spent the first visit trying unsuccessfully to change their plans. The second visit was devoted to trying to design a viable operation using their plans. We gave up and withdrew from the race, letting Firestone and an Indian industrial group win by default. The plants operated a few years and were shut down because of the high costs.

Although the trips to India were not a business success, they left many pleasant memories. I still have some admiration for the Indian civil servants with whom we dealt. Our difference was not over how to make synthetic rubber but on what raw material to use. Since I was handling this part of the project, most of the arguments fell to me. In time I realized that these people were technically competent and well versed in the economics of synthetic rubber production. However, like an attorney representing a client he knows is guilty, they would not give the faintest sign that they thought their political bosses had made the wrong decision.

The Goodyear representative in India, Niku Prakash, was the son of a longtime friend of Nehru's, one with whom he had shared a prison cell. Through Niku I had several opportunities to visit Nehru in small groups and in private. He was then not far from the end of his career and of his life. In private he was a kind old man who slumped

and talked in a low, expressionless voice. A minute later in front of an
audience, even a few people, he was transformed. He was erect, alert,
and spoke with animation.

We called on him in his office just off the floor of the parliament
while it was in session to make an appeal to the highest authority to
convince the Indians to change their plans. He let me talk about ten
seconds before saying that he understood all the issues and that the
decision was final. Then, possibly to make his refusal a little less blunt,
he reminisced about Bareilly (the city where the plant was to be located). It was there that he spent his first time in a British prison.

My one trip to Bareilly was in a Pullman car of about 1920 vin-
tage. There were berths but no bed linen. You rented a sleeping bag
in the Delhi Station and returned it at the other end. About dawn
the train stopped on a bridge over the Ganges. The noise that woke
me could have been made by a flock of birds, but it was made by the
thousands of Indians who had come to bathe in the holy water of the
river. The town, the proposed plant site, and all the other things
have faded from memory. However, I clearly remember a visit to a
sugar mill where they were using a sulfur burner of the type I had
invented and patented years before (see note on page 57).

My memories of India are clearer than my other thirty-five-year-
old memories. As a boy I read everything of Kipling's I could find. I
was more likely to imagine myself as a young British lieutenant riding
through the Khyber Pass with Kipling's "fuzzy-wuzzies" shooting at
me than as a cowboy dodging western Indians. One of my most vivid
memories of India is of getting up early to see the sunrise over the
Taj Mahal, when the water in the reflection pool is still enough to
create a perfect mirror image of the building. En route to the Taj
someone showed me the Maharaja of Jaipur's duck blind. It was a
small stone castle in the middle of a lake with a turret on each corner
of the castle from which he shot.

Seeing the Vale of Kashmir, visiting the gardens of Shalimar, and
having dinner on a houseboat on the lake were a prelude to a trip
into the Himalayas. Lucia and I went on ponies up a trail that was in

such poor shape that it would not permit carriage travel. At the end was Gulmag, what Kipling would have called a hill station. In the old days the upper-level British officials sent their wives and children there for the summer and joined them for their vacations. There were twenty or thirty large, one-story cottages with verandahs on all sides, as well as smaller cottages and servant quarters. Between and around these buildings were the vestiges of a golf course, and in the distance you could see the major peaks of the Himalayas. Through it all wandered ghosts of English officers, civil servants, and their ladies sipping tea and drinking gin on the verandahs.

After India I settled into the routine of making and selling butadiene and developing uses for some of the by-products from the operation. Because the synthetic rubber industry was growing both in this country and worldwide, there were many opportunities for expansion, and we took advantage of these. By the time I left Petro-Tex, it was many times its original size.

Chapter Six

Conoco

FIRST STEPS TO INDEPENDENCE

Afterr I had been nine years at Petro-Tex, the Continental Oil Company (Conoco), which was then in Houston, asked me to become head of their petrochemical operations. The man in charge had died suddenly with no apparent successor, and although this operation was smaller and less successful than Petro-Tex, I would be the head. I took the job, which turned out to be a very good decision. The business I took over in 1964 was losing about $2 million a year and was riddled with problems. The staff was very good but discouraged and only needed direction to get them moving. By the time I left six years later, the business had developed into a unit that I eventually bought for $600 million.

Shortly after I began, Conoco headquarters moved from Houston to New York City, and I obviously had to move with it. Lucia and I both liked the idea of living in New York, and the business I was running had operations in England, Germany, Spain, Argentina, and Japan, all of which we traveled to frequently.

When I took over, one man, John Burns, was just completing an assignment in the New York office. The management of Conoco regarded John highly and expected him to do well at the company. His peers in the chemical group agreed that he was very intelligent and ambitious. One of my first tasks was to find a new assignment for him. He became manager of a small plant in Trainer, Pennsylvania, and did so well that when we needed someone to start the Petresa operation in Spain, he got the assignment (see Chapter 7). His performance there led to his eventually becoming head of the entire chemical operation.

The staff was under pressure from top management and needed clear direction. The top management of Conoco themselves needed to regain confidence. In its earlier years the company's imaginative management team had sponsored creative research and had started several promising projects, the most important of which involved biodegradable detergents.

The first synthetic detergents had been more effective cleaning agents than soap, but the bacteria in the sewage disposal plants that destroyed soap would not eat the detergents. The discharge from the sewage plants, though harmless, carried a cover of foam from the detergents. Then Monsanto's James Roth discovered that if the arrangement of the carbon atoms in the detergent molecule was in a straight rather than a branched chain, the cleaning characteristics would be unchanged, but the bugs would literally eat it up. At the first sign of the problem and its possible solution, Conoco research developed a process to make one type of biodegradable detergent and found a process in Germany to make another type—straight-chain alcohols. Shortly before I arrived, Conoco had undertaken the job of transforming the sketchy German laboratory reports into a commercial process. Because of the transfer of key people to the oil side of Conoco and the untimely death of my predecessor, carrying these good ideas to a successful conclusion had been delayed.

Conoco's chemical business when I took over included a plant in Baltimore that was one of the first in the world to make biodegradable detergents. The plant was having the usual problems of working with a newly developed process. In addition, a plant in Lake Charles, Louisiana, was making straight-chain alcohols, also biodegradable, from ethylene by the German process. This plant was running but with more difficulties than usual for a new plant. Conoco also had two other small detergent specialty plants, one near Chicago and the other near Philadelphia.

Condea, a joint venture between Conoco and Deutsche Erdol (DEA), located near Hamburg in Germany, had a straight-chain alcohol plant identical to the one in Lake Charles, but it was running about six months behind the Louisiana plant. One of my first assignments was to travel to Germany to decide whether to continue or abandon this operation. An objective analysis indicated that it should be shut down. Pride, unwillingness to admit to our German partners that we had made a mistake, and the fact that it would cost us about $4 million to get out led to the decision to stay. After three years of good work by able German scientists and engineers, guided by my Conoco associate Augie Kellermann, it became a successful operation—so successful that DuPont decided not to include it in the package they later sold to us and which eventually became Vista Chemical (as described in Chapter 7). Good people and hard work can make silk purses from some unlikely raw materials.

PASA: AN EARLY LEVERAGED BUYOUT

In 1964 Conoco had a 25 percent interest in PASA, Petroquimica Argentina S.A. PASA is important to this story only because when I left Conoco in 1970 I agreed to continue to represent Conoco as a director of PASA and was chairman of the board from the mid 1970s until 1984. This arrangement spanned the DuPont acquisition of Conoco in 1980 and the formation of Vista in 1984, which included PASA. It continued because no ambitious Conoco executive wanted to be responsible for an operation that might go belly up any day. The PASA connection kept me in contact with the Conoco Chemicals people, which proved useful when I wanted to buy the business. It also taught me how to operate in a highly inflationary economy and to deal with governments that could change overnight from supportive to hostile.

PASA had been started in 1952 by Ray Fish of Fish Engineering. Because of his personal friendship with key executives in Conoco, Cities Service, UniRoyal Corporation, and Witco, Ray had brought them in as partners. Delays in getting permits and financing resulted in the start of operations twelve years later. When PASA got up and running late in 1964, it was the largest petrochemical operation south of the equator. It took natural gas and refinery liquids from the Argentine national oil and gas companies and produced synthetic rubber.

Within a year death, retirement, and old age removed from the company the five men who had organized it. In my first meeting of the board of directors of PASA in Buenos Aires a few months after I went to work, the five representatives of the partners were all there for the first time. To compound our ignorance, the five original organizers had been good friends, and many of their agreements had not been in writing. In addition to these problems the country was in a serious economic slump, and relations between the PASA management and key government people were poor.

On my first visit in 1964 I found an organization headed by an American with sixty-two Americans in key positions. The construction of the plant was going well, and production was expected to begin in about six months. The plant had been financed with $5 million in equity and $90 million in debt, a leveraged buyout (LBO) before the term was coined. The project had dragged on for years to the point that the senior people in our respective companies were tired of hearing about PASA and its problems. We were each told there was no more money or loan guarantees for PASA. We had to make it succeed with the resources at hand.

We obviously needed a competent, well-connected Argentine as the head of PASA because good relations with the Argentine government and its many agencies, particularly the national oil and gas companies, were essential to success. Equally obvious was the need to replace the North American engineers and supervisors with Argentines. Fortunately, we found Carlos Dietl within a year. Within three years he had replaced all the North Americans except one with competent Argentines. Carlos was an engineering graduate who had been to the Harvard Business School Advanced Management

Program. He was an Argentine of Swiss extraction and like many Argentines resembled his forebears rather than the stereotype of a Latin American. He had worked for the Argentine branches of several U.S. companies and was well attuned to the problems of U.S. corporate life.

For the first half of his twenty years as head of PASA, Carlos's main job was to keep the company out of the hands of its creditors. By the late 1970s all the debt had been repaid, and the principal problem was making a profit in periods when inflation ran above a thousand percent a year. The government solved its financial problems by printing more money, not by collecting taxes and reducing expenses. Today, PASA is a successful operation, largely because of Carlos Dietl's guidance.

For twenty years—from 1964 to 1984—I was a director of PASA and the chairman most of the time. The job required me to travel to Argentina from one to four times a year, and during this time I met every Argentine president who lasted more than six months. This succession started with a kindly country doctor and went through several generals, with Eva Peron in the middle. The pattern was the same. Each announced an austerity program to control inflation, then after a few months resumed printing money. When inflation rose to a thousand percent a year, a new general would come into power, and the cycle started again.

The return of the Peronistas brought only one change. For the only time in my Argentine experience I was approached by Argentine government officials with a proposition. Many good things would happen for PASA if $2 million were deposited in a certain London bank account. Apart from the ethical considerations, the two conspirators seemed too clumsy. I turned down their offer, and a few months later they were out in a change of government.

None of these things were serious compared with traveling to Argentina during the time the Monteneros were kidnapping Argentine and U.S. businessmen. The Monteneros were an underground group that may have had a Communist connection, but the people

The PASA plant in San Lorenzo, Argentina, on the Rio Paraná, which flows into the Rio de la Plata.

were all native Argentines, many from well-known families. They committed many crimes, and the army and police responded with violence in what became known as the "dirty war." The manager of the Exxon refinery was kidnapped and ransomed. One Argentine investment banker I knew had been kidnapped and ransomed twice. Another had become a specialist in negotiating with kidnappers. My friend Carlos had a bomb planted against his garage door that was designed to explode when the door opened. Fortunately, it went off prematurely, destroying the garage and two cars but injuring no one.

Travel to Argentina in these times was worrisome. My fellow directors chose to be met at the plane by two carloads of bodyguards and to be escorted by police with sirens. When we traveled together, I went along with this arrangement. When I traveled alone, I communicated my plans to Carlos in a code only he and I knew. I arrived and moved around as quickly and inconspicuously as possible and stayed only one or two nights.

Much has been written, some of it overblown, about the problems of doing business in foreign countries. I have operated in Cuba, Mexico, Argentina, England, France, Spain, and Germany and have done business in almost every other developed country except Russia. After reading any simple book about business in a particular country, a person of good manners and sensitivity to others can do very well. Interest in a particular business makes a common bond that transcends cultural differences.

"MR. MC"

My six years at Conoco gave me time to learn all about the business I later would buy. It also exposed me to two managers who influenced my approach to getting things done through an organization. L. F. McCollum, "Mr. Mc," in mid career was a bright young man in Esso (now Exxon), who was regarded as likely to become head of Esso in time. He left this promising future to head a small Rocky Mountain oil company. In twenty years he built Conoco into an international oil company ranking just behind what are known in the industry as the Seven Sisters. Mr. Mc was an ideal boss for me. If he had ever seen an organization chart, he had long since forgotten it. He was completely results-oriented and unconcerned with corporate protocol and procedure. I had gone through a succession of bosses who had low self-esteem, and I was relieved to spend my energy getting things done and not massaging a boss's fragile ego.

NORMAN FAIN

The Exxon and Shell petrochemical businesses were growing, and Mr. Mc wanted his to expand also. With his support we acquired the Thompson Apex Company, a major producer and fabricator of polyvinyl chloride (PVC), from Norman Fain in Rhode Island. This experience was an eye-opener and my first view of how a good owner operates a business. The acquired business was about the same size as the business I was running, but it was managed by a fraction of the number of people I had. There were no committees and very few meetings. The employees worked harder at lower salaries than our people, but in good years their bonuses gave them total compensation well above what people at Conoco received. Like Mr. Mc, Norman was completely results-oriented, and his people were comfortable working with him.

The acquisition of this PVC business was challenged by the Federal Trade Commission (FTC) on the theory that Conoco was a potential producer of PVC and, consequently, was barred from going into the PVC business by means of acquisition. This novel legal theory survived only as long as Lyndon Johnson's Great Society.

We settled the case by divesting parts of the business we did not want. The settlement was reached in a few days after a long period of intense and sometimes heated negotiations. We learned later that the impetus for settlement came not from the persuasiveness of our legal or economic arguments but rather from the fact that the two key FTC lawyers received attractive offers from private law firms and wanted to settle the case and move on to more lucrative fields. Little did I know that almost exactly twenty years later I would be back, with the FTC behaving no more rationally than in this case.

Even before Conoco became a large, successful oil company, it started behaving like one. Prior to my arrival the company had been recruiting top-quality engineering and MBA graduates. I was fortunate to take over a group of very able people. My job, as it had been at Camp Rucker, was to make this collection of individuals into an effective organization. Long before I went to Conoco, I had realized that my military-model manager did not fit the civilian scene. I suspect that in Conoco I became a pale copy of Mr. Mc.

After a few years Mr. Mc retired. His first successor lasted a year or two. After that the guardians of the status quo took over the operation of Conoco, and it became obvious that the big expansion program I had under way would not continue. I started thinking about what to do next.

LOSING LUCIA

In the fall of 1966 Lucia developed what initially seemed like a modest intestinal upset but turned out to be a cancer in the pelvic region that required major surgery. There was chemotherapy and radiation and the devout hope that all the cancer had been eradicated. For one and a half years it appeared that her health was restored, but in the spring of 1968 the cancer recurred. She had a second operation, but the cancer continued to grow. For five months Lucia was in and out of the hospital. I slept every night in the hospital with her, and her mother stayed with her during the daytime. During that period I gave up business travel and stayed in New York. One night, five months after the recurrence of the cancer, I came to the hospital in the evening to spend the night and found that she was having difficulty breathing. Instead of sleeping on a cot in the room, I sat by her bedside and must have dozed off. I awoke because I no longer heard her labored breathing and realized that this woman who had meant so much to me and who had done so much to brighten my life was no longer with us.

My restlessness in my job was magnified by Lucia's death. I entered a period of hectic travel, visiting the foreign countries I had neglected for the past year while Lucia was ill. I called on the big customers and visited all the U.S. plants. However, I could not arouse any interest in continuing to work at Conoco. Two factors reinforced my lack of interest: I did not like my new boss, and the company had made a clear decision not to invest any more capital in the chemical business.

If I had any doubt about leaving, it was resolved by one incident. I bought a small business that made plastic bottles. The business cost $40,000, well within the amount I was authorized to spend. The principal reason for buying it was to gain some understanding of the bottle business, which then was developing into a good market for PVC. The business was expected to lose a few thousand dollars a month, but this amount was less than a research project on plastic bottles would have cost and a lot more productive. After writing the third or fourth report explaining why I had purchased the business, that it was losing money, and what the plans were for making it profitable, I said "The hell with it!" and left.

Without any clear plans for the future, I quit my job at Conoco in mid 1970 and returned to Houston. I had several reasons for making this decision, but the most important were that I did not want to finish my career presiding over the status quo; my failure in the perlite business left me with a strong need to prove that I could be an entrepreneur; and I had the suspicion that except during the war my talents had not been fully utilized, and I wanted to find a place where they could be.

LESSONS FROM TURNAROUNDS

Within days after I announced that I was leaving Conoco, I started getting phone calls from investment banker friends, most of whom I had met while trying to make acquisitions for Freeport and FMC. Each needed help on a troubled investment. Because I had nothing better to do, I agreed to take on one of these and then another and another. Without realizing it, I had embarked on a career of managing troubled enterprises that would last ten years.

The first of these were new, high-technology ventures. One manufactured a collision-avoidance device for ships, one made a computer control system for process plants, one made gas chromatographs, one built test instruments for the Air Force, and one produced radioactive materials. Initially, it was contemplated that I would act as senior advisor and chairman of the board of each, but the troubles were deep enough that I had to get heavily involved in all of them. At one time I was the active head of three of these businesses. I acted concurrently as a consultant for Petro-Tex—my old company—and for FMC, and I continued to represent Conoco in Argentina. It was a full schedule, but I needed to be busy after the loss of Lucia.

MARY

After I returned to Houston in the early 1970s, my friends there—especially the married ones—felt a strong urge to see that this single man did not stay single long. Friends introduced me to many attractive women, with no lasting result. A few days before the Fourth of July 1971, one of my long-term friends, Betty Lou Bayless, the wife of one of my investment banker friends, Jim Bayless, asked me to go to dinner with the two of them and a lady they wanted me to meet. The lady was Mary Buxton, and again I had no doubt on the first date that this was the woman I wanted to marry. Because I was older and slower, a month or more passed before we talked seriously about marriage, and months of heavy courting were needed to convince her. We became engaged and were married the following April. Mary, like Lucia, was a warm, outgoing, friendly person, who brought into my bachelor life all the things that I had been missing. Now over twenty years later I can say that we will live happily ever after.

When I arrived at Mary's house for our first date, I had first to circumvent two motorcycles at the front door. I was then jumped on by two hunting dogs and greeted by three boys in their late teens with long ponytails and by a wayward niece. One boy was Mary's son Jimmy, who is today a successful foundation executive and a very conservative husband. The other two were her stepsons, who had stayed with her instead of accompanying their father after the divorce. The only normal-looking member of the household was her daughter Peggy, who was working and putting her new husband through law school. I decided that it was my mission to rescue Mary from all of this.

Mary was running the Houston Museum of Fine Arts. She had been with the museum in various capacities for about twenty years when the director, James Johnson Sweeny, left on short notice. She ran it for three years until Philippe de Montebello was made director. Mary bridged the gap between two very well-known figures in the art world, but she did more than that. She originated exhibitions—Louise Nevelson, Montibu Mabe, and Hans Hartung especially—that are still remembered by museum goers.

The first years of our marriage must have been difficult for her. I had an irregular schedule and many problems with and disappointments in the various companies. I was making enough to live on but not adding to my reserve. Mary bore all this with no sign that she ever doubted that things would turn out all right.

Mary brought so much to my life that I did not realize I was missing. She reawakened in me an interest in art, particularly in primitive art, a field in which she was very knowledgeable. She brought me the security of a comfortable home and a cheering section when things were difficult, as they often were. She knew that at times I was betting our future comfort on my ability to close a deal, but she never showed concern. I had grown up in a big, close family. Lucia and I were very close, but we had no children and were not near our families. I did not realize until Mary and I married how much I had missed being part of a close family. When Mary's children Peggy and Jimmy both married and in due course had children of their own, I discovered that being a grandparent is much more fun than running chemical companies.

A TEMPTATION FROM OXY

One incident early in our marriage might have been an omen of things to come. Occidental Petroleum needed a man to run its chemical business, and someone suggested to Dr. Armand Hammer, then head of Occidental, that he consider me. I knew that I did not want to give up my new career as an independent, but when Dr. Hammer offered to send a plane to take me to Los Angeles and back, I could not resist the opportunity to meet him.

We met in his home in Beverly Hills. Early in the meeting he must have decided that he wanted to hire me. He had answers for all the objections I raised to taking the job. I had invested in some small companies; he would buy my interest. I did not want to move to Los Angeles; he would move the chemical headquarters to Houston and give me a plane. He learned of Mary's interest in art and said that he would start by taking us to Russia to see his exhibit at the Pushkin.

My resistance to taking the job almost disappeared, but I managed to ask for time to talk to Mary. I left the house with the then No. 2 and No. 3 men at Occidental, who had been sitting quietly on the sideline. It was the day before Thanksgiving in 1972. As we walked away from the house, the two, who were on either side of me, were discussing whether they dared to go out for Thanksgiving dinner or whether they should stay home in case Dr. Hammer called. Both decided to stay at home to be available if he did call. I simultaneously decided not to take the job.

PETRO-TEX REVISITED

Around 1976, just about the time my various high-technology ventures were being sold, Petro-Tex ran into serious trouble. The two owners—FMC and Tenneco—were at odds. The company was losing money, and there was talk of liquidating it. The owners decided that the only solution was to hire someone that they both trusted to run the operation. I made a deal that I would be the chairman of the board of Petro-Tex and spend about half my time looking after its affairs and trying to get it out of trouble.

At this point the company's prospects were poor. Because of the ill will between the two owners, critical decisions had been postponed. I started making all the decisions that should have been made much earlier, and everything I did turned out right. We had been making about eight hundred million pounds of butadiene a year and losing money because we were saturating the market and driving the price down. We cut the production from eight hundred million to one hundred million pounds a year and created a shortage. Prices went up, and we began making money.

We then sold the neoprene rubber business that we never should have started to a Japanese company for more than enough to pay off all of the Petro-Tex debts. At the end of two years Tenneco bought FMC's interest—which was considered worth nothing when I came on board—for about $35 million. Petro-Tex was much like Conoco Chemical. Both had good people, and both suffered from lack of direction at the top. Tenneco suggested that I stay and run Petro-Tex, but I had been my own boss too long to be part of a big company.

ALASKA

Somehow whenever I run out of a job, another appears. In 1978, about the time I started thinking about leaving Petro-Tex yet again, a Houston company then called Alaska Interstate began a new venture. This small conglomerate owned the gas distribution system in Anchorage and southern Alaska. The Alaska state legislature passed a bill authorizing the state to sell its 150,000 barrels per day of royalty crude coming from the North Slope on a long term contract, which would go to the bidder whose proposal created the most jobs in Alaska. This would require building a sophisticated refinery with some petrochemical production.

The terms of the legislation dictated that the successful bidder be chosen by the Alaska secretary of natural resources, approved by the governor, and ratified by both houses of the state legislature. Alaska Interstate was one of the bidders, along with several other oil and engineering companies. In 1978 there was still a worldwide shortage of crude. A contract to buy 150,000 barrels a day of crude at the market price could be valuable. Knowledgeable financial people were confident that with such a contract it would be easy to finance the refinery.

My involvement in the Alaska project started before I left Petro-Tex. One of the directors of Alaska Interstate was Jim Bayless, then president of Rauscher Pierce Securities and the man whose wife had introduced me to Mary. Bill Anderson, the chief financial officer of the company, had been an investment banker with whom I had worked several times in the past. Pat Dwyer, the general counsel, had been the attorney for Petro-Tex when I was consulting for them. With so many friends involved who knew nothing about refining or petrochemicals, it was natural for one or more of them to invite me to lunch to get my advice on their Alaska venture, Alpetco.

Had fate not intervened, Alaska would be a faint memory of a few pleasant lunches. A few months after I first heard of Alpetco, the man who was running the Alaska project for Alaska Interstate had a heart attack and died in the San Francisco airport. Initially, I agreed to spend half time at Petro-Tex and half time holding the Alaska project together. A few months later, attracted by the fishing in Alaska, I agreed to become president of Alpetco at a respectable salary and a half-million-dollar bonus if the contract was approved by the state legislature.

The first step was to develop a project that would involve the maximum upgrading of Alaska crude into products that could be sold on the West Coast, in Hawaii, and in the Pacific Rim countries, mainly Japan. At the same time the project could not be so complicated that it could not be financed. Because we expected to sell part of the output to Japan, we decided to try to raise part of the capital there. This meant frequent trips to Japan, on which Mary accompanied me. On one trip we met the prime minister, a meeting that served no purpose except to let our Japanese representative show how influential he was. In fact, none of the trips to Japan accomplished anything, except perhaps to introduce us to the excellent French and Italian restaurants in Tokyo. We finally financed the venture in Germany.

In between trips to raise money we, along with the other bidders, presented our plans to various legislative committees and to influential groups in Fairbanks, Anchorage, Juneau, and Valdez, the port where the plant would be located and the name of the notorious tanker that years later would run aground and spill oil in Prince William Sound. One such meeting in Fairbanks was uneventful, but the trip back left a lasting impression. We were flying from Fairbanks to Valdez in the first of two Twin Otters, considered by the Alaskans to be the safest plane in the air. A big storm came up with strong head winds. In the flashes of lightning we could see peaks of mountains around us at our elevation. We were navigating through the mountains by radar.

Just when things were at the worst, Mary and I overhead the pilot say to the copilot, "We are not going to make it." Then realizing that we might have heard him, he added, "Because of the head winds, we won't make it before dark, and they don't have runway lights on the Valdez airport." Then he told us not to worry without telling us why. Both pilots were too busy navigating through the mountains for much conversation. We sat trying unsuccessfully to obey the pilot's instruction "not to worry." To our relief the Valdez airport came in sight with brightly lit runways. The illumination came from the automobile headlights of the people of Valdez, who had responded to a radio summons from our pilot. We landed safely, and the people with the automobiles drove away before we could thank them.

The meetings were intended to get influential groups to support our project rather than our competitor's. After two years the state secretary of natural resources recommended our project to the governor, who approved it and sent it to the legislature. Legislative approval was orchestrated by Cathy Chandler, our attorney at the time and now the wife of Senator Ted Stevens. The Senate approved the contract. The House did not, and its members were beginning to drift homeward in anticipation of adjournment. We sent an airplane to Fairbanks to bring back two absent members, only to find they were such enemies that they would not ride on the same plane. We sent another plane.

One Eskimo legislator was on a plane to go back to the Aleutians with his wife, mother-in-law, and their house plants. Cathy literally took the group—with their house plants—off the plane. When she found all the hotel rooms in Juneau taken, she gave them her room. One of our supporters spent so much time in the Red Dog Saloon that he pushed the wrong button on the voting machine and voted against us. In spite of all this, the approval of our contract passed with a good majority. Shortly afterward, we sold the project to the Charter Oil Company.

After the Alaska project was finished late in the spring of 1980, I spent two fairly quiet years punctuated with some travel. PASA, the Argentine chemical business that I was managing for Conoco, was having problems that required frequent trips to Argentina. Bill McMinn, then at FMC, asked me to help him develop a co-generation plant to supply power for their phosphorus furnaces in Idaho. I agreed to help the Hudson's Bay Oil & Gas Company develop a petrochemical business in western Canada; that project required frequent trips to Calgary. During this time I started another project, in which I was involved for ten years.

THE STERLING GROUP

In late 1982 I was approached by a young man named Frank Hevrdejs. Frank had worked as a junior partner of a two-man firm that acted as a broker in the sale of oil-field–related businesses to the several oil field industry conglomerates. A severe heart attack had forced the senior partner to retire, leaving Frank without the resources to continue the business, until he asked me to join him and finance it. I agreed to pay operating expenses for a year, but nothing to him except what he could earn in the business.

At the end of 1983, when my commitment to finance Frank's enterprise ended, I was just out of the hospital after heart surgery. I had entered negotiations with DuPont on the purchase of Conoco Chemicals (discussed in Chapter 7), but the deal was balanced on the fence. I thought I could make a deal with Allied Chemical to go into the fertilizer business, but had nothing firm (see Chapter 10). All Frank's original deals were dead, but he had two good prospects. I agreed to finance the partnership, now called The Sterling Group, for three months more.

Just before the three months were up, we closed our first deal—Balco, a business in Wichita that made expansion joints for concrete floors and roofs and related building products. It was typical of many such businesses—started by one man in his garage and now worth enough to make the owner independent for life. The owner had no heir and no one in the business capable of replacing him.

The legal and economic aspects of such transactions are minor compared with the emotional ones. The seller wants the freedom and independence the sale will give him but cannot part with the business he has worked on most of his active life. In this case several closings were aborted before the owner could bring himself to sign the final papers.

In keeping with our plan to develop The Sterling Group into a brokerage business, we found a prospective buyer, who backed out at the last minute. In desperation we called potential investors we already knew and found three who would join us in buying Balco as well as a lender to put up part of the money. This was The Sterling Group's first LBO.

We resolved to give up the brokerage business and do LBOs, a resolve that lasted about a month. We had been working on the purchase of three businesses from U.S. Steel: steel tire cord, wire and cable, and siding. One of the investors we asked to join us in making this LBO decided he wanted the entire deal and offered us $350,000 to turn it over to him. Because we had put all our Balco fees back into that deal and I was running low on funds, we took the money. The Sterling Group continued to do LBOs—about forty-odd, including helping me make the Sterling Chemical, Cain, Fibers, and second Arcadian acquisitions (see Chapters 8, 9, and 10). I concentrated on the chemical and related businesses and withdrew from active participation in the group at the end of 1992.

LOOKING FOR AN ACQUISITION

My spare time in the early 1980s was spent trying to find a small chemical operation that I could buy. One of the first prospects was the Harshaw division of Gulf Oil. In the mindless rush to diversification that swept U.S. industry in the 1960s and 1970s, Gulf had acquired Harshaw, an inorganic chemical company in Cleveland, Ohio. Harshaw made electroplating chemicals, pigments for paints and ceramics, and catalysts.

Such acquisitions are usually sold shortly after the manager who bought them retires. Gulf first offered Harshaw for sale in 1980 at a price about 25 percent more than it was worth. No one would buy it. It was reoffered at about one-year intervals thereafter. Each time the asking price was reduced by less than the value of the company had gone down. After several years Chevron Oil, the successor to Gulf, merged Harshaw into a small company and got a fraction of the original asking price. This strategy and its results could make a good business school case study illustrating how not to sell a business.

Another prospect was the Tenneco chemical business. There I was competing with the management, who were trying to do one of the early management buyouts. They prevailed because I could judge the business only on its history; they had a better understanding of its potential.

The lesson here is that getting some part of the current management on your side is a big help. But one can get too much of a good thing. While keeping some of the current management is an asset in an LBO, taking a complete management staff can be a liability. In an LBO a complete change must be made from the culture of a large corporation to that of a lean, entrepreneurial organization. Effecting this kind of change is difficult in a group that has worked together for a long time.

My next venture was to try to buy the carbon-black businesses of both Conoco and Phillips Petroleum Company. My plan was to combine the two units into a company that would be about the same size as each of its three largest competitors. I could pay off the debt out of the savings resulting from the combination. I signed a letter of intent with Conoco and had a verbal agreement with the management of Phillips. The Phillips board would not approve the agreement because it would result in reporting a loss on the sale, so my plan failed. This result provides more material for the business school case writers on the extent to which appearances rather than reality influence corporate decisions.

My search for a small chemical company might have gone on indefinitely but for my habit of playing golf every Saturday morning when I was in Houston (discussed in Chapter 7). In the meantime some changes had taken place in the business and financial worlds that would allow me, a purchaser with very little capital, to buy a business worth hundreds of millions of dollars.

ON LBOS AND JUNK BONDS: NOT ALL BAD

Leveraged buy-out, or LBO, is a term used to describe a purchase where a high percentage, usually over 80 percent, of the purchase price is borrowed. Although LBO is a relatively new term, it is not a new idea. Most purchases of houses involve a high percentage of debt.

There are two reasons to use a high percentage of debt. First, it is cheaper than equity because interest on debt is deductible for tax purposes and dividends on stock are not. Second, if the project does well, the leverage of the debt makes the value of the equity increase disproportionately. Of course, if it does poorly, it will be in financial trouble quickly.

In general, banks and other secured lenders will lend as senior, secured debt about 65 percent of the purchase price on the usual transaction. To give a return commensurate with the risk, the equity must be low, usually about 10 percent. With 75 percent of the purchase price coming from secured debt and equity, the other 25 percent must come as debt subordinated to the secured debt. The availability of this subordinated debt made LBOs possible.

In a few cases—the first sale of the Arcadian fertilizer business, for example (discussed in detail in Chapter 10)—an eager seller will take subordinated notes as part of the purchase price, but these situations are rare. A second source of such capital is the insurance companies and big pension funds that have huge amounts of money to invest and want to put a small part into higher-risk, higher-return investments. Prudential and seven other insurance companies made such an investment in Vista Chemical (discussed in Chapter 7). The total such capital available was only a fraction of that needed for the LBOs done in the 1980s. Therefore, it was necessary to develop another source of subordinated debt if the game was to continue.

Non-financial people tend to think of investments as either high-grade bonds that offer low yield and low risk or common stock that offers high yield from capital gains and high risk. If investors fell into only two categories, these two types of investments would be sufficient. However, a substantial body of investors want a higher yield than AAA bonds can give, and they are willing to take some added risk but do not want the risk of equities.

But for the provision of the Internal Revenue Code making dividends paid on stock nondeductible for taxes, this need for an intermediate risk investment could be filled by preferred stock. Preferred stock generally pays a fixed dividend, and it has a claim on the corporate assets junior to any bonds or bank loans but senior to the common stock. In some cases it can be converted into common stock or has warrants attached that give some of the benefits of common stock. But for the Tax Code, preferred stock would be a much bigger part of the capital structure of corporations today, and there would be fewer bonds.

With such a clear need it was inevitable that someone would develop a security with the characteristics of preferred stock but classified as debt so that the interest paid would be deductible. Unfortunately, this type of security was given the name "junk bond." I must confess a bias for the bonds because they made possible four very successful LBOs with which I was involved—Sterling Chemicals, Cain Chemical, Arcadian, and Fiber Industries. The junk bond holders were paid off with a premium, and the stockholders, including all of the employees and me, made a lot of money.

Long before anyone had heard the terms "LBO" or "junk bond," there were bonds on which interest payments were made regularly. But the bonds sold at a discount because of uncertainty about the assets that secured them. Such bonds were known in the trade as "fallen angels." The discount gave a higher return, and the uncertainty meant greater risk.

An MBA student at the Wharton School, Michael Milken, wrote a thesis in which he demonstrated that an investment in these fallen angels over a certain period would give a higher return than an investment in AAA bonds. The higher yield more than made up for any default of the fallen angels. College theses generally molder in the files, but not Milken's. On finishing Wharton, Milken went to work for an investment banking firm, Drexel Burnham. There were not enough fallen angels for his purpose, so he starting creating the equivalent, that is, high-risk, high-yield "junk" bonds. A big market existed for such bonds, and they permitted doing deals that could not have been done otherwise. In the course of this activity Milken made himself and many others rich and made Drexel—at least for a time—a major factor in the financial world. A jury of Milken's peers decided that he violated some of the very complicated securities laws and put him and Drexel out of business.

The fall of Milken and Drexel stopped the junk bond market temporarily, but it had such an obvious place in the financial world that it recovered after a few years. Now transactions are being done with junk bonds at a volume greater than in the 1980s. I was a slow learner and did not get comfortable with junk bonds until my third LBO.

II.
LBO Stories:
no two plots
the same

The Lake Charles plant in about 1984, when Vista purchased Conoco Chemicals from DuPont. Among the plant's products were biodegradable straight-chain alcohols made from ethylene.

CHAPTER SEVEN

VISTA
CHEMICAL

CORPORATE GIANT EDUCATES NOVICES

AT THE RIVER OAKS COUNTRY Club in Houston is an institution known as the "breakfast club." Such country clubs have two types of golfers—those who live predictable lives and play golf every Saturday morning in the same foursome and those whose business and travel do not permit such a regular schedule. Members of the second group spend a good part of Thursday on the telephone trying to set up a foursome for Saturday. Even the casual golfers try hard to arrange a foursome. The penalty for failure is spending Saturday morning at home with the risk of being pressed into domestic chores.

Such problems usually generate a solution. The solution at River Oaks is that the lost golf souls start assembling at 7:30 A.M. on Saturday morning for breakfast at the club. There is a drawing to set up the foursomes, and each player puts ten dollars in the pot for the winning team. The original informal arrangement now has a chairman each Saturday to supervise the drawing. The one or two foursomes of the early days of the breakfast club have grown to twelve or fourteen. For four hours each Saturday one has three friends who are keenly interested in one's well-being insofar as it may help win the money.

Most of the players arrive by 7:30 A.M., with breakfast over by 8:00 A.M. and tee-off time at 8:30 A.M. The eager ones fill the thirty-minute gap by rushing to the practice tee, while a few stay and chat with friends over coffee. In the late summer of 1982, in such a chat with John Burns, Vista Chemical was conceived. John had worked with me when I was at Conoco and at the time of our chat was running the Conoco Chemicals business for DuPont. I had a hunch that DuPont might be willing to sell this business. It did not fit with any of the other parts of DuPont, and large companies were just beginning to consider disposing of units that did not fit in their core business.

When I raised the subject of this purchase before our Saturday morning golf game, John responded immediately. DuPont had acquired the chemical business he was running when they acquired Conoco in 1980. John was concerned that DuPont might break up his unit and assign the parts to different departments of DuPont. I was still trying to buy a small chemical business, but the prospects for success were looking poorer each day. In the back of my mind was the thought that I might be more successful with a business I knew thoroughly, even if it was much bigger than I had planned. Further, I sensed something that became obvious later; large deals are easier to do than small ones. Both John and I used the term "LBO," which was just becoming part of the vocabulary of people on the fringe of the investment world. Neither of us had more than a vague idea of what was involved.

Neither John nor I knew that we were starting on a nineteen-month-long journey that would teeter on the brink of failure many times, led there usually by the capriciousness of some individual or institution. But then we would be rescued by someone with a vested interest in our success.

I had been through the mechanics of buying companies at both Conoco and Petro-Tex, but both times with the support of a large corporate staff and with someone else worrying about the source of money. My experience in running small, troubled companies had given me some appreciation of the problems hiding in environmental, tax, employee benefits, and other such specialized fields, but I had little competence to deal with them. I needed expert help when these matters arose, and I would have to pay for it out of my limited financial reserve.

GETTING STARTED

John wanted to talk to firms such as Kolberg, Kravis and Roberts or Gibbons Green, which were just then becoming known as sponsors of LBOs. I wanted to work with E. F. Hutton. At that point Hutton was a very successful retail brokerage firm but no powerhouse in the investment banking world. My relation with Hutton had started on the Alaska project in early 1978, when we employed numerous legal, economic, political, and financial advisors; among the financial advisors were Lehman and E. F. Hutton. Although Lehman was far better known as an investment banker than Hutton, the man from Hutton, Jim Lopp, was much more effective than the Lehman men. He was young, handsome, and knowledgeable and was clearly the leader in any discussion of financing. In selecting specialists to give advice, I have always decided on the basis of the people involved rather than on the organization's reputation.

When I decided to try to buy a medium-sized chemical operation, it was logical that I approach Jim Lopp of Hutton for help in financing my idea. By then Jim had gone on to bigger things in Hutton than working on speculative ventures with an elderly entrepreneur. He assigned a young man, Jim Gale, to work with me, who turned out to be a fortunate choice. He was intelligent, industrious, and knowledgeable about investment banking. He had an air of naïveté that disguised the fact that he was a very able investment banker. Also, he was far enough down in the Hutton organization that he was enthusiastic about being assigned to such an unlikely project.

John Burns spent about two months convincing himself that we should not work with one of the well-known LBO firms and finally agreed to try Hutton. Jim Lopp recognized that buying Conoco Chemicals was a larger project than the ones we had worked on together. He transferred Jim Gale to work for Clarke Ambrose and assigned the pair to the Conoco project. Clarke was a veteran at Hutton and in investment banking. He had the depth of experience in financing large projects that Jim Gale and I lacked. With Jim's energy and enthusiasm, Clarke's experience, and my knowledge of the chemical business, we had a good team.

Next we added the managers of Conoco's chemical business to the team: John Burns; Bob Lehmkuhl, vice president, operations; John Langford, vice president, commercial; and Johnny Weidner, who was then managing some of Conoco's human relations functions but who became chief financial officer. These men were essential to our success because they brought insight into the current conditions of the business that I did not have. They were involved in the day-to-day operations, and their presentations to lenders and investors were more effective than mine ever would have been.

The other employees had spent their careers working for Conoco or DuPont, both stable, paternalistic employers. The idea of working for a new, highly leveraged operation would disturb these people. Having the four key members of management as part of the team would reassure worried employees.

Joe Flom of Skadden Arps was Clarke Ambrose's personal lawyer and good friend. Irv Shapiro, the retired chairman of DuPont, was a recent addition to the Skadden Arps firm. Clarke told his attorney, Joe, of our interest in buying the Conoco chemical business, and Joe talked to Irv. Irv set up a meeting with the appropriate people in DuPont and then withdrew from any further participation. Apparently he wanted no hint of conflict of interest between his new job as a lawyer and his old job as head of DuPont.

On December 9, 1982, Clarke, Jim, and I took the train from New York to Wilmington, Delaware, where John Burns joined us to meet with Robert Richardson, an executive vice president and member of the management committee of DuPont. Dr. Richardson, a Ph.D. in chemistry, had spent most of his career in DuPont in research. He was an impressive man, somewhat aloof, who tended at least in our first meeting to make pronouncements rather than engage in dialogue. The meeting had the air of a visit by three priests from a minor Latin American country to a senior cardinal in the Vatican. Subsequent meetings were more relaxed, and in time we developed a warm, comfortable relationship with Richardson and all the DuPont people with whom we worked.

Richardson made the same speech every seller of a business makes. It starts with a firm assertion that they are not required to sell the business and is followed by an admission that because of a recent change in corporate objectives or policy they will entertain offers, provided, of course, the price is satisfactory and in cash. Notwithstanding this official coyness, Richardson had appointed a team to deal with us: Everett Yelton, vice president of petrochemicals; Dick Rea, legal; Marty Mand, financial; and George Amoss, controller of the petrochemical department. We met all of them either in Richardson's office or afterward.

Richardson told us that all requests for information should go to George Amoss and the information would then come back to us through him. He announced toward the end of the meeting that DuPont did not intend to conduct an auction of the business, but they would not sell it to us without getting a competitive offer. They intended to get such an offer from a previously selected company. We thought this was a German company, but we did not know which one. We still do not know whether another company actually made an offer, but we assumed that we had competition and operated accordingly. About a month later Richardson barred us from having any further contact with John Burns and the management of the Conoco chemical business until we had signed a letter of intent.

After about a six-week wait DuPont provided financial information for the first nine months of 1982 that evoked as many questions as it answered. We needed details to prepare financial scenarios for various economic situations. There was a series of meetings in which we discussed what operations would be included in the package being sold. DuPont management decided not to sell Condea, the joint operation in Germany, and a small operation that made a chemical that when added to crude oil made it easier to pump. Conoco earlier had sold the PVC business in England and an operation near Philadelphia that made detergents for lubricating oil.

The Japanese joint ventures I had started would be part of the package, along with the detergent alkylate plants in Lake Charles and Baltimore, a straight-chain alcohol plant in Lake Charles, PVC plants in Oklahoma City and Aberdeen, Mississippi, and an ethylene and vinyl chloride monomer plant in Lake Charles. In addition, we were to get Conoco's 25 percent interest in PASA in Argentina and a 50 percent interest in Petresa, a Spanish detergent alkylate business, if the Spanish partners agreed to the transfer. This made two logical packages. One consisted of the largest detergent raw material business in the world and the other of a PVC business that was average-sized but well integrated, from ethylene to PVC compounds. It was the same collection of businesses that I had put together in the late 1960s.

We also started trying to settle some of the major issues that would arise in the final sales contract. DuPont agreed to be responsible for correcting any known environmental deficiencies at the time of closing. Neither side realized it at the time, but this developed into a significant expenditure for DuPont.

In transactions like this both sides make a strong commitment to the proposition that the employees suffer no loss in their pensions and other benefits. Then each side spends hours trying to write the contract so that the burden falls on the other. In this and all subsequent LBOs we have committed to continuing the same wages and benefits packages for the employees and to protecting them from any loss of pension benefits. Fortunately, I had spent hours with an expert to become knowledgeable on pension plans. Our solution was fair to all parties. DuPont agreed to transfer a sum of money to our pension plan to allow the employees to receive pensions equivalent to those at DuPont.

Another major issue in such negotiations is the representations and warranties the seller makes. The buyer wants strong representations to the title and condition of the facilities, while the seller wants to sell things "as is." We could settle for less than the best representations in this case because I knew the plants that had been owned and operated by DuPont and Conoco were in good condition and free of any title problems.

Skadden Arps was our counsel in these negotiations, and they appointed Mike Goldberg and Paul Francis to the job. Mike was a very senior partner and certainly a lawyer of great ability. In the first conferences with DuPont, Mike spent all the time in another room talking on the telephone, I presume to other clients. After that he stayed in the background, and we saw him only when some major issue arose.

So our legal matters were left in the hands of Paul Francis, an associate. Paul was slim and a little below average height. He wore horn-rimmed glasses and gave the impression of being the kind of lawyer one would find deep in a legal library writing briefs for other lawyers. At first I was irritated that Skadden Arps regarded our job as being worthy of only an associate. This feeling wore off rapidly, however, as we worked together. Later, when I was better established, I paid Paul the highest compliment I could by trying to hire him, but he took a job with Merrill Lynch.

It is important to have the right lawyer. The chances are good that any partner of a major law firm will have the requisite legal skills, but more important is that the chemistry between you and your lawyer be right. He must know your position on every issue and when you are wrong guide you tactfully back on course. He must have the respect of the opposing lawyers and be able to establish a good working relationship with them. He must have a sense of humor and an ability to live for days in paper-strewn conference rooms on stale delicatessen sandwiches and lukewarm coffee. Paul Francis was ideal for this job.

The lawyers to avoid are the gladiators who feel obliged to debate each legal point, whether or not it has any bearing on the issue. Another type to avoid is one who thinks, probably with justification, that he is smarter than the client and tries to improve on the deals the client has made. Of course, some of this may be encouraged by clients who have second thoughts about the agreements they have made and use their lawyers as an excuse for changing their position.

Legal conference rooms, the main arena for combat in large business transactions, have a sameness, whether they are in large law firm offices or in corporate headquarters. They never have outside windows. The sides are glass from about waist-high up. From one to four sides are open to view, and anyone passing by can see who is in the room and whether they are talking amicably or angrily. It is no great surprise that word of many supposedly secret transactions leaks out when they are conducted in such a fish bowl.

Maintaining secrecy in such transactions, however, is both necessary and burdensome. I wanted to keep our negotiations secret to avoid encouraging any other potential buyers. In addition, most sellers prefer to keep secret that parts of their business are for sale because such information disturbs the employees, customers, and suppliers. Many deals have been aborted when one or both parties become irritated by premature publicity.

One quickly adopts the habits of a CIA agent. The answer to a question about my destination on leaving Houston to visit DuPont was "the East Coast" or, if pressed, "Philadelphia," but never "Wilmington." On the occasions when I ran into someone I knew in Wilmington, I would fabricate a logical-sounding story to explain my presence there.

These initial discussions with DuPont were intended first to give us confidence that we understood the information they were supplying, and second to determine that we did not differ significantly on major issues. Meanwhile, as I attended meetings, Clarke, Jim Gale, and various Hutton people were trying to develop sources of financing.

FINANCING

We determined that the banks would lend us only 65 percent of the purchase price. To give the best possible return, we wanted to limit the equity to 10 percent, which meant that we needed to raise 25 percent as subordinated debt. This had to be high yield to sell it, and it was obviously high risk. We estimated that we would bid about $600 million for the package, which meant we needed about $150 million in subordinated debt.

Because of their relation with Hutton, Manufacturers Hanover and Bankers Trust agreed to be co-agents to put together a bank syndicate to provide the senior debt. My only contribution was to meet occasionally with bank officials to explain some aspect of the business.

Junk bonds were around in the spring of 1983, but they were not part of Hutton's or my repertoire. The conventional wisdom at the time was that there were only three sources for the amount of subordinated debt we needed: Metropolitan Life, the Teachers Retirement Fund of New York, and Prudential. Hutton could not arouse any interest at Metropolitan. They did get Teachers and Prudential to listen to our story. I spent three or four meetings at Teachers explaining the business, but I evidently was not a good teacher of Teachers. After about two months they said that the business of converting ethane to ethylene, ethylene to vinyl chloride monomer, vinyl chloride monomer to PVC with some ethylene being converted, and so forth, confused them. They asked us to go away and let them invest in things they understood. I have heard that chemistry textbooks became required reading at Teachers a few years later when they learned how much was earned by Prudential and the group of insurance companies that accepted our deal.

In the meantime Clarke, Jim, and I were talking to Prudential: They covered the financial matters, and I was the chemistry professor. The man at Prudential, Dennis Murphy, had just been promoted to a level to do projects such as this and wanted to get off to a successful start. He was more patient in learning chemistry than an older hand might have been. Our negotiations went well except that Prudential knew that they were our last hope and charged accordingly. They got the right to buy 58 percent of the fully diluted equity. Prudential and the eight other insurance companies put up $17.5

million for 175,000 shares of common stock; $19 million for pre-
ferred stock with warrants for 190,000 shares of common stock; $50
million for the senior note; and $110 million for the subordinated
note; with a total of $196.5 million being invested.

Technically, Prudential was not the agent for the other companies, but the other companies accepted Prudential's lead, and we had
only a few short meetings with them. An indication of the high cost
of subordinated debt is that with the warranty the insurance companies would own 66 percent of the company.

Arranging financing for the detergent business was no problem.
It had consistently been profitable, even in recession years. On the
other hand, PVC, a plastic used to make pipe, floor tile, and shower
curtains, was also a significant part of the business, and in the previous five years this business had made as much as $25 million in one
year and lost $27 million in another. It was hopeless to convince any
bank or insurance company that the PVC business was worthy of
credit. In fact, this part of the business almost made the deal un-
financeable. We solved the problem by dividing the transaction into
two parts—a separate company for the manufacture of PVC and another one for the remainder of the businesses, which involved mostly
detergents. We borrowed over 90 percent of the total on the detergent business, and we negotiated a separate loan from the Associates, an asset-based lender with whom we had worked on smaller
Sterling Group deals, for only the amount that could be secured by
the liquid assets of the PVC business.

These negotiations brought us to June 1983. Up to this point there
had been an air of unreality in the proceedings. No one on our side
had more than a faint hope that we would be successful. Then DuPont
started to press us to give them a bid, while we wanted to know if we
were in the same ballpark on price. We received special dispensation
from DuPont to talk to the management group because they would
be significant stockholders and should take part in deciding the price.
John Burns, Bob Lehmkuhl, and John Langford came to New York,
where we spent most of a day deciding what we should offer DuPont.

The indices by which companies judge capital projects—discounted cash flow or internal rate of return on investment—were not useful in this case. We could have determined what the business might have been worth as a public company and discounted that. At that time, however, chemical companies were not a stock-market favorite, and no one thought that taking this company public was one of the options. Instead, we decided to bid the maximum amount that would let us service our debt and stay comfortably within the covenants of our loan agreements. If we barely accomplished that, we would still have an attractive return on equity because of the high leverage.

In our discussions the management of Conoco Chemicals wanted to bid significantly less than I did. This might have been a surprise at the time, but it no longer is. In subsequent deals involving management the price has always been more than management thought it should be. In the RJR Nabisco deal, as disclosed in *Barbarians at the Gate*, the lowest value of any was put on the company by its chief executive officer.

Richardson telephoned to say that he was coming to New York and wanted to see Clarke, Jim, and me. His message was that DuPont did not intend to haggle over price and that we should make our best offer first. We would not have a chance to change it.

On June 6 we gave them a written proposal to buy the business for $600 million, adjusted for changes in working capital and subject to agreeing on a letter of intent and later a definitive sales contract. Part of the sum would be a $25 million note secured by the PVC business. Six weeks of negotiation followed, with DuPont wanting a larger, all-cash offer. We had already bid as much as we thought we could finance. On July 21 we made a final offer of $600 million, all cash.

After about a week, during which we sweated and they got approval from their executive and finance committees, they verbally accepted our offer and asked that we start drafting a letter of intent. For the first time we began to feel that we might be successful. In hindsight I do not recall why it took from July 21 to October 17 to write a relatively simple letter of intent. Fortunately, during that time we also wrote and agreed on a memorandum outlining how we would settle many other matters that were pending. With the signing of the letter of intent in October we were given full access to the management.

Conoco's Lake Charles chemical plant was separate from its Lake Charles refinery, but they had many ties. They shared barge- and ship-loading facilities, and their steam systems were tied together. Under certain conditions the chemical plant bought steam from the refinery; under other conditions it sold steam to the refinery. Several streams of petroleum liquids and gases moved between the two plants. In all, over thirty agreements—appendices to the final contract—had to be negotiated and written covering the relation between Conoco's refinery and what was to be our chemical plant. It seemed desirable to let the chemical group management, who were familiar with all the details, handle these negotiations.

AN INTERRUPTION IN THE PROCESS

Early on the morning of November 1, I was jogging on a track on the roof of our apartment building when I felt a sharp pain in my chest. I slowed down and it disappeared; I sped up and it returned. I determined that above a pulse rate of 130 a minute, pain; below 130, no pain—likely symptoms of angina. Later that day I was in the hospital having an arteriogram done, which showed blockage of two of the arteries leaving my heart. After consultations the next day with several doctors, including my brother Frank, I accepted the unanimous recommendation that I have bypass surgery and a pacemaker installed. My operation was scheduled for 11:00 A.M. on November 3. There was nothing to do until then but worry. Mary got permission to take me to a movie, and I spent my free time just before surgery seeing *Beverly Hills Cop*.

I can vaguely remember Mary squeezing my hand in intensive care as we had agreed earlier that she would do. My first clear memory after surgery was of hearing the doctor and nurse debating whether to take a tube out of my nose. I tried to cast a vote for, but it did not get recorded. Around me I could hear my fellow victims being made to sit up and told to cough while they were pounded on the back. I remember being concerned about all the pounding so soon after having the chest cut open and wondering when I would get pounded. Evidently this procedure happened to me while I was unconscious.

My recovery was rapid and uneventful except that my heartbeat did not have the proper rhythm. The cardiologists said that this might correct itself. If it did not do so in two weeks, then one of my options was to do nothing, which meant that I would operate at half the capacity thereafter. The other possibility was to undergo electric shock. There was some danger in this procedure, and it might not be effective, but the prospects were good that it would work. I chose to take the treatment. Two weeks later I bounced about six inches off the table when the current hit me, but my heart resumed the proper beat and has kept it since.

I stayed in touch with my associates by telephone both from the hospital and from home, and it was apparent that things were not going well. In nearly two months of negotiations with the Conoco refining people on the thirty-plus contracts that affected the Lake Charles plant, the management had made no progress. The reasons lie in the history of the refining business.

In general, oil refineries are a necessary evil in the oil industry. Oil companies are in the business of finding and producing crude oil, and they are run by exploration and production people. Refineries and filling stations are only devices to dispose of crude. Filling stations are an interface with the public, and company pride requires that they be kept in good condition. Refineries are hidden away behind chain-link fences, with no pressure to spend money on them. Consequently, at budget time the refineries' budgets are cut if money is short. The Conoco chemical management had been negotiating with refinery personnel who for years had lost all the debates on budgets and transfer prices for hydrocarbons being used for chemical feedstocks. The refinery people vented their years of frustration in these negotiations.

Signs of great irritation were coming from Wilmington at the lack of progress. In January everyone involved in the project was summoned to Delaware for a summit meeting. In the meantime Richardson had left DuPont to become head of a Canadian telephone company, and Dave Barnes, another member of the executive committee, presided. He announced that unless the Lake Charles contracts were completed within a month, DuPont would withdraw from the deal. I asked that a higher-level official of Conoco be assigned to negotiate for them and that a senior DuPont officer be appointed to referee disputes. Dino Nicandros, head of Conoco, designated Don Clark, one of his senior executives, to negotiate for them, and DuPont appointed Ernie Ruppe as referee. I was to negotiate for our side with the help of John Langford, vice president of the chemical business.

We returned to Houston and resumed negotiations, with me taking the lead for our side at first but with John Langford taking over as we proceeded. Most of the subsequent differences arose from the Alice-in-Wonderland nature of refinery economics. A refinery converts crude oil into salable products such as gasoline, fuel oil, and jet fuel, plus by-products, some of which may be used as fuel or recycled to make other salable products. Because of the complicated arrangement of a refinery, a clever refinery engineer can arrive at any answer he wants in calculating the cost of a particular product.

The detergent alkylate plant took ordinary kerosene from the refinery and paid the posted price. The straight-chain molecules in the kerosene were removed to make biodegradable detergent alkylate. The remainder was returned to the refinery to make jet fuel. We could prove conclusively that what we returned was more valuable as jet fuel feedstock than the kerosene we took. Their engineers could prove conclusively that the reverse was true. The result was that Don Clark and John Langford generally ignored these arguments between our respective technical people and settled on what seemed reasonable.

The pressure by DuPont to expedite matters caused me to do a very stupid thing. On my first trip back to Wilmington after the ultimatum I had planned to take Mary with me. Ernie Ruppe's wife had agreed to take Mary to visit Winterthur, and Mary was looking forward to seeing this magnificent home with its great collection of Americana.

We arrived at the Houston airport to board our plane to Philadelphia to find the pandemonium that accompanies a major disruption of air travel. A heavy snowstorm on the East Coast had closed all the airports from Washington north. Just as we were leaving the ticket counter to return home, an announcement was made of a flight leaving for the East Coast. The prospects were best to get into Boston, but the flight would land at the open airport closest to New York.

I decided that it would be better to be somewhere on the East Coast where I might be able to get a train to Wilmington than to stay in Houston. I hastily sent Mary home and rushed to catch the plane. She still reminds me that I abandoned her in the Houston airport. Relying on me, she had paid no attention to where we parked the car and had to get an airport policeman to help her find it. She got home safely with nothing damaged but her confidence in her husband's judgment.

MIDNIGHT IN NEWARK

As we neared our unknown destination, the crew announced that we would land in Newark. I relaxed. I could either spend the night at a hotel at the Newark airport and take the train to Wilmington the next morning or take a taxi or bus to New York and the train to Wilmington the next day.

The best laid plans . . . Every hotel in the Newark telephone book was full. No one knew when or if there would be a bus to New York. None of the few taxis would go to New York at any price. Finally, a sullen taxi driver agreed to take me to the Newark train station. I expected that I would arrive at a well-lit station with a clerk or some other railroad employee around to tell me the schedule and the track the train would be on, and that I would then take a train either to New York or Wilmington.

Instead, the taxi driver let me out at the entrance to a dark tunnel and insisted that this was the station. The tunnel ran under the tracks of the main line of the Pennsylvania Railroad from New York to Washington. From the tunnel several stairs rose to the train platforms above. It was almost midnight, and there was no railroad office open in the darkened tunnel. I entered the tunnel to try to find a sign to tell me which staircase to take, but the light was too dim to see any signs, and there were no railroad employees around. I had to guess which staircase to take.

At first I was concerned about being in such a place alone. Then halfway into the tunnel I became more worried when I realized that I was not alone. People were sitting on the stairs and stretched out where the walls of the tunnel met the floor. Some of them muttered as I passed by. The smell of stale smoke, probably marijuana, hung in the air. Thinking there would surely be railroad personnel on the platform overhead, I guessed which stairway might lead to the southbound trains and went up, passing prone and sitting figures on each landing.

The train platform was deserted, no dark figures, no railroad people. I was alone at midnight in a Newark train station with no indication when a train might come or where it might go. My alternatives were to stay and take my chances on a train or to retreat down the stairs through the tunnel past all the mysterious figures to a hotel I had seen a few blocks away. It had no vacancies, but possibly I could persuade them to let me stay in the lobby.

I was spared having to make the decision when a dozen sailors came up the stairs. They were young, noisy, slightly tipsy, and in another time and place might have been irritating. But at that moment they were the best-looking group of young American men I had ever seen. I attached myself to them, determined to go where they went. Our destination turned out to be Philadelphia on a local train that arrived a few minutes later.

I spent the remainder of the night in the Bellevue-Stratford Hotel in Philadelphia and arrived for my meeting at DuPont the next morning a little ahead of schedule. It was the end of the month that DuPont had set as the deadline to finish the contracts, and we were only half done. The matter of missing the deadline was never mentioned.

THE FINAL PROBLEMS

During this time Clarke and Jim were in touch with the bankers and Prudential, and things were going smoothly. Then the Federal Reserve wrote to all of the money center banks, requesting reports on highly leveraged transactions. Some banks treated the letter as a simple request for information, but others thought the sky was falling and pulled out of all their highly leveraged transactions. This event caused a few revisions in our bank syndicate, but after a week or two a revised syndicate was formed with Manufacturers and Bankers Trust still co-agents.

After we signed our letter of intent, DuPont would at intervals make a telephone survey of the institutions that were to finance the project. They obviously did not want to continue if our financial support was weakening. On the morning of Good Friday in 1984 DuPont made one of their regular telephone surveys. Everyone, including Bankers Trust, gave them good reports. Then that afternoon Bankers Trust called us to say that they were pulling out of the deal. At a minimum Bankers Trust spoiled the Easter weekend for all of the groups involved in the LBO. We were close to a panic at the prospect of months of hard work going down the drain.

After Easter we met with Bill Buxbaum, chief financial officer of DuPont, and his aide, Marty Mand. Up to this point DuPont had played the role of a reluctant seller. Selling or not selling this small chemical operation was not a critical matter to their overall business. They were not concerned about losing the deal, but they were irritated at having spent more than a year working on a project only to have it aborted by the whim of one banker.

DuPont did two things. They made it known in the banking community that they wanted to close this deal, and then they gave us a "guarantee." At the top of the paper the word "guarantee" appeared, and at the bottom it was signed by DuPont. In between it said as little of substance as a good DuPont lawyer could write and still fill the space. The document guaranteed only part of the total we were to borrow and only under unlikely circumstances, but the name on the bottom was all that mattered.

Manufacturers Hanover formed a new bank syndicate, including Chase for the first time, but excluding Bankers Trust. Bankers Trust wanted to get back in, and to everyone's great irritation, someone at Hutton agreed to allow this for a small amount. During this time Prudential and the insurance companies stood in mild amusement at the antics of their banking friends.

As noted above, we had planned to finance the PVC purchase with a loan of $50 million from the Associates. The new bank syndicate decided they wanted to handle this part of the financing also. Our position was not strong enough to refuse, so with embarrassment we pulled out of the earlier deal. I subsequently made up for it by giving the Associates first crack at other deals.

From this point on we had only to finish a very complicated sales contract and put out the fires along the way. Some of the small fires involved pipeline rights-of-way. But another small fire, if left untended, could have developed into a major blaze.

One of the things we were to buy was a 50 percent interest in Petresa, a successful detergent alkylate business in Spain that I had started in the late 1960s. The other owner of the business was CEPSA (Compania Española de Petroleos), the only private Spanish oil company. We wanted Petresa because it was successful and complemented our domestic detergent alkylate business. In addition, the plant was located within sight of Gibraltar, and when you visited it, the only place to stay was at the Soto Grande Golf Club. I had been there and had visions of plant inspections that might take days while I spent my spare time on the golf course.

The contract between Conoco and CEPSA provided that if Conoco ever sold its interest in Petresa, CEPSA would have the right to buy the Conoco interest at the designated sales price. This provision did not apply if the entire business was sold, but no definition of "entire business" had been provided. We were confident that the provision gave us the right to buy the interest in Petresa without offering it to CEPSA on the "right of first refusal" provision of the contract. However, our banks insisted that we get a release from CEPSA of their right, even though we thought they had no such right.

Initially, DuPont thought that getting this release would be a simple matter easily handled by their representative in Spain. Months went by with no results. Then John Burns, who had started and run Petresa and who knew the CEPSA people well, tried and failed. These negotiations were all with Juan Antonio Lliso, the head of CEPSA and a good friend of mine and of all the Conoco Chemicals management. In early May, John Langford and I flew to Madrid to talk to Juan Antonio. He agreed to give us the release subject only to concurrence by his bankers, which he thought would be no problem. John Langford and I returned, happy in our success, only to find a telex from Juan Antonio withdrawing from the agreement.

Obviously, Juan Antonio was not in charge. I telephoned and asked him to make an appointment for me with Señor Escamez, head of the Banco Central, to which CEPSA was heavily in debt. The meeting was scheduled, and John Langford and I returned to Madrid to see Escamez. Even after this long I still feel irritation and resentment toward this arrogant old Spaniard. He treated my good friend Juan Antonio as a careless child who had been discussing matters he had no right to discuss. Escamez talked of CEPSA business as if it were his company and Juan Antonio were part of the furniture. We established that we wanted either a release of their doubtful right to buy the DuPont interest or for them to buy it for $50 million, which was the value we had put on the property in arriving at the total price, although its real value was much higher. Escamez said that he would send a car to pick us up at the Ritz the next day, which was Friday, at 3:00 P.M. to bring us to his office for his answer. At that time the next day no car appeared. A call to his office evoked the response that he was gone for the weekend.

Partly in irritation and partly because I had other commitments, I returned to Houston. John Langford had other business in Europe and stayed. On my arrival in Houston I received a cable from Juan Antonio asking us to return. We went back to Madrid, not to see Escamez, but only to have Juan Antonio repeatedly tell us over several days that the answer we wanted was still not forthcoming. John and I spent the return trip planning ways to get the banks to close without a release from CEPSA. We arrived home to find a cable saying that CEPSA would buy the 50 percent interest in Petresa from DuPont for $50 million. Our purchase price went down by this amount.

THE NEW COMPANY

Petresa was the last problem of any consequence. Even with good lawyers and careful preparation, the closing of deals like this is a time of many small crises. For the last few days dozens of lawyers rush around finishing the various attachments to the contract. Invariably, some important but not vital piece will be missing. It is a tribute to the integrity of the legal profession that many multimillion-dollar deals are closed with important parts of the documentation missing, secured only by some lawyer's commitment to supply it later.

The Vista closing in the summer of 1984 followed the usual pattern. Most of the documents are signed before the closing day, leaving only one or two essential documents to be signed on the morning of the closing. As soon as these are signed, calls go out to young lawyers and paralegals stationed in courthouses, where real property is changing hands, for them to make the appropriate filings. Then there is a tense time until calls come back reporting that the filing has been done. Invariably, delays occur: The only clerk who can do the work has taken a coffee break, or the only telephone is tied up. Just before panic sets in, the call confirming that the last filing has been made comes in, and at last the money changes hands.

The worst part is moving money by the Federal Reserve wire system. The system operators can document that only a fraction of one percent of the transfers ever go astray. However, some evil spirit has made this small fraction fall in my deals. Now I try to avoid using the Fed wire systems on the closing day, whenever possible.

This time a wire transfer of $50 million out of our total $560 million was lost. Repeated telephone calls to trace it were unsuccessful, but fortunately just before the banks closed, Manufacturers Hanover put up the missing amount. It is ironic that the missing wire was from Bankers Trust. It was as though they wanted to get in one last lick.

The initial purchase price was $600 million, which was reduced $50 million by the sale of Petresa. Then after a reduction in working capital of $43 million, the final purchase price was reduced to $507 million. The reduction in working capital resulted partly from operating like an LBO rather than a big company and partly from carrying the obligation to Conoco for feedstocks as a payable. It had been carried as an intercompany transfer. Table 1 shows where the funds required to complete the purchase were obtained, and Table 2 shows the division of equity.

Selecting a name for a new company is more difficult than it sounds. In the early legal documents the lawyers use a name like "Newco," but somewhere along the way some filing requires use of the real name. There is usually only a few days' notice, and a scramble to select a name ensues. It cannot be in use by a similar company in any of the states in which the new company will do business.

Many people use the same process that we did to select a name. Suggestions are collected from many sources: secretaries, wives, and, of course, management. The lists are consolidated, and the names you know are already in use as well as the clearly unsuitable ones submitted in jest are dropped. Vista was one of the four or five names that survived all the checks and was so clearly the best of the lot that the choice was unanimous.

Getting the Vista deal closed was like getting back to solid ground after spending two years on a high wire. For that time I lived with the knowledge that any small slip of mine or any whim of a key banker could abort the whole project. During those two years I gave up most of my paying jobs. Our living expenses plus my considerable travel, legal, and accounting expenses came out of my savings. Had the Vista deal not closed, I would have been a seventy-two-year-old man without the funds to maintain my current lifestyle. Mary knew this but never gave the faintest sign of anything but full confidence in my ability to keep us afloat.

For the first few months of Vista's life none of the parts of the business did any better than expected, and the PVC business fell well short. No one close to the business was concerned, because slumps in PVC sales in late summer were common. There was some unease, however, among the bankers.

During these first months all officers of Manufacturers Hanover who had worked on the deal left the bank. Their replacements seemed to start with the conviction that the bank had made a bad deal and

TABLE 1.
FUNDING FOR ACQUISITION OF VISTA CHEMICAL

Sources of funds	
Bank term loan and revolver	$345,000,000
Insurance companies	
Senior note	50,000,000
Junior note	110,000,000
Preferred stock	19,000,000
Common stock (10,800,000 shares)	36,000,000
Total	**$560,000,000**
Uses of funds	
E. I. du Pont	
Property, plant, and equipment	$306,163,000
Inventory and accounts receivable	157,800,000
Patents and intangibles	52,811,000
Working capital	43,226,000
Total	**$560,000,000**

TABLE 2.
DIVISION OF EQUITY IN VISTA CHEMICAL

Ownership from Initial Sale of Stock	Original Offering	Incentive Options	Warrants	Total	Percentage of Total
	(Number of shares @ $100 a share)				
Common stock					
Management group*	55,000	28,915	7,000	83,915	10.7
Directors and other investors†	130,000	—	7,000	130,000	16.6
Institutional investors‡	175,000	—	190,000	379,000	48.4
Preferred stock					
Institutional investors‡	190,000	—	—	190,000	24.3
Total	550,000	28,915	204,000	782,915	100.0

* Included 39 Vista managers, which represents total employee ownership.
† Included Gordon Cain, E. F. Hutton, Capital Southwest, and James E. Barnes.
‡ Included Prudential and eight other institutions, primarily insurance companies.

that their job was to limit the damage. About the same time Chase, which was a latecomer to the deal and had only a small part, started getting active. The Chase team of David Willetts, Mark Hughes, Susan Lintott, and Paul Beckwith took over all routine banking functions, such as letters of credit and interest rate protection, the banking services that Manufacturers would normally have handled. Chase has continued as Vista's banker, and Chase and I started a relation that has been very profitable for both of us.

Conoco Chemicals had an autonomous management, except that the financial, controller, and shipping functions were handled by Conoco headquarters. We were able to persuade the men who had been handling the chemical division functions in the headquarters to transfer to Vista. The major jobs in establishing the new company were to set up new employee benefit plans and develop our own accounting and computer systems. These tasks were all done under the able direction of Johnny Weidner, the new chief financial officer of Vista, with the help of Electronic Data Systems (EDS).

New companies also need directors. I started with the conviction that a high percentage of the boards of U S companies are a disappointment. It is a continuing surprise to see the number of men of good reputation and impressive records, who for a modest fee, a few perks, and another entry in *Who's Who* become rubber stamps for a management. One example is the directors of all the U.S. steel companies, who after World War II let our steel industry fall so far behind that we had to buy technology from abroad to catch up. Another is the directors of the automobile companies who allowed their companies to build shoddy vehicles until the Japanese manufacturers almost took over the U.S. automobile market. One gets the impression that the directors of RJR Nabisco took independent action only after being warned by their lawyers of the consequences of inaction—and after they had created the largest private air force in the corporate United States.

In addition to the three members of the Vista management—John Burns, John Langford, and Bob Lehmkuhl—we chose directors who had no special ties to the management or to me. The new directors were Jim Barnes, chief executive officer of Mapco; Clarke Ambrose of E. F. Hutton; Bill Thomas, chief executive officer of Capital Southwest, a public venture capital company; John Morrow, former chief financial officer of Conoco; and Norman Hackerman, president of Rice University. The group made a hard-working, effective, independent board. I was the chairman.

CASHING IN AND OUT

The financial performance of Vista improved, and by our second anniversary in July 1986 we were all thinking about cashing in some of our winnings. The members of management had borrowed heavily to buy stock and had been living on reduced budgets to pay interest on their loans. I sensed then what later became obvious—that success in an LBO can bring almost as many problems as failure.

There were two camps on the board and in the management: the large majority who wanted to go public and a small minority, including me, who wanted to borrow money, re-leverage the company, and declare a dividend. The fact that the management was unanimous in wanting to go public decided the issue. Its members were all products of a big company environment and were entrepreneurs by accident, not by choice. They had won one big bet, and they did not want to risk their winnings.

Hutton took Vista public in December 1986. After a 30-for-1 stock split the stock sold for $17, or 5.1 times, the initial price. The management sold about 25 percent of its stake. By agreement with the board I sold all my stock and resigned as chairman and member of the board. By this time I had become more interested in doing LBOs than in being a part-time chairman. The $5 million I made on Vista should have been my retirement fund but became instead my capital to do more LBOs.

In the initial capitalization of the company the thirty-nine key employees bought $5.5 million worth of stock, about 10 percent of the initial, fully diluted equity. In addition, they received options on about the same number of shares. These key employees, at the initial public offering (or IPO, the initial sale of stock made when a company first goes public), had stock and options worth about $50 million. If they kept their stock until the sale of Vista to a German company, RWE AG, in 1990, the stock and options were worth $198 million.

I wanted to include an employee stock ownership plan (or ESOP, a trust authorized by federal law to buy stock for the benefit of the employees) in the initial capitalization. The ESOP would borrow money to buy stock for all the employees, and the loan would be repaid by the contributions made by the company. Contributions to the Conoco Chemicals Thrift Plan had previously been invested in the Magellan Fund, which had been so successful that the management thought that replacing the Thrift Plan with an ESOP would be unpopular. In addition, the union at the Lake Charles plant opposed the substitution of an ESOP for the Thrift Plan. There was no ESOP until the 1989 recapitalization, when an ESOP was established that bought 6.3 percent of the outstanding stock. These ESOP shares were worth $47,000 to each craftsman or operator when the company was sold in 1990.

In 1985 the trustees of the Thrift Plan bought on behalf of 485 non-management, non-union employees the equivalent of 801,000 shares (after a 30-to-1 stock split) from E. F. Hutton for $6.133 a share, or $4.9 million total. At the time of the 1986 recapitalization this value had increased to $13 million. Between the initial stock purchase in 1985 and the recapitalization in 1989, Vista employees accumulated about 1.1 million shares in their Thrift accounts with a value of over $60 million.

My interest in offering ESOPs and profit sharing to the Vista employees came primarily from my conviction that success was more likely if everyone had a stake in the business. I was not interested in social theory but was convinced that the combined knowledge of all involved would achieve better results than relying only on the skills of a few.

IN RETROSPECT

Late in 1985 Monsanto offered its Texas City plant for sale, and I was the successful bidder. This deal closed in July 1986, and the company became Sterling Chemicals, Inc. (discussed in Chapter 8). Forming Sterling, of which I became chairman, was added reason to get out of Vista. The two businesses had some small conflicts of interest, which were manageable as long as Vista was private but were a potential problem after Vista became a public company. More important, the excitement of doing deals was much greater than that of running a business.

My decision to get out of Vista was prompted by a change in my goals. I was no longer interested in being a part-time chairman of anything; I wanted to do deals. I also developed a clear idea of how I wanted to do them. I wanted to operate with minimum overhead, not only to save money but to shorten lines of communication and give the management less time to think about anything but the business. All the key people would buy stock with their own money. In addition there would be an ESOP, a conventional stock option plan, and a profit-sharing plan that covered everyone.

My opposition to Vista going public was intuitive. After I read "Eclipse of the Public Corporation" by Michael C. Jensen of the Harvard Business School,* I was able to rationalize my position. There are two reasons for going public: to raise capital for expansion and to give stockholders liquidity. Vista did not need to raise additional capital, and we could have given the stockholders limited liquidity through dividends and stock repurchases. Was the increased liquidity from going public worth the cost?

One of the minor costs of going public is the time managers must spend on stockholder matters. The major cost comes from the managers' tendency to run the business to keep the public stockholders happy. In a stable, growing business this attitude is no problem, but in a cyclic business it is a problem, and Vista and all commodity chemical businesses are cyclic. The average stockholder, even the institutional ones, judge performance by next quarter's earnings and are unhappy with big changes. To keep peace, managers try to produce uniform earnings from what is basically a cyclic business. No business with an economic cycle longer than a year should be public unless it has some way to hedge major changes in its product or raw material prices.

I was also disappointed that I had little effect on the corporate culture of Vista. Operationally, the Vista people took to an LBO situation very well. They reduced working capital substantially, cut down the number of railroad cars required by 20 percent, and made numerous other improvements. In fact, they did everything possible to improve the operation except to reduce the size of the management staff. By Conoco–DuPont standards the organization was lean. By

---

* *Harvard Business Review* 67:5 (Sept./Oct. 1989), 61–75.

the standards established later in Sterling Chemicals and Cain Chemical (discussed in Chapters 8 and 9), it was overstaffed, with the cost and inefficiencies that come from overstaffing.

I must give Vista credit for making me aware of Dr. W. Edwards Deming and his work. Shortly after the formation of Vista we were informed by the Ford Motor Company that we must have a statistical quality control program if we were to sell our products to them. They suggested that we use one of Dr. Deming's disciples to help us put in a program. Deming was a Ph.D. in mathematics and a specialist in the application of statistics to quality control problems. He went to Japan in the late 1940s and is credited with having changed "Made in Japan" from a symbol of shoddy merchandise to one of high quality.

Deming measured and recorded on a graph the quality of output of each operation. Then he determined the extent to which the variations were a result of human error and which resulted from other factors such as the equipment or the raw materials. Then with the help of the people involved in the operation, he determined the changes to be made. The involvement of the people doing the work is an important part of the process. They know things that no one else knows, and if they are involved in developing the solution, they are more likely to make it work. I left Vista before the Deming programs were in full operation, and it was not until the formation of Sterling Chemicals and Cain Chemical that I saw what a powerful force Deming's ideas could be in improving operations.

Among the things I took away from the Vista experience were a modest (at least by later standards) amount of money, a great admiration for the DuPont company and its people, and many good friends, some of whom I first met as adversaries across a conference table. The regrets are minor—that I did not oppose more effectively Vista's, and later Sterling Chemicals', going public and that I did not in the Vista case establish an ESOP at the beginning, which I have in all subsequent deals.

Because of my lack of experience the Vista deal took at least twice as long as it should have. We succeeded because of the patience of the DuPont people, the skill of Clarke Ambrose and Jim Gale in raising money, and the excellent Vista management, which gave lenders confidence that we would do what we promised. With such a learning experience I could go on to doing other deals with confidence.

CHAPTER EIGHT

STERLING
CHEMICALS

FIRST JUNK BONDS

In mid 1985 Monsanto decided that its Texas City plant no longer fit its corporate objectives. The plant produced only commodity chemicals used as raw materials—for example, styrene, acrylonitrile, acetic acid, and plasticizers. Styrene is used to make polystyrene, which appears as foam cups and food containers; many rigid molded products; and synthetic rubber. Acrylonitrile is used to make wool-like synthetic fibers and is the "A" in ABS resin, which is used for large, strong, molded products (e.g., television sets and canoes). Acetic acid, the main component of vinegar, is used to make many types of adhesives and water-based paints. Plasticizers are what the name implies, chemicals to make plastics more flexible. Monsanto wanted to move away from these commodity-type products to more specialized, higher-margin chemicals. Divesting the plant was a logical step in implementing the new policy.

Although the chemical business is a large industry, its management personnel form a small community in which news travels fast. Word of Monsanto's decision, together with the fact that they were already talking to several major companies, including Amoco and Sohio, reached me quickly. My first inclination was to treat the story as an interesting news item and to conclude that against such impressive competition trying to acquire the plant was a waste of time.

This particular plant has a special place in my memory. In April 1947 I was flying into Houston from New York when I saw in the direction of Galveston a tremendous fire. On landing we were told that a major explosion had occurred in the Monsanto plant in Texas City. The story was not quite accurate. A ship loaded with ammonium nitrate, moored to a public wharf adjacent to the Monsanto plant, had a fire in the hold. People from the town and the Monsanto plant had gone to the area to watch the firefighters work. The ship exploded, devastating the Monsanto plant and killing more than 500 people, of whom 145 were Monsanto employees. The fires raged out of control for days.

Ammonium nitrate is a powerful oxidizing agent and has ambiguous properties. It is a commonly used nitrogen fertilizer applied in solution or mixed with other plant nutrients. Mixed with oil, it is an explosive used in strip mining of coal and iron ore. Mixed with any combustible material, it has the potential to explode. One possible explanation for the Texas City explosion is that this load of ammonium nitrate had somehow been contaminated by oil. None of this should have been a surprise to an industrial historian. A few years after World War I, a warehouse full of ammonium nitrate exploded in the BASF plant in Ludwigshafen, Germany, killing several thousand people. A more recent example of the chemical's explosive properties is the 1995 Oklahoma City disaster.

In addition to its place on the list of industrial disasters, the Texas City plant has an important place in the history of the U.S. petrochemical industry. It was one of the first such plants built in 1943 on the Gulf Coast to supply styrene monomer for the government's synthetic rubber program. Many of the processes that are common to the industry were pioneered in the Texas City plant.

GETTING STARTED

My call to Monsanto in the fall of 1985 brought word that the sale of the plant was being handled by Earl Brasfield, an executive vice

The fire that destroyed the Monsanto Chemical Company in Texas City, Texas,
April 16–17, 1947. A ship carrying ammonium nitrate moored next to the
plant and later exploded, setting off additional explosions that killed more than
five hundred people. Courtesy AP/World Wide Photos.

president, and he would call me later. When he called, he was friend-
lier and more encouraging than my prospects of buying the plant
warranted. (I learned later that Earl had been the Monsanto representative in a joint venture with Conoco Chemicals. The Conoco
Chemicals people, now Vista, had given him reports on how well
that deal had gone.) He agreed to send a copy of the prospectus to
me and to arrange a visit to the plant.

By this time I had confidence that I could do a major LBO without an investment banker partner. Through Vista I had developed a
good relation with Chase Manhattan Bank, which could be a source

of senior debt, and with Prudential Insurance Company, which could be a source of subordinated debt. By then it was apparent that getting equity for an LBO was no problem.

I called David Willetts of Chase and Dennis Murphy of Prudential and asked them to join me in the investigation of the Texas City plant. David and Paul Beckwith of Chase came, and Dennis sent two men from Prudential. The five of us made a good team.

The financial record of the Texas City plant was discouraging. In the past five years it had made a small profit half the time and lost a little the other half. Over those five years the plant had more or less broken even. This type of record did not encourage lenders, but the whole story was not presented in the profit-and-loss figures. The financial records showed that Monsanto had been allocating $27 million a year in overhead to this operation. I was confident that the overhead could be cut to $7 million a year or less, which constituted a $20 million a year improvement in EBDIT (earnings before depreciation, interest, and taxes), helpful but not enough to get Prudential or Chase to sign up on a deal that would cost over $200 million. Something more had to be done.

I had a vague hope that we might be able to get a contract for all or part of the output of one of the units, which might help in the financing. However, it could not be merely a conventional chemical sales contract; it had to be a bankable contract. Styrene, plasticizers, and acrylonitrile all had erratic histories, fluctuating from profits one year to losses the next, and no buyer wanted to be tied to a contract for a product with such a variable history. Our best possibility for a product that would provide a financeable contract was acetic acid.

On the other hand, our best prospect for increasing earnings lay in the styrene plant, which at that time was about breaking even. The plant had a capacity of 1.5 billion pounds a year and was one of the lowest-cost producers in the world. Even a small improvement in the styrene margin multiplied by a billion and a half would significantly add to profits.

The domestic styrene industry was operating at 89 percent and the world styrene industry at 83 percent of "name-plate" capacity— the capacity that the builders of the plant announced it would have. For the previous decade the consumption of styrene had grown at the rate of 1.6 percent a year domestically and 3.6 percent abroad. With no new capacity being built or even on the drawing board, the present rate of increase in consumption would mean a styrene shortage and higher prices in about five years—far too long to interest investors.

What factors might cause this process to accelerate? First, the effective capacity of the styrene industry might be less than its name-plate capacity. Second, polystyrene competes with paper, wood, and aluminum, and price was an important factor. The recent drop in oil prices had reduced the cost of raw materials going into styrene by eight cents a pound, bringing the price of styrene down from twenty-four cents a pound to sixteen cents a pound. This drop in price would make styrene more competitive and increase its use. If these two assumptions were correct, the styrene shortage and higher prices could come within a year.

The first meetings with Monsanto in St. Louis answered the many questions we had about the information they gave us. We also discussed some of the critical issues of the contract, such as the handling of environmental liabilities, employee pensions, and so on. Earl Brasfield handled the discussions, with the help of Dick Stohr of Monsanto's legal department. As always with big companies there were six or eight other people in the room. John Bland of the Houston law firm of Bracewell & Patterson and I represented our side.

I started working with John on some of the smaller deals that were done in The Sterling Group, and he proved to be the ideal lawyer for me. We share the same values. We have worked together so much that each knows where the other stands on every issue. In addition, he works well with other lawyers, and on many occasions when I made a mistake, John either set me straight without letting it be obvious or took the blame.

NEW PARTNERS

About this time in late 1985 two important things happened: Prudential withdrew, and Virgil Waggoner joined the project. Although the withdrawal of Prudential seemed like a disaster, I was later glad they were out. They called to say that their management had decided not to make any investments in commodity chemicals. Decisions to "redline" areas or industries may make lenders' jobs easier but may also keep them out of some good deals. Had Prudential made the same investment in Sterling Chemicals that it made in Vista, their investment of $100 million in July 1986 would have been worth $600 million two years later.

With Prudential out we needed help in raising subordinated debt and started talking to investment bankers. The first was E. F. Hutton, but my friend Clarke Ambrose had other responsibilities in the firm, and the chemistry between the people he sent and me was not right. We talked to other investment bankers, but none made a lasting impression. In Morgan Stanley, with Charles "Chas" Phillips and Bill Laverack, we found a fit. They proposed to sell high-yield bonds for us publicly, which in this case does not mean selling to "widows and orphans" or even to the general public. It means registration with the Securities Exchange Commission (SEC) followed by sale to sophisticated investors. This was my first experience with what are commonly called "junk" bonds.

In 1950 Virgil Waggoner joined Monsanto in the Texas City plant as a research chemist out of the University of Texas. By coincidence Bill McMinn, who later became president of Cain Chemical, joined Monsanto in Texas City, and Virgil and Bill worked together as members of the research department. Early in his research career Virgil realized that he would never expand the boundaries of science and arranged a transfer to marketing, which turned out to be a good decision for both Virgil and Monsanto marketing.

Virgil rose steadily through the Monsanto management to become a senior vice president. Then an opportunity to be president of El

Paso Products Company, the chemical division of El Paso Company in Odessa, Texas, caught Virgil's attention. After a few years El Paso was acquired by Burlington Northern Railroad Company, which sold the chemical business, leaving Virgil free. When I first talked to him, he also was trying to buy the Texas City plant, and he was having misgivings about the commitment of his financial backers. Evidently he became convinced that they were not likely to go forward, and he agreed to join me.

Virgil and I made a good team, though we are quite different: The words "extrovert" and "introvert" could be defined by describing our respective personalities. I had completed two successful LBOs—Vista (Chapter 7) and Arcadian (Chapter 10)—and I had the confidence of financial institutions. I knew the multitude of administrative and legal issues that must be covered in a negotiation, but I knew little about this particular operation. Virgil had spent ten years in the Texas City plant, first in research, then in marketing, and then as the general manager. He knew the plant, the products, and the people, and he knew the questions to ask, especially about old environmental issues, that would never have occurred to me.

Acetic acid was our one hope of getting a sales contract that might support some of our financing. We initiated negotiations with USI (or U.S. Industrial Chemicals, now Quantum) and Celanese Corporation of America on acetic acid, with the aim of securing a bankable, long-term contract. We made little progress with USI, but discussions with Celanese were encouraging.

We negotiated with Aristech and BASF on plasticizers, but we clearly could not get a contract that would be helpful in financing. Moreover, both Virgil and I had been in the plasticizer business before, and neither of us wanted to get involved with it again. Such a business would take a larger marketing and distribution organization than we wanted to develop, so we wanted to get someone else to handle these functions for us.

Monsanto announced that they would take final bids in mid January. Before they would take our bid, they wanted assurance that we could raise the money if we were the successful bidder. We arranged for David Willetts and Mark Hughes of Chase and Chas Phillips and Bill Laverack of Morgan Stanley to meet with the key Monsanto executives. Both Chase and Morgan Stanley declined to give us a firm commitment but exuded enough confidence in their ability to finance the project that Monsanto accepted us as a bona fide bidder.

The first deadline for submitting bids was called off at the last minute because one of the bidders was not ready. We had to sit idly for two nerve-racking weeks, thinking that the extra time was just what someone else needed to submit a better bid than ours.

About this time either Virgil or I had what turned out to be a great idea. British Petroleum (BP) was a major factor in the acetic acid business everywhere except in the United States; they might pay a premium for quick access to the U.S. market. We called them and received a prompt response that they wanted to talk.

NEGOTIATIONS

At the end of January we submitted our bid of slightly over $200 million and were told that we were the winner, provided Monsanto could be assured again that Chase and Morgan Stanley were still confident about the financing. They were, and Monsanto accepted our bid. There followed six months of steady negotiations on contracts, the last of which was not signed until five minutes before 2:00 P.M. on the day of closing, with a 2:00 P.M. deadline to get the money transferred. In the center ring was the contract for Monsanto's sale of the property to us. On either side were the negotiations with BP on acetic acid and with BASF on plasticizers. One of the other important negotiations was with the Monsanto purchasing department on toll-processing or conversion arrangements to supply them with styrene, acrylonitrile, and tertiary-butylamine (TBA). Under these arrangements Monsanto would supply the raw materials, and we would convert them into styrene, acrylonitrile, and TBA for a fee. These contracts had value to the lenders because they gave us an assured but low return and reduced our working capital requirement on this part of the business.

Negotiating with Monsanto differed from negotiating with Du-
Pont on the Vista acquisition. DuPont came into each session with a
single designated spokesman, who had developed in advance the company positions on each of the issues to be covered. He had some
flexibility but not much. If we failed to reach an agreement on some
point, he would agree to reconsider and respond at a later time. After covering the points on which DuPont had a prepared position,
the session was adjourned.

Negotiating with Monsanto was more of a free-form exercise. Earl
Brasfield conducted the negotiations for Monsanto, but he frequently
brought in people from other parts of the company to negotiate on
special issues. Earl had one special tactic that if used by a less likable
person could have caused problems. Whenever a difficult issue was
scheduled for discussion, Earl would find a reason to be away and
leave the negotiations to Dick Stohr and John Mackie. They would
take completely unreasonable positions, and the session would grind
to a halt. We would resume later with Earl, and he would make some
concession from the Stohr–Mackie position. Although the concession would be less than we wanted, we would frequently be more
flexible than we had ever intended rather than go through another
set of unreasonable demands. Both Virgil and I were very fond of
Earl, and we usually came out of each of these episodes with more
admiration for his performance than irritation at being outnegotiated.

Environmental matters take a significant amount of the negotiating time and energy. Before making an accurate assessment of the
price one can pay for a business, an estimate must be made of the
cost of dealing with any environmental problems. First, one must
determine if the plant is in compliance with the current regulations.
In dealing with responsible operators, as I have, the plant records
and the reports to the regulatory authorities are adequate for this.
Next, one must predict the likely changes in the regulations and estimate the cost of compliance.

These issues are simple compared to dealing with past, and usually unknown, problems. In such cases as the Monsanto Texas City

A view of the Monsanto plant after purchase by the newly formed Sterling Chemicals in 1986.

site, industrial plants have been on the same site for forty or more years. Thirty or forty years ago no one was concerned if a little of a chemical leaked onto the ground or if someone piled drums of waste on an unused piece of land. None of this was illegal at the time, and even the most responsible operators were not aware of the damage that could result from such actions. Sterling Chemicals later found the ground water under its plant contaminated with a chemical that had not been used there for more than fifteen years.

Under current law the owner of the property is responsible for correcting any problem. He can get redress if he can find whoever caused the problem, if they are solvent, and if he can prove that they did the deed. Because of these problems few buyers will purchase an industrial property without getting an indemnity from a responsible seller for any preclosing environmental liabilities. More important to anyone doing LBOs is that no financial institution will lend money without a strong indemnity.

Our initial proposal, which Monsanto accepted, was based on getting a complete indemnity from Monsanto for all preclosing environmental liabilities. After the initial agreement Earl must have changed his mind or been pressured by Monsanto to change because he spent a good part of our subsequent discussions trying to limit this indemnity as much as possible without violating the initial commitment. We finally settled for the indemnity we wanted, but one that applied only as long as two out of three—Virgil, Gene Tromblee, and me—were actively involved in the management of the company. Monsanto's rationale was that they trusted us but might not trust our successors. This proved nothing except that flattery works.

We subjectively decided to make a deal with BASF rather than Aristech to market our plasticizers. BASF seemed more willing to make the deal, and we preferred a willing partner to a coy one. We negotiated toll-processing deals with Monsanto on styrene, acrylonitrile, and TBA, under which they supplied raw materials and we converted them into finished product for a fee that was related to the market price for styrene. This would give us a slightly better return than we would have received at low market prices and a lower return at high market prices.

The negotiations with Celanese and BP on acetic acid proceeded in parallel. Our aim was to get a contract that would produce enough assured income to help in borrowing money. We determined that the economic terms we could get from each were the same. However, Celanese had a rigid policy against making any contract for more than five years, and BP would make the ten-year contract that we wanted. We made an agreement with BP under which they would pay us a fixed amount of money a year for ten years for the right to use our acetic acid plant. This contract became the security for a $66 million project loan at a favorable rate of interest. As far as I know, such a contract is not common in the industry.

Two new issues came up after we signed the letter of intent and were well along in the negotiations. Monsanto decided that they wanted to sell their technology for the production of acetic acid. Theirs was the best available technology, and we did not want it sold to someone who was not in the acetic acid business and who might license the process to many companies. This problem was solved when BP, which was in the acetic acid business, bought the technology. Then Monsanto decided to sell their polystyrene business, and we wanted the purchaser of that business to honor the contract we had to sell styrene to Monsanto. Monsanto let us negotiate with Polysar, to whom they planned to sell their polystyrene business, and they waited to close that sale until we had signed a styrene sales contract with Polysar.

Completing the final documents for a transaction like this is always a bigger job than one anticipates. The day before closing, the contract with BP was not complete. At this point the negotiations were between the Chase lawyers and BP's outside counsel because the contract was security for the Chase project loan. At two o'clock in the morning a heated argument broke out between two of the lawyers on a point of law. Once things became quiet enough to permit a rational discussion, it was apparent that the legal point at issue was irrelevant to any concerns either side had. We sent the lawyers out to have coffee and finished the contract in time for me to go home and get two hours sleep. Most of the others did not get any sleep that night.

FINANCING AND THE "ROAD SHOW"

Concurrent with these negotiations Bob Santoski—who had recently joined the group and with whom I had worked on the Alaska project years before—and I were trying to arrange financing. We had no problem convincing Chase to make a $66 million project loan based on the BP acetic acid contract, which was described by one lawyer as a promissory note rather than a contract. But this amount gave us only $66 million of the more than $200 million dollars we needed.

We had to raise the balance on a business that had made no profit over the past five years. We could make a case that we could reduce overhead and that the Monsanto toll-processing contracts had value, which would give us enough to borrow an additional $20 million on a term loan secured by assets that had a replacement value of at least twenty times that amount. We also negotiated a working capital loan, but on the understanding that we would not use any of this loan at closing. So we were still $120 million short, and we had to get this amount as subordinated debt in the form of high-yield bonds, or junk bonds.

We had lost Prudential as a source of subordinated debt early in the proceedings when they decided that commodity chemicals were too risky for them. The Morgan Stanley team of Chas Phillips and Bill Laverack did not seem a bit daunted by the prospect of selling high-yield bonds for a venture that made little money. In normal times this would have been an impossible job, but the 1980s were not normal times in the financial markets.

Morgan Stanley decided that we should sell $8 million of pre-ferred stock convertible to 15 percent of the common stock and $120 million of high-yield subordinated bonds—junk bonds—and regis-ter these with the SEC and sell them publicly. They would be sold to sophisticated investors, but the fact that they were registered would permit these securities to be traded.

The first step was to prepare a prospectus, which consisted of a detailed financial history of what was to be Sterling Chemicals and some limited projections. Much work was required of our accoun-tants and Monsanto's. The business had operated as parts of six dif-ferent Monsanto units, which meant that the accountants had to reconstruct the financial record as though the separate units had been one. I incurred some substantial accounting bills before I had any idea whether we would be successful. The text of the prospectus was divided equally between a description of the new Sterling Chemicals and disclaimers that any and everything in the description might be wrong and one should not rely on the information to make an in-vestment decision.

Then came visits to the rating agencies. Earlier, I commented that much of the financial community regards symbols as reality. This view is especially true of rating agencies. Among them all we found only one analyst—at Moody's—who was interested in anything but numbers. Issues such as the costs relative to the competition, whether the markets were growing or shrinking, and the safety and environmental record were of little interest; only the numbers mattered. We worked to get a B rating. We got a CCC+ rating from Standard & Poor's and a B– from Moody's, the group that showed some interest in more than numbers.

With little effort Morgan Stanley sold to three institutions the $8 million of preferred stock. Selling the bonds required a major effort, starting with a "road show," a part of selling securities that must be experienced to be believed. In getting the "show" to the most places in the least time, firms like Morgan Stanley have developed great logistical skills that equal those of the military. The objective of a road show is to cover the U.S. buyers of this type of security in one week. Big markets like Boston and New York might take a full day each, but typical of other days might be a breakfast meeting in Minneapolis, a lunch meeting in Chicago, and a dinner meeting in Cleveland.

The selling team consisted of me and one or two people from the company to help me explain the business, Phillips, Laverack, and two or three senior Morgan Stanley bond salespeople. At each stop the local Morgan Stanley salespeople would join the group. Somewhere in the background was a pleasant, competent young woman from Morgan Stanley who appeared when last-minute changes had to be made.

At the end of the week you have been to so many places in such a short time and answered the same questions so often that you are in a fog. Then, based on the response to the road show, the interest rate for the bonds is set, and the underwriter's sales force starts trying to get orders. If you have done a good job and if the market is favorable, word comes back in a day or two that the issue is oversubscribed.

A brief feeling of satisfaction lasts only until you talk to some of the bond buyers over a drink, when you learn they remember nothing you said. They know you make chemicals but have forgotten which ones. They bought the bonds for two reasons. First, they had money they needed to invest, and second, they were satisfied with the last issue they bought from Morgan Stanley. The lesson is that the promises you make today are much less important than how well you delivered on yesterday's promises.

With all the parts coming together—the Monsanto contract, the BP contract, the bank loan agreement, and the high-yield bonds—the next step was the closing. Maybe some day I will orchestrate a closing with no last-minute problems, but it has not happened yet. The crisis between the BP and bank lawyers was resolved at 2:00 A.M. the morning before closing, and I thought the last issue was settled. But I was wrong.

CLOSING

Months before, the contract with BASF for them to operate the plasticizer business seemed important, and signing it was a condition of the bank loan agreement. As the negotiations proceeded, the BASF agreement became irrelevant because the plasticizer business it covered became a small part of the whole deal, but it remained a condition of closing. We wanted to take it out of the contract, but the bank people said that it would take days for them to get approval from their lawyers. BASF did not want to sign our contract until they had a contract with the Ethyl Corporation to buy the raw material they needed to produce plasticizers. On the morning of closing we persuaded friends from Ethyl to come to Houston to complete their contract with BASF. Five minutes before two o'clock that afternoon a contract with BASF was signed. Fortunately, we did not depend on the federal wire system to transfer the money. This time it was all in an account at Chase, and we transferred it directly to Monsanto's account at Chase by 2:00 P.M. on August 1, 1986. Table 1 shows the type of funds we had at closing and how this money was

TABLE 1.
FUNDING FOR ACQUISITION OF STERLING CHEMICALS

Funds at closing

Senior debt

Project loan	$66,000,000
Term loan	20,000,000
Revolver*	0
Subordinated notes	120,000,000
Preferred stock	8,000,000
Common stock	5,000,000
Interest	80,000
Inventory sale to BASF	7,146,000
Total	**$226,226,000**

How the funds were used

Monsanto[†]	$195,000,000
Chase Manhattan commitment fee	2,500,000
Other bank fees	1,435,000
Primex[‡]	1,650,000
Preferred stock placement fee	320,000
Bracewell & Patterson[§]	920,000
Coopers & Lybrand[¶]	90,000
Deloitte Haskins & Sells[‖]	180,000
Morgan Stanley	3,545,000
The Sterling Group, et al.[**]	2,450,000
Johnson & Higgins[††]	1,515,000
Miscellaneous	378,000
Total	**$209,983,000**

[*] Consisted of a $60 million line of credit not used at closing.

[†] Our agreement with Monsanto provided for a payment of $216 million adjusted for working capital. The working capital had been reduced by $21 million at closing.

[‡] Because of the tight liability insurance market, Sterling became part of an offshore insurance company, Primex, organized by several chemical companies. The company started with $16,243,000 in working capital. Our initial capital contribution was $1,650,000.

[§] Sterling's lawyers.

[¶] Sterling's auditors.

[‖] Monsanto's auditors, who prepared historical financial information.

[**] Included Virgil Waggoner and Camp, Ross, Santoski & Hanzlik.

[††] Initial insurance premiums.

TABLE 2.
INITIAL SALE OF STOCK IN STERLING CHEMICALS
(IN CURRENT SHARES AFTER A 75-TO-1 SPLIT OF INITIAL STOCK)

Ownership	Original Offering	Incentive Options	Warrants	Total	Percentage of Total
	(In thousands of shares)				
Officers*	6,186	3,188	1,762	11,136	18.5
Senior management	2,712	3,562	—	6,274	10.5
Middle management	2,149	—	—	2,149	3.6
ESOP[†]	9,000	—	—	9,000	15.0
Total employee ownership	20,047	6,750	1,762	28,559	47.6
Directors	7,576[‡]	—	2,755[§]	10,331	17.2
Founders	6,877[¶]	—	2,233	9,110	15.2
Institutional investors	3,000	—	—	3,000	—
Preferred stockholders	9,000[‖]	—	—	9,000	15.0
Total	46,500	6,750	6,750	60,000	100.0

* Five officers.
[†] ESOP shares were owned approximately 35 percent by salaried employees and 65 percent by hourly employees.
[‡] Of which 6,421 were bought by Gordon Cain.
[§] All to Gordon Cain.
[¶] The Sterling Group and associates, excluding Gordon Cain.
[‖] Preferred stock (sold to institutional investors) was convertible into the remaining 15 percent of common stock.

used. We were left with a cash balance in the company of $16,243,000 for working capital. The initial sale of stock is shown in Table 2, with the figures in current shares after a 75-to-1 stock split before the IPO.

ORGANIZATION — EVERYBODY WINS

By the time the Sterling Chemicals deal was closed, I had developed strong ideas on how companies should be organized and operated. Fortunately, Virgil and I were in agreement. First, there should be maximum ownership by the employees, and to do this, we established a leveraged ESOP that borrowed $1.2 million and bought 24 percent of the initial common stock offering (15 percent on a fully diluted basis). The five officers—Virgil Waggoner, CEO; Gene Tromblee, vice president of manufacturing; Doug Metten, chief financial officer; Bob Roten, vice president of sales; and David Heaney, vice president of administration—bought 10.3 percent of the stock and got options on 8.2 percent, and eleven senior management people bought 4.5 percent and got options on 6.0 percent (all based on fully diluted equity). Stock was offered to forty-three middle managers, and all but one bought it. This group bought 3.6 percent of the common equity.

Thinking that the payoff from an ESOP might be too slow to be of immediate value as an incentive, we also developed a profit-sharing plan. This plan has several characteristics that reflect the strong prejudices I had developed as a participant in several corporate bonus plans. The plan does not favor the more visible people at the expense of the anonymous workers in the back room, as does the usual bonus plan. It covers everyone. If anyone gets anything, everyone does. A rivalry is not set up between people or groups. Sterling is in a business where one person alone cannot make a difference because any improvement requires the help of many people.

The payoff is based only on results—in this case, cash flow in excess of what we told the bank we would make. The distribution was made on the basis of salary, and everyone at the same salary level received the same amount. Initially upper-level people received a higher percentage of their salary than people at lower levels did. We distributed the shared profits this way because we paid completely competitive compensation up to about $75,000 a year. Above that amount we paid less than the competition, with the gap widening at the top. Virgil Waggoner, the CEO, received a salary less than half the average for comparable jobs, but he got a higher percentage of salary in profit sharing. We wanted a large part of the key people's compensation to depend on the results. At first, we paid the profit sharing annually in Sterling Chemicals but changed to quarterly payments at Sterling and in subsequent operations.

Much of U.S. industry is badly overstaffed with managers. Employees, at least the kind we were taking over, did not need all of the supervision they had been getting. I was determined to have only a fraction of the usual overhead, not only to reduce costs, but also because fewer managers mean fewer levels of management and shorter lines of communication. Busy people have no time for empire building and interdepartmental squabbling. The controls that are such a big part of most corporations were not necessary in organizations where the managers have a big stake in the success of the venture.

Having a lean organization does not necessarily mean that the people in the organization work harder or longer hours, but it does mean that they do not waste time on unnecessary tasks. For example, Sterling is a large producer of plasticizers. Selling plasticizers requires a large selling organization, technical service, and terminals at strategic points. BASF would perform those functions for us for about the same cost we would incur if we did them ourselves. By having BASF market plasticizers, we saved the working capital that would have been tied up in plasticizers as well as a lot of management effort that would have gone into this low-margin business.

Safety has always been a major concern. Once years ago at Petro-Tex I had to wake up a wife with two small children and tell her that her husband had been killed in an explosion. One does not forget such an experience. Sterling not only has a safety department, but all managers know that their safety record is a major factor in promotions and pay increases. The Texas City plant had a good safety record under Monsanto, and it has improved under Sterling. In a meeting of two hundred petrochemical companies in San Antonio in 1989, there were fifteen safety awards, three of which went to companies in which I was involved.

Our agreement with Monsanto required that we offer jobs to the plant manager and all the plant people. Monsanto had done a good job of reducing the plant staff to a minimum, and we were pleased with the organization. The overhead functions of this business had been performed by various groups in Monsanto, so we did not have to take a separate overhead organization. This freedom allowed us to establish the kind of organization we wanted.

We made Gene Tromblee, who was plant manager, vice president for operations, but also left him as plant manager. With only an hour's drive between the plant and the corporate office, an operations or manufacturing man was not needed in the office. We made Doug Metten, who had been plant controller, vice president of finance and chief financial officer (CFO). Doug was one of the few finance people we have found in a big corporation who had broad enough experience to handle the total finance job. He established treasury, risk, and cash management functions in the corporate office but left all the comptroller and accounting functions at the plant.

Doug had one of the most difficult jobs in the new company, that is, separating the accounting and management information systems from Monsanto. As noted above, this plant had been part of several different divisions of Monsanto, and each used a slightly different system. With Monsanto's help we were able to have our own systems in operation in less than twelve months.

The other key members of the management were Bob Roten and David Heaney. Bob had been at Monsanto with Virgil and then followed Virgil to El Paso, where he became vice president of sales for the El Paso chemical business. When Virgil left El Paso, Bob also left and set up a very successful chemical brokerage business, where his principal enterprise was reselling styrene. David was a partner of Bracewell & Patterson, the law firm that has handled many of our deals, although David never worked on them. He had told the firm that he wanted to leave law and get into business and was actively looking for a business opportunity. We took a chance with David that turned out very well for both. He became the vice president of administration in charge of everything the other three were not doing.

Encouraged by my experience at Vista with Deming's statistical quality-control program (discussed in Chapter 7), we started such a program at Sterling immediately. Virgil was sold on the idea and did a good job of selling the rest of the organization. All the top officers took a four-day course; then we worked from the top down through the organization.

All of the people in these organizations were good, well-trained employees who had been well treated by their employers, but they had been working in units that were known to be for sale, and they were discouraged. Their attitude was "If it ain't broke, don't fix it." Our job was to convert them into motivated employees who were convinced that everything could be done better.

The Sterling plant, the Vista plants, and the plants we acquired later in Cain Chemical and Fiber Industries were all originally designed and operated by very competent organizations: DuPont, Monsanto, Imperial Chemical Industries (ICI), Celanese, and others. These plants did not have quality problems in the usual sense of making off-specification product. They had been so finely tuned that there was no room to improve energy or raw material efficiency. At first glance there seemed to be little opportunity to improve such well-designed and well-operated plants.

On the other hand, we found many things outside of the process that could be improved. By better scheduling we were able to reduce the number of railcars used to deliver product by 20 percent, a change that saved many millions of dollars a year in railcar rent. We reduced inventories by as much as $40 million and reduced working capital by scheduling payables better and getting invoices out quicker and with no errors. The list could go on, and the process still continues at Sterling over a decade later. All of these improvements were suggested and implemented by people on the job.

The economic results are impressive, but even more impressive is the way it has changed the organization. I thought that making all of the employees stockholders through an ESOP would make them involved and motivated, but I was wrong. The announcement of the ESOP made hardly a ripple of interest. The change came when we started involving employees with the Deming Total Quality Program.

When a suggestion for an improvement is made, it is examined by a team of the employees involved. If they decide that the idea has merit, then they refine the solution. A supervisor is involved, but only as a facilitator to get the necessary money appropriated and to be sure the solution will not interfere with some other operation.

The team consists of the people who can contribute and includes members from different departments and levels of management, which has some beneficial side effects. People on the job feel that someone is listening to them, and they are. The members of the team come from any part of the organization that can contribute, and then by working together, barriers between departments are broken. Problems that once went to the top of the chain of command of one department and then over to another department and down its chain of command are now solved by the members from various levels of both departments as they work on a team.

The new philosophy of management has improved the operation of departments, but it has been even more effective in improving interdepartmental cooperation. Sterling had a working capital loan with a provision that the maximum amount borrowed had to stay outstanding for sixty days. Because large payments to several suppliers frequently came at the same time, we often had a larger working capital loan than we needed. The solution required cooperation from four departments: shipping, purchasing, operations, and treasury. An ad hoc team was formed, and they worked out a way to reschedule the payables so that the maximum working-capital borrowing was reduced by more than $10 million. Thus funds became available to pay off debt.

Each quarter Virgil or one of the senior officers talks to all the employees, who are assembled in small groups. He explains the results of the previous quarter and invites a discussion of ways we can improve.

PAYOFF

We arranged financing on the assumption that we would have an EBDIT of $40 million a year. For the first few months after closing we ran at the forecast rate. By the end of the calendar year 1986 it was apparent that although styrene demand in the United States had not increased in 1986, the demand worldwide had increased 5 percent. As a result, by late 1986 we were operating the styrene plant at full capacity to meet the demand from Europe and the Far East. It also became apparent that the effective capacity of the styrene industry was only 93 percent to 94 percent of the name-plate capacity. We announced the first styrene price increase for September 1, 1986, only one month after closing the acquisition, and prices continued to increase during 1987 and 1988. This increase in styrene consumption resulted from such changes as the replacement of paper cups and plates in fast-food stores with polystyrene cups and plates.

During this time the cost of the raw materials used to make styrene increased but less than styrene prices increased. Table 3 shows the price and the margin between raw materials and sales prices for different years in cents per pound.

With these margins on styrene and good prices for acrylonitrile, by the beginning of 1988 we were generating cash at six to seven times the $40 million rate we had forecast. At this point the principal consideration was how to reap some of the rewards of this success. The management people had all borrowed money to buy stock, and their entire financial estate was in Sterling Chemicals stock.

TABLE 3.
PRICE AND MARGIN FOR RAW MATERIALS, 1987–1995

Year	Contract Gross Margin	Spot Gross Margin	Export Spot Price	Contract Sales Price (average)	Stock Price at Sept. 30
	(Cents per pound)				(U.S. dollars)
1987	8.32	22.04	51.51	36.54	—
1988	18.48	36.67	69.21	45.23	16.00
1989	15.46	13.22	34.81	41.58	8.75
1990	7.67	16.11	43.16	41.77	6.00
1991	6.62	3.14	37.26	37.64	5.13
1992	1.49	(0.53)	22.25	24.27	4.00
1993	0.48	(1.63)	20.47	22.58	3.63
1994	2.60	1.60	22.50	23.50	13.50
1995	12.20	0.80	23.90	35.30	8.25

We paid a premium to buy back the last of the subordinated debt and repaid all bank debt except the acetic acid project loan. We then had funds to pay an $80 million dividend ($100 per share on stock that had cost $10) in April 1988 and a $100 million dividend ($125 per share) in September 1988.

At this point there were three possibilities: We could sell the company, go public, or stay private. We had a discussion with a few people who had expressed an interest in buying the company, but none of them seemed likely to pay as much as we could get in a public offering. The dividends we had declared let the management pay off their loans and had given them some significant cash above that. Some of the management wanted more liquidity, so we engaged Goldman Sachs to do an IPO after declaring the $100 million dividend.

The stock, which we initially thought would sell at $20 a share, sold at $16. In 1989, much earlier than anticipated, styrene prices started to slide, as did the profit and the price of the stock. The stock slipped below $4 in 1993, but shortly thereafter started to rise again with the improvement in styrene prices. In the spring of 1995 styrene and acrylonitrile were both in short supply, and the stock went just above $14. By the fall of 1995 it was slightly above $10. Then the styrene price and the stock started down again.

In spite of this the employees of Sterling have done well. The five officers bought 6,186,000 shares of Sterling stock and got options for 3,188,000 shares. They received $33 million on the sale of 25 percent of their stock at the IPO and still own stock worth $86 million at $12 a share. In addition, each owns $1 million worth of stock in the ESOP, and the five have received $50 million in dividends and $2.4 million in profit sharing.

The eleven managers at the next level have stock worth $60 million. In addition, they have received $34 million in dividends and $4.2 million in profit sharing and still have over $2.5 million in the ESOP. The forty-three middle managers were offered stock, and all but seven bought a total of 2,086,000 shares. At the IPO they sold about 25 percent of their holdings for $7.3 million, leaving them with 1,602,000 shares worth $19.2 million at $12 per share. In addition, at the IPO this group held 610,000 shares in the ESOP. Currently, thirty-six of these middle managers are still with Sterling (some have been promoted) and own 635,000 shares in the ESOP. During the period from 1987 to 1993 the forty-three middle managers received $14.1 million in dividends and $4.6 million in profit sharing.

A typical craftsman or operator who earns about $40,000 a year received $35,000 at the IPO, has collected $52,000 in dividends and $17,000 in profit sharing, and has $120,000 worth of stock in the ESOP. The initial buyers of common stock have received about one hundred times their investment.

In 1992, in an attempt to diversify, Sterling bought a sodium chlorate business from Tenneco for $202 million. Partly as a result of better management and partly because of an improvement in the market, the annual EBDIT from this business has increased from $38 million at the purchase to an estimated $61 million for the fiscal year starting October 1, 1995.

Looking back, most of the key people concluded that whatever additional liquidity they gained from going public was only marginally worth the burden of public ownership. Sterling Chemicals has otherwise been an unqualified success. The company has demonstrated the results that a highly motivated, involved group of employees can achieve—and that an organization can be managed, and managed better, with a fraction of the overhead usually employed by larger corporations.

Two lessons can be learned here. First, many U.S. businesses could reduce costs and potentially improve productivity if they reduced overhead and increased the effectiveness of the remaining overhead people. Second, very cyclic businesses like Sterling probably should not be in the public market.

———

Postscript: In early 1996 Sterling Chemicals signed an agreement to sell its stock to The Sterling Group, the organization I helped start but withdrew from in 1992 (see Chapter 6). The transaction is scheduled to close in August 1996. The initial investors will receive about one hundred times their investment. A craftsman or plant operator who has been employed since the start of Sterling Chemicals received $35,000 at the IPO in 1988, $52,000 in dividends and $17,000 in profit sharing over the twelve years, and has assets in his ESOP account worth $190,000. Further the buyer of Sterling Chemicals has agreed to keep all the present employees or pay any that are laid off two years' salary.

Chapter Nine

Cain
Chemical

WHERE NOTHING WENT WRONG

In 1980 the Corpus Christi Petrochemical Company brought on stream a plant capable of producing 1.2 billion pounds per year of ethylene. Ethylene is by far the most important petrochemical, both in terms of volume and value. Its uses include polyethylene, which is the largest volume plastic and is used for food containers, pipes, grocery bags, flexible moldings, pliable film, and rigid sheet. The plant was jointly owned by ICI (37.5 percent); Champlin Petroleum, a subsidiary of Union Pacific (37.5 percent); and Solvay, a large Belgian company (25 percent). The builders had the benefit of ICI's many years of experience in constructing ethylene plants and incorporated the most advanced technology in equipment and operations. However, it was the last ethylene plant built in the United States for more than ten years.

Before this plant began operating, ethylene prices went down, and the entire ethylene industry experienced losses until after we bought the plant in mid 1987. Not surprisingly, the owners were unhappy with the operation and with each other, so they retained Jack St. Clair, a retired president of Shell Chemical, to assist them in selling the plant. They could not have made a better choice. Jack was very knowledgeable, highly respected in the industry, and uniquely qualified to handle the difficult task of getting three parties with widely different interests to agree on a common course.

The owners were unhappy because the plant had lost money from the start. Further, they did not have a common interest: Champlin supplied feedstock but took no ethylene; Solvay was the largest purchaser of ethylene but owned the smallest interest in the company; and ICI was the builder and operator of the plant but only a modest buyer of ethylene. As losses mounted, each owner concluded that it had made a bad deal and wanted to get out. To the credit of the owners' representatives, none of these problems resulted in any personal acrimony.

I first met with Jack St. Clair about the Corpus Christi plant in mid 1983, when I was about halfway through the DuPont–Vista deal and just beginning to suspect that doing LBOs might be more interesting than running a chemical company. Jack explained that it was not officially for sale, but the owners had retained him to try quietly to find a buyer. The plant had been financed with loans guaranteed by the owners, and because it was not profitable, they were repaying the loans as the installments came due. The owners were determined not to sell for less than the unpaid balance of the loans, an amount much more than the plant was worth. In hindsight I was lucky that the number was not lower. Like a dog chasing an automobile, I would not have known what to do with it if I had caught it. Given the state of the ethylene business at that time, I could not have raised the money to buy it at any price.

At intervals of six months to a year I would see Jack and inquire about the plant. The price remained out of my range until the fall of 1986, when he told me that the unpaid balance of the loan on the plant was down to $250 million. This amount was about what I thought the plant was worth, and Jack thought that the owners would sell for that.

I then had the problem of raising money to buy a plant that had never made a profit. I had purchased Monsanto's Texas City plant and formed Sterling Chemicals only a few months before, but there were already signs that the styrene demand would reach capacity in a few months, as I had speculated. My claim that the same thing might happen in the ethylene business was more credible than it would otherwise have been.

For three years I had been studying reports on the supply and demand of ethylene. I thought that some of the same factors that caused a greater-than-expected increase in the demand for and price of styrene might apply to ethylene. These factors were fivefold:

- A decline in oil prices had reduced the price of ethylene-derived plastics and made them more competitive.
- General prosperity in the United States and abroad was increasing the demand for consumer goods made from ethylene.
- Many of the plants had never been pushed and might not produce their stated capacities.
- No new capacity was being built or being planned.
- A sharp decline in the use of ethylene to produce ethanol, acetaldehyde, and acetic acid had masked the large increase in ethylene consumption for other uses.

My theories gave me encouragement but had only a limited effect on our bankers, Chase Manhattan, and investment bankers, Morgan Stanley. We had worked very effectively together on the Sterling Chemicals deal, and I had no inclination to break up a winning team, so I did not approach any other banking companies.

David Willetts, Mark Hughes, and Paul Beckwith of Chase listened to my reasoning about the ethylene supply-and-demand balance with interest but said they would not finance a one-plant, one-product operation. Their advice was to find something to combine with it, which meant finding operations that would use some of the ethylene produced in Corpus Christi. Thus began the assembly of the pieces that became Cain Chemical.

DUPONT AGAIN

The first possibility that came to mind was half of an ethylene glycol plant in Orange, Texas, which DuPont owned jointly with Pittsburgh

Plate Glass Company, or PPG. Ethylene glycol is used for automobile antifreeze and for making polyester fibers. Ethylene glycol plants also make and sell ethylene oxide, which is used in the manufacture of many types of liquid detergents. It seemed likely that DuPont might sell their half of the plant, even though ethylene glycol was an important raw material for their polyester fiber business. I called Ernie Ruppe at DuPont (with whom I had dealt on the Vista transaction) and asked him to determine if the glycol plant was for sale.

In a few days I received a call from Bill Simeral, an executive vice president and member of the DuPont Executive Committee. Bill said that the glycol plant probably was for sale, and he would put us in touch with the proper people. However, he added that DuPont had decided to get out of the high-density polyethylene business and to sell their ethylene plant in Chocolate Bayou and their high-density polyethylene plants at three Texas sites—in Orange, Victoria, and Bay City—as well. The decision to sell these plants was prompted by the same desire to get out of the commodity chemical business that had led Monsanto to sell its Texas City plant. Bill said that a DuPont team had already made presentations to several prospective buyers, and I asked him to add us to the list.

A short time thereafter the DuPont team of Bill Simeral, Bob Bradley, and Bruce Bachman arrived in my office. Bill was a little earthier and more informal than the usual DuPont senior executive. Bob Bradley was in charge of the polyethylene business, which included the business being sold. Both Bill and Bob planned to retire after they finished the sale of the business. With DuPont's permission and encouragement after the sale was completed, Bob became a valuable director of Cain Chemical.

All our subsequent negotiations with DuPont were represented by Bruce Bachman, who at that time was financial officer of the DuPont plastics business. Bruce represented DuPont ably and fairly. We met many times, usually in Wilmington, and I can recall no time when we did not accomplish amiably what we set out to do. We negotiated not only the agreement to buy the plants but also an agreement for DuPont to buy a substantial part of our polyethylene output and agreements on how the Orange and Victoria plants, which were inside larger DuPont plants, would be operated.

OUR TEAM

Bob Santoski, Bill Barnwell, and I started and finished the negotiations that led to the formation of Cain Chemical. Early on we brought Chase and Morgan Stanley into the picture, with either David Willetts, Mark Hughes, or Paul Beckwith of Chase and Bill Laverack of Morgan Stanley as part of our team from the beginning. In making a decision we always considered its effect on our ability to raise money. John Bland of Bracewell & Patterson was the other member of the team from start to finish.

Bill Barnwell had worked with me at Petro-Tex. He had followed Bill McMinn as head of marketing when McMinn went to FMC. Barnwell left Petro-Tex subsequently to join Oxirane, one of the few cases where a scientific entrepreneur developed a major chemical enterprise in a short time and made a lot of money.

That entrepreneur was Ralph Landau, a Ph.D. in chemical engineering from MIT, who after a few years with a major engineering company started his own. In addition to developing a successful company, he and his people were very creative: They developed new processes and catalysts to make a number of important commodity chemicals, and he had a profitable business licensing these processes to other companies. However, when he developed a special process to produce propylene glycol, he exchanged this technology for half interest in a new company, Oxirane, which he formed with Arco. Oxirane was very successful, and in a few years Arco bought Ralph's and his associates' interests for about $300 million. Oxirane then became what is now Arco Chemical.

Barnwell was a vice president of Arco Chemical when he took early retirement a few months before the Cain Chemical project started. He returned to Houston, where we made a deal that I have subsequently made with several other people: We provide an office with The Sterling Group and reimbursement for any out-of-pocket expenses incurred for our account; if an outside opportunity comes up that interests the person in question, he or she works on it and shares in the rewards, if any, on a basis that we determine after the fact. Barnwell's first job was to help me decide whether buying ethylene and ethylene-derivative plants was a good idea, and if it was, to help me convince financial institutions that we were right.

I knew that I wanted Bill McMinn to run the operation if we were successful in putting it together. Bill and I met in 1957, when I hired him to be the third member of our newly organized sales force at Petro-Tex Chemical. He subsequently left Petro-Tex to run the chemical business of the FMC Corporation, one of the owners of Petro-Tex, and he was instrumental in hiring me to run Petro-Tex in 1976 when it was in trouble (see Chapter 5). That job put me back into the chemical business after being on the fringe for six years. In 1985 Bill retired from FMC when he reached fifty-five and saw that he was not likely to become CEO.

As soon as we started to negotiate on the high-density polyethylene business, we found that we did not know enough about this area. We began looking for a consultant to help in the negotiations, one who had the prospect of becoming part of the operating organization if we were successful. We received many suggestions and invited several candidates to visit us. Fortunately, the first to come was John Luchsinger. He was so obviously what we wanted that we called the others and told them not to come. John began as a paid consultant, but within a short time he decided to give up his pay and join the rest of us as an unpaid entrepreneur.

John had spent his career in Union Carbide, largely in the plastics part of the business but also in ethylene glycol. Like Bill McMinn he had reached the level just below the top in his company, decided that he was unlikely to get the top job, and retired early. If we were successful, he was to run the plastics business.

Russell Bowers had been in charge of operations at Petro-Tex when

I went there in 1976, and he became president after I left in 1978. He subsequently moved from Petro-Tex to Tenneco (co-owner of Petro-Tex), where he became head of the Tenneco chemical business. Shortly before I started this exercise, Tenneco sold their chemical business, with Russell still on the Tenneco payroll wondering what he would do next. He joined our group as an unpaid consultant on petrochemicals and subsequently became the head of the ethylene and glycol parts of the business.

Bill Barnwell and I spent hours poring over charts and tabulations of ethylene production and consumption, feedstock costs, and margins for the previous twenty years. We started with several well-known facts. The industry's capacity for producing ethylene had been greater than the market had required for a number of years. Competition had driven the price so low that no new ethylene plants had been built in the United States since 1980. With the demand for ethylene increasing, it was only a matter of time before the demand equaled supply. The question was when, and if we thought the answer was soon, could we convince financial institutions that we were right?

Late in 1985, about a year before we started this project and with the industry operating at slightly above 90 percent of capacity, ethylene prices fell one-quarter to one-half cent per pound. Both the Corpus Christi and the Chocolate Bayou plants had the lowest margin above raw material cost they had had in years and operated at a loss. At the time I was negotiating, the industry was operating at 94 to 95 percent of capacity, and the price of ethylene was only six to seven cents above raw material cost. A margin of ten to twelve cents a pound is necessary to give a satisfactory return on investment.

An antitrust expert might conclude that ethylene prices are controlled by an oligopoly, but an oligopoly of buyers, not sellers. One explanation for ethylene prices staying down even though the industry was operating at such a high percentage of capacity is that the producers had tried to raise prices and had been disappointed so many times before that they were afraid to try to raise them again. Another explanation is that the ethylene business was dominated by oil companies, and oil companies could never be convicted of being astute marketers.

With the Sterling Chemicals deal I had had some misgivings about my predictions that styrene prices would increase within a year. In the case of Cain Chemical it was crystal clear that ethylene prices would rise almost immediately, even though the sellers of ethylene seemed afraid to raise them. My main concern was that prices would go up before we closed the deal and that some of the sellers of the plants might back out. At any rate ethylene was so obviously likely to be in short supply in the near future, bringing a price increase, that we had no trouble getting financial institutions to lend us money—even though people in the business were cutting prices.

CLOSING

Our negotiations were going well, except that our attempts to buy half of the DuPont glycol plant went nowhere. The sale of this plant was handled by the DuPont department that operated it, and we needed a contract to sell glycol to the DuPont textile department. The selling department set a price for the plant, and the textile department set a price they would pay for glycol. The glycol price was not high enough to justify the price of the plant. After months of unsuccessful attempts to reconcile the difference and to get the top level of DuPont to intervene, we finally gave up. In the meantime, however, we had found two other ethylene-consuming plants that were for sale.

PPG owned the other half of the glycol plant with DuPont. At the time we started negotiating with DuPont, PPG was negotiating to sell their half of the plant to Texaco. Shortly thereafter, we heard that these two companies had suspended their negotiations, so we approached PPG.

The second glycol plant, in Bayport, Texas, was owned by ICI. In the course of our negotiations with ICI on the Corpus Christi ethylene plant, we inquired about the glycol plant and determined that it was also for sale. We were thus negotiating concurrently with DuPont to buy one ethylene and three polyethylene plants, with a different part of DuPont for half a glycol plant, with PPG for the other half of the glycol plant, with Jack St. Clair and the representatives of the owners for the Corpus Christi ethylene plant, and with ICI for their glycol plant. At times I felt like a juggler with five balls in the air.

With Chase as agent, the formation of the bank syndicate went smoothly. Most of the banks had also been in the Vista and Sterling Chemicals deals. Morgan Stanley sold high-yield bonds. By now we knew the routine. Visits to the rating agencies were followed by a "road show" to talk to bond buyers. Again I came away from the experience with the feeling that all our carefully rehearsed presentations were unimportant. The fact that many of these buyers had bought Sterling Chemicals bonds and were happy with them *was* important.

We decided to close the PPG deal first because it appeared to be the easiest. Their people were very competent and committed to getting the deal done, and I have no recollection of anything but smooth going. We were all so confident that the closing would go forward that we celebrated the evening before closing rather than afterward. At the last minute Chase asked what would happen if we closed the PPG deal and failed to close any others. They reminded me that they had said from the first that they did not want to lend to a one-plant, one-product operation, and this deal consisted of only half a plant. We ignored the question, they forgot it, and we closed the deal.

Closing the DuPont deals went equally smoothly but was much more complicated. We had to negotiate the contract for the sale of the four plants, plus operating agreements for the two plants that would continue to operate inside larger DuPont plants. DuPont wanted to buy back some of the ethylene and a large quantity of polyethylene, and these contracts had to be negotiated as well.

At the same time we were negotiating with the owners of the Corpus Christi plant and with ICI for their Bayport glycol plant. On the points on which they all agreed, the owners of the Corpus Christi plant left the negotiation to Jack St. Clair. However, there was enough disagreement among the three owners on other points to require several meetings with them. They worked out their differences while they negotiated with us. Lee Marshall represented Champlin and Harry Corliss represented ICI in the Corpus Christi plant negotiations and in the sale of the glycol plant.

In all of these transactions Solvay was the least willing seller. Their attitude was more from a general reluctance to sell anything than from a conviction that ours was a poor deal. They went along partly because they wanted to oblige their partners and partly because we agreed to pay a portion of their selling price in convertible preferred stock in the Corpus Christi operation. This deal would give them less money at closing but ultimately more money if we were successful. Whit Sadler represented Solvay and was largely responsible for their taking the preferred stock. This decision would be worth over $100 million to Solvay less than a year later, when we sold Cain Chemical to Occidental Petroleum Corporation, familiarly known as Oxy.

We closed the PPG deal on April 30, DuPont on June 9, and Corpus Christi and ICI–Bayport on July 7, 1987.

THE ORGANIZATION

While the negotiations were in progress, Bill McMinn, John Luchsinger, and Russell Bowers were busy setting up the organization to operate the new companies. We took all of the Corpus Christi organization, but in the other acquisitions we took only the plant managers and employees below that level. David Burgess, who had been general manager of Corpus Christi, was put in charge of the ethylene businesses, with Gene Chambers from the Chocolate Bayou plant as his principal associate. John Luchsinger persuaded Dave Porchey and Don Brewer of the DuPont plastics business to join us as sales and distribution managers. In addition, we were fortunate to persuade

Cain Chemical management. Front row, Gordon Cain and William McMinn; back row, Russell Bowers and John Luchsinger.

Ray McLaughlin, who was then CFO of Lyondell Petrochemical, to become our CFO.

We took our cue from Sterling Chemicals' success in hiring David Heaney from the Houston law firm of Bracewell & Patterson as general counsel and vice president of administration. For the same position in Cain Chemical, we hired Gary Rosenthal, a partner of Vinson & Elkins and one of David's friends and contemporaries, who wanted to change from law to business. David recommended Gary highly. The change worked well for both Gary and the company. We recruited the remainder of the corporate staff from outside, largely from people recommended by the key officers. We also took the entire DuPont research group that had been working on high-density polyethylene and moved them to Chocolate Bayou, and we used the Corpus Christi accounting department as the framework for the corporate accounting system.

Then overnight this heterogeneous lot of people, none of whom was paid before closing, had to become a cohesive organization. Starting with nothing at 12:01 one night, this group, many of whom were strangers to one another, would be responsible for running a billion-dollar business. They had to buy supplies, ship product, pay employees, and file a multitude of reports to various government agencies. The four different medical and hospitalization plans had to be merged into one, and claims had to be paid on schedule. Bill McMinn and his people miraculously accomplished these tasks without any noticeable bobbles.

The entire corporate overhead, including marketing and research, was lean, with a total cost of less than 2 percent of sales, about one fourth that of the competition. All the key people bought stock, and we instituted an ESOP that made all the employees stockholders. Including the 10 percent incentive stock options that went to the management and the ESOP, the employees owned 44 percent of the company. Bill Barnwell became our in-house expert on ESOPs, profit sharing, and executive compensation.

OPERATIONS

Early in the year, when it appeared that we would close all of these deals by June 1, Mary and I planned our first cruise, to the Baltic. I scheduled our departure from Copenhagen on July 8, confident that there was at least a month's leeway. As we slowly lost ground on the schedule for closing, the prospects for the cruise faded. After the last

TABLE 1.
FUNDING FOR ACQUISITION OF CAIN CHEMICAL

Sources of funds	
Senior debt	
Term loan	$578,000,000
Revolver	28,000,000
Subordinated notes	350,000,000
Preferred stock	
Class A*	15,000,000
Class B	85,000,000
Common stock	24,000,000
Total	$1,080,000,000

Uses of funds	
Du Pont	$507,000,000
Three high-density polyethylene plants	
One ethylene plant	
ICI-Champlin-Solvay†	303,000,000
1,280-mile pipeline	
One ethylene plant	
ICI: One ethylene-glycol plant	95,000,000
PPG: One half of an ethylene-glycol plant‡	51,000,000
Fees and expenses	56,000,000
Cash and short-term investments	52,000,000
Prepaid insurance and other	16,000,000
Total	$1,080,000,000

* Paid to Solvay.
† ICI: Imperial Chemical Industries.
‡ PPG: Pittsburgh Plate Glass Company.

closing I caught a plane and met Mary in New York; we flew to Copenhagen and caught the ship only because they held it for about thirty minutes. I left with complete confidence that McMinn and colleagues could get the new company under way without me. Table 1 shows the sources and uses of funds at closing, and Table 2 shows the distribution of stock.

On my return it was evident that our bet that ethylene, polyethylene, and glycol prices would increase was paying off. All the plants were running at capacity; ethylene prices were up about one-and-a-half cents per pound, and polyethylene and glycol prices were up two to three cents per pound. The reported financial results for the first few months were too distorted by start-up costs and other un-usual expenses to be meaningful, but it was obvious we had a winner.

The first full quarter, October to December of 1987, showed that earnings before interest, taxes, depreciation, and amortization were 50 percent more than we had forecast. Part of this increase came from the improvement in the market and part came from the un-usual organizational spirit that had developed. All the employees knew that we could sell everything we could make, and they each did what they could to make more. Within a few months the polyethylene plants were running at 20 percent above name-plate capacity. Usu-ally when the new shift arrives for work, the people being relieved go home immediately, but not these employees. The old shift stayed to be sure the relief shift understood exactly what was happening.

One outstanding example of this employee spirit manifested itself when the Corpus Christi ethylene plant had to have a seven-week outage for maintenance in the fall of 1987, a time when we needed every pound of ethylene we could produce. Workers from the Choco-late Bayou plant came uninvited and unpaid to help on their days off.

TABLE 2.
DISTRIBUTION AND VALUE OF STOCK AT CLOSING

Initial Sale of Stock	Original Offering	Incentive Options	Warrants	Total	Percentage
		(In U.S. dollars)			
Common stock*					
Management	6,100,000	1,678,000	—	7,778,000	28.3
ESOP	3,500,000	—	—	3,500,000	12.7
Total employee ownership	9,600,000	1,678,000	—	11,278,000	41.0
Directors					
The Sterling Group	4,600,000	—	—	4,600,000	16.7
Institutional investors	9,800,000	—	—	9,800,000	35.6
Preferred stock					
Institutional investors	—	—	1,850,000	1,850,000	6.7
Total	24,000,000	1,678,000	1,850,000	27,528,000	100.0

* Before management stock options.

Through the efforts of the people on the job, the seven weeks' outage was cut to five weeks with a saving of about $5 million a week. Under the profit sharing plan 10 percent of this $10 million saving went to the employees. With 1,337 employees, this averaged out to $750 per employee.

THE PAYOFF

By January 1988 it was evident that the EBDIT for the calendar year 1988 would be at least twice what we had forecast. It was only natural that there be speculation about what we should do. Someone had the idea that we should combine Sterling Chemicals and Cain Chemical and take the combination public. Because I was a major stockholder in both, I left the negotiations to the managements of the two companies, but even after several weeks they were unable to reach an agreement. Each management was more optimistic about their own business than about the other. We started a discussion with Arco about the possibility of combining Cain and their Lyondell Chemical. This leisurely discussion was preempted by another event.

Nalco Chemical has a hunting lodge at Hawkeye in East Texas. Each year in February they hold a quail hunt to which they invite key people from the chemical industry. I was invited in 1988. I had attended twice before and had enjoyed the previous hunts. The management of the chemical industry is a closely knit group brought together by a common interest in safety and environmental protection. For no obvious reason a high percentage of these managers are hunters and fishermen.

W. H. Clark, Jr., CEO of Nalco—always known as "H"—and Jerry Waters, manager of the Hawkeye lodge, are fine hosts. The guests were the top people in the chemical industry, many of whom I had not seen in years. Among the guests was Dale Laurance, executive vice president of Occidental, who after dinner asked Bill McMinn and me to meet with him in one of the conference rooms near the main lounge. I had previously met with Dale in Houston in early

Gordon Cain at the ethylene plant in Chocolate Bayou, Texas. Originally owned by ICI and Solvay, it was acquired in 1987 as the nucleus for Cain Chemical, then sold in 1988. Photograph by Will van Overbeek.

January, and he had voiced his interest in buying Cain Chemical, but so casually that I did not take him seriously.

Dale started this meeting by saying that Occidental had wanted to buy the Corpus Christi ethylene plant but had not pursued the effort as diligently as they should have, and thus gave us the chance to buy it. Now they wanted to buy all of Cain Chemical. Bill and I made the usual protestations that it was not for sale, but he persisted. We insisted that he give us a price, and he said that Oxy was willing to pay between $800 million and $850 million for the equity, about twenty-eight times the original cost, depending on what they found on due diligence. Both Bill and I said that at that price we were not interested, and the meeting broke up. We thought we had heard the last from Occidental.

Over the next two months we had a few telephone calls from Dale, who asked questions about the business, our relations with DuPont, and the deal we made with Solvay to give them preferred stock as partial compensation for their interest in the Corpus Christi plant. At no point did he give any indication that their ideas about the price had changed.

The prospects for public offering looked good, so with Goldman Sachs's help we started studies to estimate the value of the company in a public offering. We called them "studies," but the price at which a stock is likely to sell is at best a guess. It depends on the state of the stock market, the public perception of the industry, and general business conditions at the time.

Estimates of the value of the equity of Cain Chemical in a public offering varied from $1.5 billion to $2.5 billion, depending on the estimator's view of the long-term prospects of the business. Those of us who had been through some of the cycles of the chemical business were inclined to be at the lower end of the range. My own estimate was $1.5 billion. Within the past five years I had worried about paying the rent, and now I was speculating about whether I owned 8 percent of a $1.5 or $2.5 billion business. Had nothing interfered, we would very likely have gone public in October of 1988.

The National Petroleum Refiners Association (NPRA) meets in San Antonio each spring, but I seldom attend because the event is too crowded. A few days before the 1988 NPRA meeting Dale called to ask if I would meet with him in San Antonio. On March 23, with Bill McMinn and Gary Rosenthal, I met Dale Laurance and Roger Hirl at the San Antonio airport at the fixed-base operator where the Occidental plane landed. The meeting was relatively short. Dale offered to give us forty-five million shares of Oxy stock for our equity in Cain Chemical. Their stock was selling for $25 per share, which

gave the offer a $1.125 billion value, but there would be some re-
strictions on when we could sell it. They would buy the Solvay preferred stock separately. We asked for a few days to consider the offer.

Back in Houston the next day I called a meeting of McMinn,
Luchsinger, Bowers, Rosenthal, and McLaughlin. Although we were
considering a decision that would make all of us very rich, there was
no great joy at the prospect. In the meantime Occidental changed
their offer from stock to cash and raised it slightly. We agreed that
$1.2 billion in cash was better than Oxy stock or $1.5 billion in stock
that we might get in a public offering and could sell only over a long
time.

I had made some money in Vista, and it was apparent that I would
make more from Sterling Chemicals. I felt no financial pressure to
sell. Cain Chemical was an unusual organization with high morale
and a high level of motivation. Frankly, I had a strong inclination not
to sell. I wanted to see if we could continue this kind of organization
and how it would fare over the long run.

My colleagues recognized my reluctance and did not press. Finally, I agreed to recommend to the board that we sell, much to their
relief. I decided to do so because I could not keep so many people
from making a lot of money simply to prove that some of my ideas
about organizations were correct.

From this point on Gary Rosenthal, with some help from McMinn
and McLaughlin, handled the details of the closing. From a verbal
offer in San Antonio on March 28 to the exchange of $1.2 billion on
May 2, 1988, thirty-five days passed, a record for such transactions.
It went so quickly and smoothly because both sides wanted the transaction to close and because both were experienced and did not let
small matters get in the way. Each share of common stock that initially cost $1 was worth $44 at closing. I came out with about $100
million and a very high regard for Dale Laurance, who represented
Occidental and handled the transaction very smoothly.

The management and the employees (not including me) owned
44 percent of the equity and divided $535 million. This total was

divided about equally among the ESOP, the seventy-seven managers who received options, and the key people who bought stock. An operator or craftsman in the plant who had the full amount in the ESOP received $112,000. These employees had already collected $24,000 as part of the profit-sharing program. In the following week I received many letters from employees who paid off their mortgage, sent their children to college, or took their first real vacation from the sale of their ESOP stock.

A few weeks after the closing a full-page advertisement appeared in the *Wall Street Journal*. It simply said "Thanks," and was signed by all 1,337 employees.

LET NO GOOD DEED GO UNPUNISHED: A FOOTNOTE TO SUCCESS

One day in May 1991—three years after the sale to Occidental—I was sitting smugly in my office, admiring a facsimile of the *Wall Street Journal* ad, hung on the wall. My speculations about where to have lunch were interrupted by a constable bearing a summons. We were being sued.

The plaintiffs comprised about fifty employees of the Cain Chemical Corpus Christi plant. The defendants were all of the officers and directors of Cain Chemical as well as all of the people who received stock options, totaling almost one hundred. The employees in Corpus Christi who were not named in the suit suggested that it was filed because some of the management who received stock options boasted too loudly of their good fortune.

The suit was filed both in Texas state court and in federal court. Texas state judges commonly take campaign donations from lawyers who practice before them. Although we had no indication that the employees' lawyer was connected to any state court judges, no one was eager to be a party in a lawsuit that might be held before a judge who had accepted donations from opposing counsel, as had occurred in the Texaco vs. Pennzoil suit. We were successful in consolidating the state court case with the Corpus Christi federal court case. The plaintiffs' complaint was that they should have received more of an equity interest in Cain Chemical than they did, without specifying why. These were some of the same people who had signed the *Wall Street Journal* advertisement thanking us.

In response to the plaintiffs' request, we delivered pertinent records, and the plaintiffs' attorneys retained the dean of a Texas law school to review them. Evidently the dean decided that there was no case, because shortly thereafter the attorney recommended to his clients that they drop the suit, which they did on May 19, 1992.

In early May 1992, when it was evident that the Corpus Christi case was to be dropped, another constable appeared with a summons.

The plaintiffs in this case were employees of the Chocolate Bayou plant. The directors and officers of Cain Chemical were again defendants. This case was similar to the first except that the plaintiffs more specifically claimed that we had known about the sale to Occidental when the shareholders approved the ESOP and that this fact should have been disclosed when the shareholders approved that plan. In effect, I was charged with reducing the value of my stock and that of the other directors by 10 percent.

We were successful in removing the case to federal court as we had with the Corpus Christi lawsuit. By early September 1992 our attorneys had taken depositions from some of the plaintiffs with no unexpected developments. My deposition was set for the afternoon of the day I was scheduled to leave for Europe. The plaintiffs' lawyer was a nice-looking man in his mid forties who tried to start a conversation. I was in no mood for light chatter and avoided shaking hands with him.

The basis for his case was that at a meeting I had with Dale Laurance of Occidental on January 8, 1988, we had reached an agreement to sell Cain Chemical; further, that this fact should have been disclosed to the stockholders before they ratified the stock option plan on January 28, 1988; and that by putting in the stock option plan, we had reduced the value of the ESOP stock by 10 percent.

In my deposition I was able to testify that the stock option plan was similar to ones in effect in many other companies; that such a plan had been promised to all the new people we hired; that the board, without any optionees (those receiving options) voting, approved the plan in September 1987; and that the voting directors represented well over a majority of the stock. It was difficult to make a case for fraud when the major shareholders—in this case Chase, Morgan Stanley, and I—all of whom were represented on the board, knew they would gain nothing and would lose 10 percent of the value of their holdings by approving the option plan.

The questions for the first two hours were relatively routine, presumably in preparation for hard questions to come. After the second hour, when I expected the really tough interrogation to start, the questions became innocuous. By the time the deposition was over, I thanked the plaintiffs' lawyer for completing the process in a timely fashion to let me catch my plane. He thanked me for being a responsive witness. We shook hands and parted, if not friends, at least friendly adversaries.

After we separated, one of our lawyers said that our opponent had decided to drop the suit at the last break in the deposition. He was correct. In a few days the plaintiffs' attorney offered to drop the suit if we would agree not to try to recover damages from them for filing a frivolous suit. We agreed, and the matter was closed.

It was closed legally, but I still needed to understand how in the eyes of many employees I could have been transformed from Santa Claus into Scrooge. An easy explanation is that the lawyers had encouraged the suits, but there was no evidence of that. The lawyers in both cases were intelligent professionals who, when they understood the facts, got out. The motivation for both suits clearly came from someone else.

I asked the personnel departments of each plant to give me a résumé of the leading plaintiffs. All were considered good employees. The only common denominator was that each group contained a supervisor who did not get options and who seemed to be the leader. Each of these supervisors received a little under $200,000 from the ESOP and nothing from options. Supervisors of slightly higher rank, who did receive options, made almost $1 million each. The motivation for the suits was not the 10 percent reduction in value of everyone's stock, but rather the perception that the difference between the amounts received by the optionees and their non-option peers was too great.

With a fixed number of shares available for options, we needed to limit the number of people on the option list to give each person enough shares to induce him or her to work for us. The seventy-eighth person in the hierarchy did not get options but had responsibilities that were not greatly different from the seventy-seventh, who did get options. Had things proceeded normally, the difference between what the two received would not have been noticeable. Instead, there was nearly a million-dollar difference, and this disparity caused unhappiness, which I understand. If I had been given the foresight to predict that in nine months the stock of Cain Chemical would appreciate forty-four times in value, I would have handled the options differently. Also, I would have bought more of the stock myself. But foresight would not have been enough. I would have needed to convince the optionees that their stock would appreciate forty-four times in nine months and that they should take fewer options so more people could be included.

The cost to the plaintiffs to file these suits was a few dollars for filing fees plus a small amount of the lawyer's time. The cost to the defendants, most of which was borne by Occidental, was over a million dollars. This expenditure may seem excessive, but anyone who knows what kind of awards juries have given will not take such a suit lightly. I also suggest that fewer such frivolous suits would be filed if the plaintiffs were required to bear some of the costs.

IN RETROSPECT

The entire Cain Chemical transaction can best be described as low key. There were no late-night sessions, no overeager lawyers, and no financial institutions changing their minds at the last minute. I worked with lawyers and commercial and investment bankers with whom I had worked before. The sellers were represented by competent professionals who were not inclined to play games. In selling to Occidental and Dale Laurance I was dealing with a company and a man who had successfully done many such transactions.

Sixteen years before, Armand Hammer had offered me the job of running the Occidental chemical business. The Occidental people were careful not to let him know until after closing that he was paying over a billion dollars to the man who turned down his earlier offer.

Some of the success of this venture can be attributed to the improvement in the market for ethylene-based chemicals. Some was a result of the economies of operation effected by combining seven plants that complemented each other into a single economic unit. Finally, the plants were operated better than they had ever been because everyone involved had an economic stake in their success.

Occasionally I have a small bit of regret that we sold Cain Chemical to Oxy rather than releveraging and continuing to operate with the same management. I could have demonstrated conclusively the validity of my ideas on employee involvement, profit sharing, and ESOPs, but at the risk the employees would not receive the substantial amounts of money that they did from the sale of the company.

Oxy was happy with the deal. Ethylene prices stayed high long enough for them to get most of their money back. However, as far as I can determine, they made our operations fit into their authoritarian, centralized organization and gave up profit sharing and employee involvement.

CHAPTER TEN

MORE LBOs

MANAGEMENT MAKES A BIG DIFFERENCE

WITH MOMENTUM FROM THREE successful LBOs behind me and a smoothly working team of professionals around me, it was only natural that we continue to do LBOs.

FIBER INDUSTRIES

In 1986 Celanese merged with Hoechst, a German company with extensive U.S. operations. Both companies were in the polyester fiber business in this country, and the FTC approved the merger, with the condition that the merged company divest part of their polyester business. The FTC retained the right to approve the divestiture.

Hoechst-Celanese decided to sell its plants at Darlington, South Carolina, and Fayetteville, North Carolina, both of which had been part of Celanese. I visited these plants and started negotiations with Ernie Drew, president of Hoechst-Celanese, and Frank Pizzatola of Lazard Freres, his financial advisor. Fortunately, we were able to get Al Dragone, a former president of Celanese, to join our team. Al proved to be a real asset because of his thorough familiarity with the polyester business and with the people running it.

After a few months Hoechst-Celanese asked for sealed bids on the polyester business, and seven or eight bids were submitted. Ours was accepted; then followed the time consuming task of getting the FTC to approve the transaction, an exercise that involved many trips to the FTC offices and conferences with and presentations to the staff and the commissioners. The staff wrote reports that were generally favorable but included enough caveats to give any of the commissioners a basis for asking questions.

No logical basis existed for opposing the transaction. The problems arose from a suspicion of business ingrained in the FTC, which seemed stronger with the commissioners than with the staff. The FTC required that the divested part of Hoechst-Celanese, the part we wanted to buy, be a viable competitor. Celanese had chosen two of their four plants to be divested. The FTC commissioners concluded that since Celanese had chosen these two plants they must be the poorest of the four.

On the other hand, we had studied all the plants and concluded that the two being sold were the best and the ones we wanted. My job was to convince the commissioners that we would not invest $245 million in these particular plants unless we were certain we could be a viable competitor. Each of the five members of the commission seemed to have his own agenda, and we had to meet with each one separately. The staff openly disliked the chairman, who, in turn, seemed to have no influence on the other commissioners. After months of negotiation they accepted our arguments and approved the transaction.

While I was busy with Cain Chemical and the FTC, Dragone, Bill Barnwell, and Willard Hanzlik (with whom I had worked on the Alaska deal described in Chapter 6), were organizing the team to run the new company, which was named Fiber Industries, Inc., or as we called it, Fibers. Hoechst-Celanese gave us freedom to select people from their organization. With Al Dragone's knowledge of the people, we were able to select a good group, headed by Tony Champ. The organization was lean, with the minimum number of management levels, and in setting it up, we ignored what the previous management had done. We started with the CEO and let him pick his five or six key managers. Then we reminded these key men that they would be spending their own money and let them choose their own employees. An informal contest developed to see who could get the best people and still be the leanest.

We asked Morgan Stanley to take the job of raising subordinated debt for us, but they declined. They were involved in the acquisition of Burlington Mills, which was a customer of Fibers, and thought this would be a conflict of interest. We went to Goldman Sachs, who helped us on this transaction, the Sterling Chemicals IPO, and the reorganization of Arcadian (discussed below). Chase arranged the senior debt.

Finally, FTC approval came, and we closed on January 28, 1988. Table 1 shows the sources and uses of funds at closing, and Table 2 the sale of stock.

TABLE 1.
FUNDING FOR ACQUISITION OF FIBER INDUSTRIES

Sources of funds	
Senior debt	
Increasing rate note*	$120,000,000
Term loan (Chase)	125,000,000
Revolver (Chase)†	0
Preferred stock	20,000,000
Common stock	8,250,000
Total	$ 273,250,000

Uses of funds	
Hoechst-Celanese	
Fixed assets	$217,144,253
Inventory	25,000,000
Bank fees	7,651,888
Sponsor fees and expenses	3,934,056
Legal fees and expenses	867,500
Accounting fees	100,580
Insurance and appraisal fees	334,796
Total	$255,033,073

Note: The $18,216,927 difference between sources and uses of funds became part of the working capital for the company.
* Placed by Goldman Sachs, which subsequently replaced these with high-yield bonds.
† A $10 million line of credit not used at closing.

TABLE 2.
DISTRIBUTION AND VALUE OF STOCK

Sale of Stock	Original Offering	Incentive Options	Warrants	Total	Percentage of Total
	(In U.S. dollars)				
Common stock					
Senior management	1,576,750	1,062,500*	—	2,639,250	25.4
Middle management	623,250	—	—	623,250	6.0
ESOP	1,350,000	—	—	1,350,000	13.0
Total employee ownership	3,550,000	1,062,500	—	4,612,5000	44.4
Directors	850,000	—	—	850,000	8.1
The Sterling Group	2,000,000	—	—	2,000,000	19.3
Institutional investors	1,850,000	—	1,062,500	1,850,000	17.9
Preferred stock	20,000,000	—	—	1,062,500	10.2
Total	28,250,000	1,062,500	1,062,500	10,375,000	100.0

* For all managers.

Collectively, the management and the directors owned just under 32 percent of the fully diluted common equity. The ESOP owned 13 percent, giving the employees and directors 45 percent of the fully diluted equity. Later stock option plans brought the total employee ownership up to 50 percent.

We instituted a profit-sharing plan with 10 percent of any cash flow in excess of what we told the financial institutions we would make going into a pool. This amount was divided among all the employees, with each employee getting the same percentage of salary.

Part of the success of both Sterling Chemicals and Cain Chemical could be attributed to an improvement in operation under new management. However, both companies were also beneficiaries of significant improvement in their respective markets. With Fibers, sales volume and prices improved only modestly in 1988 and early 1989. The substantial improvement in results came largely from programs we instituted, which involved all employees, to improve productivity and the quality of the product. In productivity, for example, we increased the output of the plants by 10 percent.

Early in 1989 a Taiwanese and a Japanese company separately

approached us about acquiring Fibers. Each was in the synthetic fiber business in its home country and wanted to use an acquisition to get a foothold in the United States. Asian companies have become major factors in the industrial world, but one thing none of them has learned is to make major decisions quickly. Discussions with both companies might still be ongoing if an American company had not entered the picture.

Late in 1989 Al Dragone started a discussion with Wellman, Inc. Wellman had developed a very successful business that recovered used polyester bottles and recycled them into low-grade fiber. They now had more bottle scrap than they had capacity to make fiber and were looking for additional ways to increase that capacity. Wellman's desire to expand led them to offer $341 million for the equity of Fiber Industries, half in cash and half in Wellman stock. Because the Wellman stock increased in value between the offer and closing, the total consideration increased to $361 million. Each Fibers stockholder—who had paid $1 per share less than two years before—received $34 per share when this deal closed.

Half the total, or $180 million, went to the employees. Of this the seven officers made a little under $9 million apiece; the twenty-three senior managers received a little over $1 million each; and the fifty-two supervisors averaged about $300,000. A worker in the plant received from $55,000 to $60,000. With the low wages typical of the textile industry, this amount came to about three times the annual salary. The balance of the total went to the other stockholders, Goldman Sachs, Chase, and the members of The Sterling Group.

I took only a passing interest in these matters. I had already given away all my stock to family and charities.

ARCADIAN: GETTING A CRITICAL MASS

Arcadian, the oldest name in the U.S. fertilizer business, was registered as a trademark on September 1, 1914, by a coal company that later became part of Allied Chemical. They were recovering ammonium sulfate from coke oven gas for use as fertilizer. In 1913 Fritz

Haber in Germany, whose work was subsequently taken up by Carl Bosch, developed what became known as the Haber-Bosch process for making synthetic ammonia, which is vital to the production of explosives. This development gave Kaiser Wilhelm the confidence to start World War I. Neither the world nor the fertilizer business has been the same since Haber's invention.

THE FIRST DEAL WITH ARCADIAN

Some time after negotiations with DuPont for Vista started late in 1982 (discussed in Chapter 7), I had the idea that there might be an opportunity in the fertilizer business. It is almost completely dependent on the U.S. government's agricultural subsidy program. In 1983 this program was changed from cash payments to a payment-in-kind, or PIK, program. The government paid farmers not to raise particular crops by giving them from government storage the crop they were paid not to raise: They gave corn farmers corn and wheat farmers wheat, and so on. The result was smaller inventories of all grains, which pointed to a major increase in acreage to be planted in 1984. The fertilizer business would benefit from the increased demand.

Although I had never been in the fertilizer business, I had grown up on a farm, my father was an agricultural expert, and I have owned a farm since I first accumulated enough money to buy one. I called my old friend Dave Bradford, who had been in charge of the Conoco fertilizer business when I was there. He had left Conoco and become president of Allied Chemical, a job from which he had recently retired. Together we visited several owners of fertilizer businesses and found that in spite of the better prospects for the industry, most of them were interested in selling. However, the most eager was his old company, Allied, which had a special reason for wanting to sell.

Allied was more concerned (as are many companies) about its reported earnings than the actual results. At the end of 1983 its fertilizer business had lost a substantial amount. If management could sell the business before they closed their books for that year, they could show the fertilizer business as a "discontinued operation." Under standard accounting practice the losses of this discontinued operation would not be charged to the current earnings. We had not only a willing seller, but one that wanted to close soon.

We closed the Arcadian deal in May 1984, about two months before the Vista closing. My contributions to forming the new Arcadian were the idea that the time was right to go into the fertilizer business and the foresight to bring Dave Bradford into the deal. Because I was heavily involved in the Vista deal at the time, all of the negotiations with Allied and with the sources of money were conducted by Hutton, Dave Bradford, and Herb Kirby, who was managing the business for Allied and who became president of the new Arcadian.

We paid $76 million for Arcadian, including its plants in Geismar, Louisiana, and Omaha, Nebraska; some fifty fertilizer terminals located generally east of the Rockies; and a plant in Helena, Arkansas, that had been shut down. Production capacity consisted of 520,000 tons per year of ammonia, nearly 1.7 million tons per year of nitrogen and phosphate fertilizer solutions, and 500,000 tons per year of diammonium phosphate. The Helena plant was subsequently sold, and the purchaser tried to go into business using the plant and failed.

Table 3 shows the sources of funds for the purchase of Arcadian. Allied helped in the financing by taking a partial payment of preferred stock and a subordinated note; only eager sellers will do that. I wanted to institute an ESOP, but the bankers were averse to this liberal idea, and I was not strong enough then to prevail.

TABLE 3.
FUNDING FOR ACQUISITION OF ARCADIAN

Common stock	$3,300,000
Junior preferred stock	1,700,000
Preferred stock to Allied	10,000,000
Note to Allied	10,000,000
Term loan (ITT)*	20,000,000
Revolver (GE Credit)†	31,000,000
Total	$76,000,000

* International Telephone and Telegraph Finance Corporation.
† General Electric Finance Corporation.

As we expected, corn acreage increased in 1984. Fertilizer prices
and the volumes sold were good, and the business had an EBDIT of
$21.2 million for the last seven months of 1984. In 1985 grain inven-
tories increased, the acreage had decreased, but Arcadian still had an
EBDIT of $13.5 million. In 1986 corn stocks increased and corn
acreage was further reduced. The Eastern bloc countries dumped
urea and nitrogen solutions into the United States at very low prices,
so Arcadian had a deficit EBDIT of $5.5 million.

In 1986 I resigned from the board of Arcadian. Herb, Dave, and
Clarke Ambrose were doing a good job of running the company, and
I was becoming involved in the Sterling Chemicals operation and
was beginning work on the formation of Cain Chemical.

In 1987 fertilizer prices and volumes continued to be low. Arcadian
would have shown a loss of $5.4 million except that the company
bought back the $20 million Allied note and the preferred stock at a
discount, for a profit of $5.9 million on the retirement of the Allied
note. Thus they were able to show an EBDIT of $500,000 for the
year.

In 1988 grain stocks were greatly reduced because of a severe
drought, which caused fertilizer demand and prices to increase sharply.
Also, Arcadian brought on stream a co-generation unit at Geismar
that reduced electric power costs by $4 million a year. The EBDIT
was $25.5 million. In addition, in 1988 Shearson Lehman acquired
Hutton, along with its 29 percent ownership of Arcadian. Because
Shearson was uncertain of its investment, Arcadian negotiated the
purchase of Shearson's stock in Arcadian for $5.2 million in July 1988,
which would be worth $30 million a year later. In mid 1988 Arcadian
management made an unsuccessful attempt to sell the company, and
in late 1988 Arcadian was again offered for sale, this time through
Merrill Lynch, without any takers.

THE NEW ARCADIAN

It was then I concluded that the nitrogen fertilizer business had nowhere to go but up and decided to build a major nitrogen fertilizer

A field of corn treated with fertilizer made by Arcadian.

business using Arcadian as the nucleus. As in the styrene and ethylene industries, the excess ammonia capacity was being used by the 2 to 3 percent a year increase in worldwide consumption, and not enough new plants were being built. Again, it was only a matter of time until the demand caught up with the supply.

The first step was to buy Arcadian by creating a new company to buy out the stockholders who wanted to sell. This maneuver allowed me and the Arcadian employee shareholders to exchange our stock for stock in the new company, which was also named Arcadian. The original stockholders received thirty times their initial investment. The seventy-five officers, managers, and supervisors received $58 million for their stock and stock options. The original Arcadian deal was my first LBO, done when I was new at the game and beholden to bankers who regarded ESOPs as socialistic nonsense. With the new

Arcadian I was in control and could go to my pattern of ESOPs, profit sharing, and a Deming quality program. This first step in the formation of a new Arcadian was closed on May 31, 1989, my seventy-seventh birthday.

We were successful in finding a number of fertilizer operations that were for sale at reasonable prices. Table 4 shows a list of acquisitions, including the dates purchased and prices paid. Nitrex had an ammonia and urea plant in Memphis and a solutions plant in Wilmington, North Carolina, which had been built and operated by W. R. Grace and was subsequently sold to a group headed by Jim Shirley, who then sold the plants to us. Jim became a stockholder and director of Arcadian. Olin Corporation was an ammonia and urea plant in Lake Charles, Louisiana. Hawkeye Chemical Company was an ammonia, urea, ammonium nitrate, and solutions plant in Clinton, Iowa, which had been purchased from Texaco a few years earlier by The Sterling Group and Unicorn Ventures. Frank Diassi of Unicorn had been the Hawkeye CEO and remained a stockholder and director of Arcadian. Columbia Nitrogen Corporation in Augusta, Georgia, was an ammonia, urea, and solutions plant.

The only plant that we tried to buy without success was an ammonia complex in Lima, Ohio, owned by British Petroleum. We agreed on the price but were unable to agree on how to handle the major environmental problems at the plant.

We financed the initial purchases with a bridge loan and refinanced the loan just before the end of 1989 with increasing rate notes (IRNs).

TABLE 4.
ARCADIAN ACQUISITIONS

Company	Date Acquired	Price
Arcadian	5/31/89	$150,000,000
Nitrex	7/21/89	103,000,000
Olin	8/18/89	21,000,000
Hawkeye Chemical	9/15/89	24,000,000
Columbia Nitrogen	11/7/89	166,000,000
Total		$464,000,000

A condition of the sale of $20 million of notes to one Japanese buyer
was that we arrange for him to play on the Augusta National golf
course. We did, and he bought the notes. Table 5 shows the sources
of funds for the refinancing and for working capital. We planned to
replace the IRNs with high-yield bonds, but the high-yield bond
market was poor, so we had to leave the notes in place.

The results for 1989 were too confused by all of the acquisitions
and refinancing to be meaningful, but they were generally not as
good as expected. We moved the headquarters from New Jersey to
Memphis to be closer to the market.

The year 1990 was not a good one for the fertilizer business, and
we showed an EBDIT of only $67 million. We had organized the new
Arcadian on the assumption that we would have an EBDIT of $120
million. The most important event of 1990 was that Bill McMinn,
the former CEO of Cain Chemical, became chairman of the board.

Business improved in 1991. The EBDIT from operations was $104
million, and we made $21.6 million more by buying some of our
IRNs at a discount. In 1992, however, the EBDIT from operations
rose to $110 million, but an explosion in the Lake Charles urea plant
resulted in the shutdown of the entire plant and a write-off of $14.5
million. The main reactor in the urea plant failed because of a faulty
weld that had been made before we bought the plant. The flaw could
not have been detected by any of the customary inspections at the
time of the purchase. The top of this heavy-pressure vessel blew
straight up, and ammonia and urea were spread over the countryside
and the nearby highway. There were no serious injuries, but enough

TABLE 5.
FUNDING FOR REFINANCING AND WORKING CAPITAL

Source of Funds	Amount
Bank term loan	$250,000,000
Increasing rate notes	225,000,000
Preferred stock	25,000,000
Common stock	15,639,000
Total	$515,639,000

people got a good smell of ammonia to keep us in the courthouse for years.

RECAPITALIZING AND EXPANDING

Early in 1993 Doug Campbell became president and CEO, and we decided to reduce Arcadian's debt in preparation for further acquisitions. We normally would have gone public and sold common stock, but we decided to take advantage of the provision in the tax code that permits fertilizer businesses and only a few other businesses to operate as master limited partnerships (MLPs). We chose this route because Arcadian's large debt would discourage buyers of its common stock.

We transferred all the Arcadian plants except the one in Savannah into an MLP, and CS First Boston Company sold 54 percent of the units to the public. After expenses this sale raised $293 million. In addition, the partnership borrowed $200 million from a group of insurance companies. The combination of the loan and the proceeds of the partnership offering permitted us to pay off all of the bank debt and the IRNs. This left the Arcadian Corporation as the general partner and owner of the Savannah plant and 46 percent of the MLP, with the only debt left owed to the insurance company.

With Arcadian's balance sheet in better shape, we were ready for further acquisitions. An obvious possibility was the BP plant in Lima, Ohio, that we had been unable to buy earlier because of environmental problems. We resolved this issue by agreeing to let BP operate the plant for us.

About this time the Trinidad government decided to sell an ammonia plant that they owned. We were the successful bidder. We financed the purchase with a bridge loan from Kidder Peabody and paid off the loan with the proceeds from a $340 million public sale of bonds. The proceeds of this sale were used in five ways: to purchase the BP plant ($100.5 million); to purchase the Trinidad plant ($168 million); for modification and expansion ($38.2 million); for expenses from the bond sale ($15 million); and as debt-service reserve ($18.3 million). Arcadian is now the largest nitrogen fertilizer producer in the United States, with 25 percent of the market and a total capacity in thousands of tons per year (see Table 6).

A modest improvement in the business occurred in 1993, with an EBDIT of $119 million. Then in 1994 came the boom that I had forecast for the fertilizer business—two years later than expected. Ammonia prices increased dramatically, giving the company an EBDIT of $178 million, and the prices continued to rise in 1995, with an EBDIT of $295 million.

Because it is unlikely that the price of natural gas in this country will remain as low as it has been, Arcadian has actively been developing ammonia production in places where gas is abundant and cheap—in Trinidad, for example.

We want to continue this program in other places where gas is cheap, which will require capital. To give us the flexibility to raise

TABLE 6.
ARCADIAN PLANT PRODUCTION CAPACITIES

Plant	Ammonia	Urea	Nitrogen Solutions	Ammonium Nitrate
		(Thousands of tons per year)		
Geismar, Louisiana*	511	410	1,125	650
Omaha, Nebraska	195	160	480	215
Memphis, Tennessee	390	415	—	—
Wilmington, North Carolina	—	—	420	212
Lake Charles, Louisiana†	—	—	—	—
Clinton, Iowa	260	70	180	167
Augusta, Georgia	545	415	640	659
Savannah, Georgia‡	—	—	—	—
Lima, Ohio	545	408	186	103
Trinidad§	1,269	603	—	—
Total	3,715	2,481	3,031	2,006

* This plant also produces phosphate products: phosphoric acid—220,000 tons; SPA—220,000 tons; and phosphate solutions—528,000 tons (10-34-0 basis).
† This plant was shut down after an explosion.
‡ This plant has been temporarily shut down.
§ The ammonia capacity will be expanded by 700,000 tons in 1998.

the additional capital, we reorganized the company in the summer of 1995. We had an IPO of common stock, and the proceeds were used to buy all the partnership units at a premium. The IPO went well, with the stock after a 3-to-1 split coming out at $15.50 and going to $21 or $22. Those who invested in Arcadian in 1984 and stayed in now have stock worth 210 times their original investment. Those who invested in 1989 and 1990 have stock worth about seven times their original investment.

———————

Postscript: On Labor Day, 1996, Arcadian signed an agreement with the Potash Corporation of Saskatchewan. Under its terms PCS will acquire Arcadian for $26 a share, payable half in cash and half in PCS stock. This price will give the original investors of 1984 a return 240 times their investment and the investors of 1989 eight times their investment. Like the contract to sell Sterling Chemical, this one has a provision that any Arcadian employee released as a result of the sale will receive three years' severance pay.

PETRO-TEX: THE THIRD TIME AROUND

My career in petrochemicals started when I helped the FMC Corporation acquire Petro-Tex in 1955. I ran Petro-Tex from 1976 to 1978, when it was having problems. It is only fitting that my last LBO be the acquisition of Petro-Tex.

Early in 1984 Tenneco, then the owner of Petro-Tex, decided to sell it as part of their program to divest businesses outside of the mainstream of their effort. At the time Tenneco asked for offers, I was at a critical point in the negotiations with DuPont on Vista and with Allied on Arcadian. I could not possibly have added a third deal to my load.

In May 1984 Tenneco sold Petro-Tex to Dave Swalm, who had been a competitor in the butadiene business and later a very successful independent broker of light hydrocarbons. Dave and I share many of the same views on how to operate a business: Petro-Tex under his leadership has a very low overhead and a generous profit-sharing plan for all employees.

Dave decided to devote his time to charitable activities, his ranch, and his golf course, which meant selling his business. Because of his concern for his employees and his desire that they continue to enjoy the same benefits they had under him, he offered the business only to me. Bill McMinn (who was with me at Petro-Tex, at Cain Chemical, and now at Arcadian) and I closed a deal to buy Petro-Tex, now Texas Petrochemicals, on July 1, 1996, for a little over $400 million. Dave paid less than $50 million for it eleven years ago.

CHAPTER ELEVEN

NEW
ACTIVITIES

MY ENTHUSIASM FOR DOING LBOs diminished as the 1980s drew to a close. The expansion of Arcadian was my last major effort. At the end of 1992, I stopped active participation in The Sterling Group, although my associates there continue to be active and have bought a large producer of special envelopes, a collection of plastic fabricating operations, and the Purina animal feed business.

Still, I have not been able to give up business, but now I only do things that interest me.

AIRLINES: A NEW FIELD AND
AN OLD LESSON DRIVEN HOME

In the early summer of 1988, shortly after the *Wall Street Journal* ad from the Cain Chemical employees appeared, our receptionist announced that a Captain Charles Caudle wanted to see me. I had no idea that the captain was a Pan Am pilot and president of the Pan Am Pilots Union.

The captain's schedule gave him an occasional layover in Houston, and every month or so he would come by and we would talk. He had an interest in ESOPs and how they worked. We also discussed the airline business and what was wrong with Pan Am. He predicted that in order to survive Pan Am would sell its shuttle, the regular hourly service between New York and Washington and New York and Boston.

Shortly thereafter he brought a group to see me that was making an offer to buy the shuttle. A West Coast financial group and Ed Acker, who had been the CEO of Pan Am about ten years before, were the principals. I agreed to become a stockholder in the group, and they made an offer for the shuttle that Pan Am took several months to reject.

A few months later someone else offered to buy the shuttle under terms that would have replaced all of the Pan Am pilots. The Pan Am Pilots Union decided to make a competitive offer and asked me to join them, which I did. Neither offer was accepted. About a year later, with bankruptcy impending, Pan Am sold the shuttle to Delta.

Through this process I started learning a little about the airline business. My intuition told me that in any business as screwed up as the airline industry change is bound to occur, and change presents opportunity if one can forecast the direction of the change. Among the possibilities were the following:

- One or more no-frills carriers like Southwest might develop.
- Someone might take advantage of the hub-and-spoke system and offer service between major cities and the large, non-hub cities.
- The big carriers like American, United, and Delta might realize that their cost structure does not permit them to operate small planes over short distances and leave this business for regional or commuter lines.
- In a business where people are so important, some airlines would discover the benefits of employee stock ownership, profit sharing, and employee involvement in the operation.

ATLANTIC COAST AIRLINE

In the summer of 1991 I was ready when Ed Acker approached me with the idea of buying Atlantic Coast Airline, a commuter line operating out of Washington-Dulles as United Express. The planes

Atlantic Coast flies as United Express.

looked like United planes, connected with United flights, and used many United services, but the company was owned independently. The owner, a West Coast line, wanted to sell because they were bankrupt. We closed the deal in the fall of 1991, but we had to let the previous owner operate it until we could get Department of Transportation and Federal Aviation Administration (FAA) approval, which came through on January 1, 1992. Kerry Skeen, who had been running the airline for the West Coast owner, became president.

The purchase price of $18,140,000 plus $4,710,000 of working capital (a total of $22,850,000) was financed with equity of $7.5 million and two loans, one of $7.5 million from Electra Corporation and one of $7,850,000 from British Aerospace, the manufacturer of the type of plane Atlantic Coast was using. Of the equity, I supplied $3.7 million; the ESOP supplied $1.5 million; and Ed Acker, the management, and outside investors supplied the balance. The loan from Electra had options to buy varying amounts of common stock depending on how long the loan was outstanding.

At the beginning of 1992 we were operating sixteen British Aerospace nineteen-passenger planes and twelve Brasilia twenty-nine-passenger planes from a hub at Dulles to cities within 450 miles. About half of the passengers connected with United flights, and half originated or terminated at Dulles. Through 1992 and the first half of 1993, United reduced its operations at Dulles, which could have hurt Atlantic Coast except that United gave us several short-haul flights into Dulles that they could not serve economically.

In the spring of 1993 United turned over to us all of the commuter flights they had been operating out of Dulles through their subsidiary, Air Wisconsin, and leased to us the planes they had been using in this service. By mid 1993 the twenty-eight-plane fleet of a year and a half before had grown to fifty-eight planes. We opened a hub in Newark that served cities in New England and Upstate New York. We also opened a five-plane operation in Orlando, Florida.

We had an ESOP and a profit-sharing plan from the beginning. We put 8 percent of our EBDIT in excess of our initial projection into a profit-sharing pool, divided equally among all the employees. The first quarterly payment of about $200 per employee was made at the end of the third quarter of 1992.

By the second quarter of 1993 our level of activity had almost doubled that of the previous year. Table 1 shows a comparison of Atlantic Coast's activity from 1992 through 1996.

TABLE 1.
ATLANTIC COAST AIRLINES OPERATIONS, 1992–1996
(SECOND QUARTER REPORTED TOTALS)

Year	Number of Revenue Passengers	Number of Departures	Average Number of Daily Flights	Earnings after Taxes (in U.S. dollars)
1992	199,056	19,158	211	460,878
1993	397,662	34,200	376	1,073,383
1994	420,974	36,404	400	180,000*
1995	372,529	32,277	355	5,121,000
1996	396,089	35,235	386	8,464,000

* The reported numbers were a loss of our $7 million, which included about $8 million in write-offs of intangibles, principally options to buy Brasilia planes.

Our record in 1993 plus the good performance of the other commuter airline stocks was enough for Alex Brown and Company and Kidder Peabody to take us public in mid July 1993. We sold 2,558,750 shares at $10 a share. Of these, 2.3 million shares were sold by the company and 258,750 shares were sold by Electra. These were shares Electra received in connection with its $7.5 million loan. With the net proceeds of $21,390,000 we paid off the Electra and British Aerospace debt and bought one Brasilia aircraft. Within a few weeks after the stock came out, it was trading in the $14 to $16 per share range, but soon thereafter it went down to $9 to $10. I kept all my stock, for which I had originally paid $2 a share.

With things going well and with encouragement but no formal commitment from United, we leased additional planes to expand into other routes out of Dulles and Newark. Shortly after we committed for these additional planes, United gave the unions control of the company in return for certain wage concessions. As part of the deal United could not permit the expansion of any affiliate carriers without union permission. They were slow giving us permission to expand, which left us paying for planes we could not use and penalized our earnings to the extent that the stock went as low as $2 per share in the summer of 1994.

We immediately started a program to reduce the size of our fleet and in the process reduce the number of types of planes we were flying. By the end of the first quarter of 1995 we had disposed of all our Brasilias and Dash 8s. From mid 1994 to mid 1995 we reduced our fleet from sixty-one planes to fifty-five and the number of types from four to two.

In order to finance these changes and the leases that resulted, we convinced British Aerospace to invest $15 million in the company. This investment was in the form of $7 million for common stock at $4.91 per share (at the time the stock was selling for $2 per share); $4 million for preferred stock convertible at $7 per share; and $4 million for a term loan. In the second quarter of 1995, earnings were about 58 cents a share, and the stock was at $8 a share. By the second quarter of 1996, earnings were over $1 a share, and the stock was selling at $15.

AIRLINE OF THE AMERICAS

In the meantime Captain Caudle lost his job when Pan Am folded, and he was looking for a new career. He found a bankrupt charter airline business in Smyrna, Tennessee, that had lost all of its planes. Its assets were a collection of Boeing 727 parts and an FAA certificate that let it operate both charters and scheduled service.

We bought these assets, gave the operation the pretentious name of Airline of the Americas, and started the process of getting the FAA certificate transferred. In order to get the certificate, we had to have on the payroll an operations officer, a chief pilot, a chief of maintenance, and a quality-control supervisor, all of whom had to be acceptable to the FAA. In addition, we had to have a plane, which meant leasing a 727, an undertaking that required a deposit and monthly payments. Our costs at this point already amounted to several hundred thousand dollars a month. We could not fly during this time because our application to transfer the certificate to the new company had not yet been approved. About the time the approval should have come, our application for transfer of the certificate was returned with a note that said we should have applied for a new certificate.

We filed an application for a new certificate, and in a few months this was returned with the message that we should have applied for a transfer. We resubmitted our original application, which was approved about six months and a million dollars after it should have been. During this time pilots and flight crews were adding to the unemployment statistics when they could have been gainfully employed. Obviously, the U.S. government could use some of Dr. Deming's ideas on quality.

This delay caused us to miss the winter charter season, which left us operating a number of ad hoc charters when Charlie had an idea that sounded good at the time. Later, however, we were sorry he ever had it.

WHITE HOUSE CHARTERS AND ULTRAIR

When the President of the United States travels, a large body of media representatives follows him in a plane chartered by the White House press office. Each media traveler reimburses the press office for his share of the travel cost. In the past Pan Am had supplied some of these planes, and Charlie knew about the business and its particular requirements.

Charlie bid on and was awarded one of the early Bush re-election campaign flights. He put together a crew of ex–Pan Am pilots and flight attendants who had had experience with these flights and who were well known to the media people. More important, he hired the caterer who had worked for Pan Am on earlier media flights and thus knew what food and drinks the passengers wanted. Because we had very happy passengers, we were given all of the Bush campaign flights.

After the election of President Clinton, we were able to book only an occasional flight for the press and some irregular charter flights. In mid November, Charlie brought in a travel agent who had handled most of the corporate travel in Houston before selling his business to American Express. This agent claimed that if we would start flights from Houston to Newark and Los Angeles with good food, good service, and plenty of space between the seats, he could put enough passengers on the planes to create a profitable operation.

Partly because he was very convincing and partly because we had idle planes and crews, we changed the name of Airline of the Americas to UltrAir and started service with two planes on each route from Houston to Newark and Los Angeles. Before starting these flights, we negotiated a contract with American Airlines to supply us with maintenance, crew training, ground handling, their reservation system, and the use of their frequent-flyer program.

Our flights were a great social and public relations success. We received many compliments on our food and service. Tony Vallone, owner of Tony's, an upscale restaurant in Houston, supervised the meal service. In spite of this the Los Angeles flights never averaged over fifteen paying passengers. We discontinued the service after a few weeks and started service to La Guardia. Occasionally on a Newark or La Guardia flight, we would have as many as forty-five paying passengers, but the average hovered around twenty. We needed an average of forty for a profitable operation, and in midsummer we discontinued it.

Why did such a promising operation fail? First, the former travel agent was much less effective than he claimed he would be. Second, we underestimated Continental's influence on travel agents. Air travel from Houston is dominated by Continental. A travel agency that books passengers on a competitive airline risks incurring lack of cooperation on its larger volume of bookings on Continental. Third, the corporate travel managers who had promised to help us had little influence on their travelers, who were accumulating Continental frequent-flyer miles to use for family vacations. Being required to take American instead of Continental frequent-flyer miles would have postponed whatever goal they had set.

THE WHITE HOUSE AGAIN

As if operating a failing airline were not enough woe, someone in the White House circulated a memorandum prepared by a charter operator who was a friend of a friend of Bill's (Clinton), charging the following:

- A complaint had been made to the Federal Election Commission that we were a Republican airline and that we had flown free for the Bush campaign as a contribution to the party.
- We were awarded contracts without competitive bidding.
- There was some improper relationship between us and the White House travel office.

The statement that a complaint was made to the Federal Election Commission is completely untrue (which could have been verified easily), as was the accusation that we flew people free as a contribution to the Republican party. In our financial state we would not have flown free for anyone. The suggestion that we are a Republican operation is equally untrue. I have never discussed politics with Charlie, but I suspect because of his union involvement that he is a Democrat. I am nominally a Republican, but I have made only modest contributions to the party. I supported two Republicans and one Democrat for Congress in the 1994 election, which is a fair indication of my political position. We followed the usual procedure in submitting bids and think that we must have been the low bidder. Certainly, we did nothing to encourage them to favor us except to give very good service.

The entire White House travel office was fired,* an FBI investigation was announced, and three Internal Revenue Service (IRS) agents arrived at the UltrAir offices in Tennessee. It is unusual for a company not old enough to have filed its first return to get so much attention from the IRS. After spending months going over the UltrAir books with no indication of any irregularity, the IRS requested my personal tax return, which I sent. Later there was the same request from the Federal Bureau of Investigation (FBI), followed by a visit from two FBI agents, who asked a long list of not very relevant questions. Now we hear that the General Accounting Office is starting an investigation. Obviously, one who takes business away from a friend of Bill's is at some risk of having every government agency descend on him. One can only hope that the White House staff can handle serious matters a little better than they handled this small incident.

In the meantime I bought out the travel agent's interest in UltrAir and shifted the planes to flying a no-frills service between JFK airport in New York and Orlando and West Palm Beach, Florida. After a few months this operation was shut down.

---

* Billy Dale, the head of the White House travel office who was charged with embezzlement by the Federal Bureau of Investigation, was acquitted.

OTHER AIRLINES

Despite these problems I helped to finance another airline. Through my interest in Arcadian I had come to know and be impressed by the top people in the government of Trinidad, where Arcadian has an ammonia plant (discussed in Chapter 10). When they decided to privatize their airline, I agreed to help with the financing. The airline, BWIA, is now operating profitably. In addition, my associate in Atlantic Coast, Ed Acker, bought and merged several small air freight lines that are now operating profitably, delivering express packages and mail from the main airports to the outlying cities for United Parcel, Federal Express, and others. I am a major stockholder in this enterprise.

If my interests in BWIA, Acker's air freight line, and Atlantic Coast are successful, I will recover my loss in UltrAir. Otherwise, I will join Warren Buffett on the list of people who have overestimated the prospects of the airline business. The lesson driven home here is that when I have worked with experienced professional managers like Ed Acker and the managers of Sterling Chemicals, Cain Chemical, and Fiber Industries, things have gone well. With this lesson on the importance of good managers in mind, I then ventured into bio-chemistry, a field in which there has been so much development that all the good managers have been taken.

AGENNIX AND LEXICON GENETICS

A compound called lactoferrin is the component of a human mother's milk that is believed to give the milk its antidiarrheal properties. It has never been available because it is too expensive to recover. The Baylor College of Medicine researchers developed a process to make lactoferrin by fermentation. The initial fermentation yielded about one-fiftieth of the amount needed for commercial use in baby foods. We formed the Agennix Corporation, and after two years and $7 million we have increased the yields about thirty times, which will allow us to sell the product for therapeutic uses and encourages us to

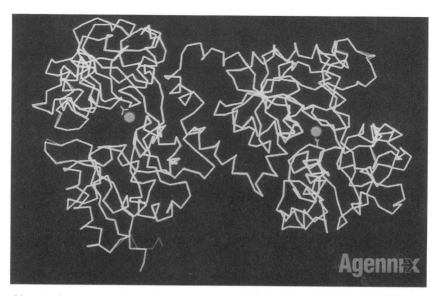

Chemical structure of lactoferrin, a compound found in mother's milk, now produced by Agennix, by a process developed at Baylor College of Medicine.

believe that further improvement is possible that will reduce costs enough that it can eventually be added to baby food.

Fortunately there is excess fermentation capacity in this country and in Europe, and we will not need to raise capital to build a plant. Zeneca, an English pharmaceutical company, has contracted to produce a ten-kilogram batch of lactoferrin for us; it is being used in various animal tests. We have sold 10 percent of Agennix to a Dutch company, Gist-Bocadges, which will manufacture additional quantities of lactoferrin for us.

This use of lactoferrin cannot be adopted until we get approval from the FDA. Their first mission was to protect us from unsafe drugs. Then Congress added the responsibility of determining the effectiveness of drugs, a job that could be done much better by the medical community. To ensure that they were performing their assignment and in keeping with the bureaucratic imperative, the FDA imposed very elaborate test requirements on new drugs that can delay their introduction for years. As a result people are dying of diseases, the cures for which are delayed by the FDA, and the pharmaceutical industry is becoming more concentrated because the FDA has made the barriers to entry so high.

The Baylor researchers also developed a technique for inducing specific genetic defects in mice. The defects make the mice particularly useful in studying the prevention or cure of the induced condition. One of our strains of mice has an induced genetic defect that makes it very susceptible to skin cancer. We formed an organization called Lexicon Genetics and are selling these mice to research organizations.

ANOTHER ENTERPRISE

I am still enough of an engineer to be a pushover for anyone who has a solution for a technical problem that I can understand. Our oil refineries produce a waste stream containing water, heavy oil, and solids that requires an expensive disposal process. A group of engineers, some of whom I had known in the past, developed a process to separate the solids and water, oil free, so that the clean oil can go back into the refinery. After demonstrating the process on a commercial scale for months in several refineries, we finally have our first customer. If nothing else, we have demonstrated that the management revolution bypassed the major oil refineries. Their decision-making processes are as ponderous as any government bureau's.

THE CAIN FOUNDATION

After the high-pressure days of staying up until 2:00 A.M. to solve a problem on a deal, I now go to the office knowing that I can decide which of several things I want to work on. The affairs of the Gordon and Mary Cain Foundation, the charitable foundation that Mary and I set up in 1989, take some time. Through it I have learned that giving away money constructively is as difficult as making it. Each day's mail brings a moving account of some person's problems that could be alleviated with a little money or of some worthy organization that is trying to solve a difficult problem and needs financial help. With limited funds we must make choices.

Because of personal interest some money goes to local cultural institutions. The money we are giving away was made by using leverage, so it follows that leverage should be a factor in giving it away. Rather than donating money to alleviate problems, it is better to try to prevent the problems. Consequently, a substantial part of our funds is going to education at all levels, from trying to improve the secondary schools to creating college scholarships.

Some money is also going to medical research, mainly projects in disease prevention. At the same time we have become less interested in supporting the national organizations devoted to a particular disease. Many of them have not yet learned what businesses learned a few years ago; that all the overhead is not necessary. Our money is going to local medical institutions that work on the same problems but do so without the big overhead. In addition, because of my philosophical inclination substantial amounts go to public-policy groups, or "think tanks," that support free-market, limited-government policies.

FREE MARKET

My own experience has convinced me that the "invisible hand" of the market is the best regulator of our economic affairs. Therefore, I am interested in the free enterprise system for the reasons given in the last part of a speech I made to the Houston Rotary Club:

> I am a beneficiary of the free enterprise system. There are those who regard making money as evidence of greed. I can live with this label when I remember that all the employees made money with me. Some businesses that might have been on the scrap pile are thriving and creating good jobs for several thousand people.
>
> My concern for the free enterprise system does not spring from materialism. Rather it comes from the lesson of history. The people

of seventeenth-century England, Germany, or France lived no better than those of Julius Caesar's time. Essentially all the economic progress we have made has been made since the start of free enterprise.

I am concerned about economic progress because all other progress depends on it. Only a prosperous society can build churches, hospitals, and universities. Only a prosperous society can do research on cancer and AIDS and can afford to be concerned about the environment or the arts or the handicapped.

To have continued progress, we must get back to what Adam Smith intended by removing as many impediments to free enterprise as possible. We must make capital available by reducing the size of government. A step in this direction would be to limit the term of our elected representatives, who the record shows spend more the longer they are in office. We must let the owners of business, the stockholders, demand performance from their managers and replace those managers that function more as bureaucrats than as owners.

Most of all, we must not limit the rewards to a few. We must extend the benefits of free enterprise to all employees through stock ownership plans, employee participation in operations, and profit sharing.

The free enterprise system is not a dog-eat-dog and every-man-for-himself world, as outsiders sometimes see it. Regardless of any personal ethics, I have a great economic interest in having my fellow workers be competent, highly motivated people, which means that they are satisfied with their work. For them to feel this way, they must have some confidence in and respect for their employer, and they will not have that unless they are treated fairly.

My well-being depends on having low-cost, reliable suppliers and customers who can buy increasing amounts of my products and pay their bills promptly. Regardless of market conditions, I cannot afford to exact from either suppliers or customers the last pound of flesh. For those who are reluctant to attribute such restraint to morals or ethics in businesspeople, another explanation is that we have learned to take a long view, and we know that if we overcharge our customers, gouge our suppliers, and exploit our associates, our businesses will not prosper.

Largely because of unwise political constraints our economy is not producing as it should. Economic growth is less than it should be, and people at the low end of the economic order are faring poorly. What is the explanation? The next two chapters address this question.

III.
REFLECTIONS:
THE HUMAN FACE
OF FREE ENTERPRISE

W. Edwards Deming, a specialist in statistical quality control, whose programs were instrumental to the success of the Cain acquisitions. Here in 1960 he poses wearing the Second Order Medal of the Sacred Treasure, awarded by the Emperor Hirohito. Courtesy The W. Edwards Deming Institute.

Chapter Twelve

Changing Management

THE BOTTOM LINE

$\mathbf{M}$AKING WHAT TO ME IS A LOT OF money has been satisfying. But being part of a business management revolution has been even more satisfying, even though, like all revolutions, this one had casualties, most of them innocent bystanders.

THE PROFESSIONAL MANAGER

As long as businesses were managed by owners, each owner managed his business as he saw fit. Employees adjusted to these methods, or they found other jobs. Inevitably, some owner-managers died or retired without a family successor to manage the business, which led to the non–owner-manager, or professional manager. This change was well under way in the last part of the 1800s and practically complete by the end of the century. Today there are only a few major enterprises managed by their owners.

With the advent of the professional manager, management began to be thought of as a separate skill. It developed its own philosophy and philosophers, special schools and literature. This concept was given greater legitimacy by the establishment of a Graduate School of Business at Harvard University on April 8, 1908. With this academic recognition of management as a separate discipline came an undue emphasis on the process at the expense of the results.

261

Since the day I walked into the U.S. Army barracks of the heavy mortar company in Panama more than fifty years ago, my principal occupation has been getting people to do things, being a manager first in the army, then in business. In business I had, as did my peers, the military as a model, which was constructed as a hierarchy with the duties and responsibilities of each job clearly defined and with the relations between positions cleanly delineated. Detailed job descriptions and organizational charts were drawn after hours of debate over which lines should be solid and which dotted. Such clarity and uniformity were required in the military because soldiers had to be interchangeable cogs, able to replace one another effectively with little or no notice. But there is no such requirement in business.

World War II increased the influence of the military on organizational practices. Many business executives had been in the military and were impressed by how well large numbers of men and tons of supplies were moved in a short time and precisely on schedule. My first management experience was in the army, and I went back to civilian life convinced that the military's organizational methods were the way to run a business. Somehow, I forgot the many defects of the military style of management.

This authoritarian hierarchy was designed for and is effective in getting people to do things they really do not want to do: fight wars, for example. The business manager's job has always been to decide on the mission of the organization, produce the highest-quality product or service at the lowest cost, and use the minimum capital. Once this was accomplished by orders from the top. Now a manager's job is not to manipulate people but to convince them that it is in their best interest to achieve a particular result. In a free society and a free market, people should do something either because their moral code requires it or because it is in their best interest to do it.

THE NEW MANAGERS

The managers of all my LBOs had spent their careers in the corporate world and without some change would have continued to be efficient corporate bureaucrats. But in an LBO the stakes are too high, the penalty for even a small decline in expected earnings too great, to permit a routine operation. A change in philosophy and attitude had to take place, and the change was effected by making all of the key people owners. Each key person had a greater stake in the success of the enterprise than in his or her own job, and all employees were owners through the ESOP.

The prevailing attitude in a company before an LBO was "if it ain't broke, don't fix it" (discussed in Chapter 8). Afterward the assumption was that anything we did could be done better—along with a determination to do it better. The attitude became "even if it ain't broke, fix it." The focus was on the results without much concern for who got the credit.

The change in management philosophy came in a roundabout way. Immediately after World War II the damage to the other industrial nations left the United States without competition in most manufactured products. Managers forgot that their only reason for existence was to serve customers, and the quality of some of our products declined, as did our competitiveness. This decline, however, did not happen in the chemical business; the industry had enough domestic competition to keep it alert.

It became obvious that some of our industries had slipped when the Japanese began producing better-quality and lower-cost automobiles than we were. To be outclassed in a typically American product hit both our pride and our pocketbooks. We started looking critically at how we were managing our businesses.

Shortly after World War II, General MacArthur took Dr. Edwards Deming, a specialist in statistical quality control, to Japan. As discussed in Chapter 7, Deming changed the phrase "Made in Japan" from one meaning shoddy, mass-produced goods to a mark of high quality. Ideas about business organizational practices were changing in the United States before Deming came on the scene, but his ideas accelerated the change. The thrust of the Deming program is the improvement of quality. This concept alone would have been an important contribution to an industry that was making shoddy automobiles, but Dr. Deming did more than that. His work provided a catalyst for changing the way we were doing things.

The Deming techniques use statistical methods for determining variations in quality and their probable cause, similar to many other such programs, but Deming differs from the others in an important particular. To effect the changes necessary to improve quality, Deming organizes teams of workers. The advantage is that the people on the job generally know better how to solve the problem than do outsiders. If the workers help formulate the solution, they are more likely to make it work than if the solution is imposed.

Another benefit is that the team that develops the solution usually includes people from different departments and different levels of management. Working together as a team breaks down barriers between departments. Ideas that originated in one department once had to filter to the top of that department, move across to the top of another department, and then percolate down to the person who could use it (who might sit across the hall from the originator of the idea). Now with these two people (the originator and user) working on the same team, communication is direct (as discussed in Chapter 8). The Deming program did as much to make my LBO companies effective organizations as did any of the financial incentives we installed, and the total positive effect was more than the sum of the two. Dr. Deming was opposed to incentive compensation, but in the one short conversation I had with him, it was apparent that he was thinking of piecework pay and individual production bonuses. He did not seem to be opposed to profit sharing for all.

The routine business of an organization still goes, and probably always will go, through regular channels. The non-routine issues of effecting change and solving problems are handled by formal teams organized for a particular mission and disbanded when the mission is completed. However, once the custom of forming teams becomes established, small problems will be handled by ad hoc groups that never become formal teams. The focus is on getting results, not on the procedure.

The concept of a team rather than a hierarchy is in keeping with our character and experience. After all, most Americans spend a part of their formative years on teams. They are accustomed to the idea that one infielder must back up another or that a football lineman must block not only his assigned man but also any other that is a threat. Men and women may bring somewhat different assets to the new system. Women, for example, usually have had less (and a less aggressively competitive) team experience than men, and they tend to be more sharing, cooperative, and nurturing in general.

The conventional structure that used the middle manager as an information go-between has become obsolete through the widespread use of computer information systems. Self-managed teams are taking much of the middle manager's supervisory role. The result is less work for middle managers and hence fewer such managers. An article by Brian Dumaine in the February 22, 1993, issue of *Fortune*, titled "The New Non-manager Managers," summarized the differences between the new and the old managers as follows:

The Old Manager	**The New Manager**
Thinks of self as a manager or boss	Thinks of self as a sponsor, team leader, or internal consultant
Follows the chain of command	Deals with anyone necessary to get the job done
Works within a set organizational structure	Changes organizational structure in response to market change
Makes most decisions alone	Invites others to join in decision making
Hoards information	Shares information
Tries to master one major discipline, such as marketing or finance	Tries to master a broad array of managerial disciplines
Demands long hours	Demands results

I would add only one point to Dumaine's description of the new managers greater concern for the customers. These changes in management style have not come easily. Not all supervisors are willing to let a team of employees make changes in the operation while they act only as a guide ("facilitator" is the "in" word). Because the first-line supervisors and the middle management are most threatened, changes happen only if a strong top management pushes the effort. The failure of a quality- and productivity-improvement program is a result of weak top management.

Much has been written in the press that suggests that a big change is coming in the relation between people and their jobs. They predict that many people will become independent contractors going from job to job. This is an exaggeration. There may be more outsourcing of non-core services, but this will be on long-term arrangements that give the people involved as much security as they ever had. Most people will continue their jobs as usual. Insecurity in employment will be a problem largely for middle managers.

Business should have copied the military in the use of staff. The military effectively uses a line-and-staff organization: A line commander is advised by specialists on his staff, who in turn have under their command troops with special skills, distinct insignia, and pride in their particular specialty. A military staff officer has no authority except over his own people. If a staff officer wants to make a change that affects anyone outside his special branch, he does this only by the authority of and over the signature of the commanding officer. When business adopted the line-and-staff idea, this limitation on the authority of staff officers was lost in the transfer.

As a result many business organizations have multiple power centers headed by staff people who have power without responsibility, who have more interest in maintaining the prerogatives of their special unit than in the success of the organization. They can stop an action by the line people without having responsibility for the results. Numerous people in these organizations can say "no," but very few can take constructive action. Some people who have dealt with the old IBM have had deals aborted because some staff department of IBM "did not concur."

We should have followed the military model and vested all authority and responsibility in the line management. Safety is too important to be delegated to a staff specialist; it must be the responsibility of the line managers. A credit analyst looking only at financial statements cannot decide whether to make a particular sale on credit; only a marketing manager who knows the customer and the market should make such a decision.

The potential for lack of adequate control in less formal organizations is a concern. The best control system is for the managers to have a substantial stake in the business, some of which can be in stock options or stock appreciation rights, but not all of it should be risk free. A significant amount should be in stock purchased with the managers' own money.

In spite of all the turmoil, there has been more improvement in the management of U.S. business in the past ten years than in any other decade. Quality programs, employee involvement, and other factors have been given credit, but another reason for the improvement has been the return of some owner influence on management. With this came the recognition that businesses exist only for the customers. The LBOs led this change.

THE WALKING WOUNDED

The new management philosophy caused many middle managers to lose their jobs. Not all these losses can be attributed to the new management style. Many of them are a result of companies finding that they were overstaffed, even by old standards. A surplus of thousands of people does not happen overnight. Some highly paid CEO and a disinterested board sat on their butts and let the surplus grow. The companies should pay for this failure of management by compensating the laid-off people adequately.

The press has chronicled the layoffs of thousands of white-collar workers. These people were not being laid off temporarily because business was slow. Their jobs are gone forever. We finally realized that these people were intermediaries, or more precisely bottlenecks, between productive workers who now communicate directly and thus more effectively. Companies must adapt to the new philosophy and to the reduced numbers of middle management.

The numbers of CEOs, CFOs, and VPs of Sales at the top of the pyramid and young engineers, accountants, and MBAs entering at the bottom will remain unchanged. But there will be fewer management levels and fewer promotion opportunities for all the people coming in at the bottom.

Up to now companies have been solving the problem of excess numbers of middle managers by keeping them on the payroll as long as times are good, then letting them go in a recession, when their chance of finding another job is poor. Many careers have been ruined and families disrupted by the failure of large, well-known U.S. companies to recognize early that they were badly overstaffed. A wise company will have a very generous separation policy for people at all levels to make it easier for managers to reduce staff. Employers must make the outplacement of surplus managers part of the usual human relations function, which would involve periodically determining the likely surplus and encouraging the excess managers to leave at a time when there are opportunities for them elsewhere.

Companies can ease the problem of too many middle managers by being more restrained in their recruiting and by establishing separate career tracks for specialists. There is already acceptance of the idea that a good research scientist should be paid more than his or her position in the organization chart would justify. We need to recognize that the same can be true of engineering, tax, environmental, and other specialists. For the individual the best solution is to recognize the problem early and be prepared to continue one's career in a smaller company, as an entrepreneur, or as a specialist. From the companies' perspective this outcome could be negative if they lose the best and brightest.

All of these concepts are based on the assumption that the reduction in middle management staff is accompanied by the elimination of work that the managers once performed. Reducing staff to reduce costs without making changes in the operation is a futile exercise. The remaining employees will feel imposed upon by being asked to work harder. Some of the best will leave. To be effective, a reduction in staff must be accompanied by significant changes—for example, a reduction in paperwork.

Reducing the number of management staff at Vista Chemical Company was difficult (as described in Chapter 7). The people there had worked together for a long time and were convinced that all the people and all the functions being performed were necessary. So I elected not to reduce staff except by attrition. Starting fresh at Sterling Chemicals, Cain Chemical, and Arcadian, with new people and no established pattern of operation, we were able to perform essentially the same management functions with a fraction the number of staff. The people we did not need either remained in the seller's employ or were worked off by attrition. Any large reduction in staff would have been evidence that I had not done a good job.

One would like to think that these reductions in staff with the attendant disruption of people's lives is a one-time event, but this is unlikely. There is a force as strong as gravity that pushes the overhead of all organizations to increase at a rate greater than necessary. Another generation of managers will make the same mistakes we have in letting overhead increase—and then they will have to rectify those mistakes.

BOARDS OF DIRECTORS

Although substantial improvement has occurred in the internal management of business organizations, there has been no corresponding improvement in the overall direction. This function, which was once performed by the owners, is now supposed to be done by the board of directors.

If the owner-manager had a board, it usually comprised his friends and associates. It did not direct the owner but was a discussion group or sounding board for his ideas. As professional managers replaced the owner-managers, the function of the board of directors did not change. Boards continued to be selected by the management to act as the CEO's advisors, not as his bosses.

The idea that the stockholders own the company and control it by electing a board of directors is part of our folklore. Instead, almost all board members are chosen not by the stockholders but because they are friends of the CEO or some member of the current board or because they have recently held a high-profile public position. The judgment to recognize bad corporate policies and the fortitude to oppose them are not required. As a result the board is the weak link in the free enterprise system. The Securities and Exchange Commission, or SEC, has been an accessory in the development of the management-dominated boards by making it difficult for stockholders to remove them.

The first step toward better corporate governance would be for the SEC to give up its policy of protecting management. It should remove all barriers to stockholders consulting with each other for the purpose of electing board members or changing the by-laws and drop the limits on how much stock a stockholder can own. Then major stockholders should unite in urging companies to drop golden parachutes, remove anti-takeover provisions from the by-laws, and change the state of incorporation to a state with no barriers to changes in control. These changes alone would make a major improvement in corporate governance. The removal of barriers to change will lessen the need for change.

The jobs of CEO and chairman should be separated to give the board some independence and autonomy. The chairman should be only part-time and should not be a candidate for the CEO position, what the British call a non-executive chairman. There should be no CEOs serving on each other's boards. If a CEO is doing his job properly, he should not have time to serve on more than one other board. The board should be small, with eleven as the maximum. Outside, independent directors are needed, with the emphasis on "independent." To be independent, a director cannot be beholden to the CEO for his job. It is not enough for the committee that nominates new directors to be outside directors; it should include representatives of major stockholders.

The term "stakeholder" is now being used to describe the people who have a special interest in the company, for example, suppliers, customers, labor, the community, environmentalists, feminists, and others. Some have suggested that such groups should be represented on corporate boards. Certainly it is desirable for suppliers, customers, and labor to be stockholders, and to the extent that they are stockholders, they should be represented. The others have special interests unrelated to the welfare of the corporation. Their interests are better served by a law-abiding company focused on producing good products at a low cost in a workplace that is clean, safe, and open to all and that has no adverse impact on the environment. Boards that try to serve too many masters will serve none of them well.

A board is no place for constituency directors representing interests other than the stockholders'. It is good to have women, minorities, labor leaders, or environmentalists on boards, but only if they are good directors. They should not be there to represent a particular point of view other than that of the stockholder whose major interest is in maximum profits over the long term, while operating within the bounds of the law and ethics. A director's job is to guide the affairs of one corporation, not to change society. Many institutions are better fitted to effect social change than a corporate board: schools, churches, chambers of commerce, and the media, among others.

Much has been written about compensating directors with stock, stock options, or stock appreciation rights to give them a greater stake in the company. Certainly these are valid ideas and should be followed. However, after having chosen about thirty directors for various companies, I conclude that compensation may attract directors, but it will not improve their performance. Some of our best directors have owned little stock or were wealthy enough that

directors' fees were of no consequence. Only by their performance
can you determine who will be a good director. Fortunately, I have
chosen my directors well and have never had the problem of removing an unsatisfactory director.

Until recently, private investors, including mutual funds, have not
been a factor in improving the operation of poorly managed companies. They either do not invest in them or they sell the stock if they
are unhappy with the management. The managers of private pension funds are beholden to corporate managers and are not a factor
in corporate governance because they are hired by company managers and are not likely to upset other managers.

The managers of the pension funds of states and universities and
other public employees were led into greater involvement in the direction of companies by an investment policy decision. To reduce
criticism of their investment decisions, almost all public pension fund
managers have become "index" investors, that is, they buy all the
stocks of the Standard and Poor's 500 Index in the proportion that
the stock is represented in the index. With this policy their investment results are always as good as the index but, of course, never
better.

To remain an index investor, the fund manager cannot sell a stock
no matter how badly the company performs. Without being able to
sell the stock, a pension fund manager has no way to protect his
investment in a poorly run company except to try to change the company. Under pressure the SEC lowered its barrier against unhappy
stockholders talking to each other. The fund managers joined forces
and beheaded a few CEOs but left unscathed the real villains, the
directors who let it happen.

Help is on the way. There are signs that large private investors are
joining the public pension funds and becoming more active in the
affairs of corporations in which they are stockholders.

On simple, easy-to-explain issues like excessive executive compensation, the business press has had some influence on corporate
governance. Beyond that the press has been a disappointment. Thus

far, few business writers have had the skill and courage to make it clear that the prominent names on the boards of General Motors, IBM, and other such companies are responsible for the decline of those companies. Many security analysts recognized what was happening and wrote about this decline, but no one had the nerve to point to the guilty parties, the directors.

The increase in agricultural productivity in this country shows the importance of owner influence in management. When the country was first settled, ninety of every hundred workers were engaged in agriculture, and we were barely able to feed ourselves. Now fewer than three of every one hundred workers are engaged in agricultural work, and we are feeding ourselves as well as supplying food to other countries. The improvement in our diet is less important than the fact that eighty-seven of every hundred workers have been released from farming to teach in universities; to do medical research; to amuse, entertain, and inform us; to do all the things that make our lives better. Much of this improvement in productivity can be credited to the fact that our farms are owner managed.

THE IMPERIAL CEO

An important part of the board's job is to choose and monitor the performance of the CEO. The selection of a person to fill a job similar to the one he or she has now is simple. You can go on their record. However, an employee's record as the number two person in a company is not a reliable indicator of how good a CEO he or she will be. In making this decision, one must look for other qualities not necessarily important in the old job but vital in the new one.

In most situations when a CEO is chosen, three or four executive vice presidents will be candidates for the job. They will have risen through the organization and are steeped in its culture. Part of this culture is to conform. When the board chooses a CEO, they will not necessarily pick the best man or woman; usually they choose the one who has spent the most time cultivating the board. Virgil Waggoner of Sterling Chemicals, Bill McMinn of Cain Chemical, and Al Dragone of Fiber Industries all provide evidence of the fallibility of boards in choosing CEOs. They were all passed up for promotion to CEO by large public companies, and yet each of them did outstanding jobs as leaders of the LBO companies with which I was involved.

Having chosen this man or woman from a group of equals, the board does something that so far only the College of Cardinals has been able to do—confer infallibility. Overnight, this person who has always had a boss is free from any control except that of a board chosen by the previous CEO for its willingness not to rock any boats. The new CEO's salary is increased to about twice that of recent peers and all other compensation—stock options, bonuses, and so on—is increased even more. Some of these people are now where they should be and thrive in the higher altitude. Others believe that their skill and judgment have increased as much as their compensation and become autocrats.

We have concluded in all our organizations that we should encourage team work and participation, with managers being leaders and not bosses, but we have gone to a "star" system at the top, with CEOs being compensated at a rate many times that of their associates. The reason given for this high compensation is that CEOs are in short supply, and the market requires high pay for those who are available. If this is true, it is only because many potential CEOs retire early, unrecognized by their boards.

One result of this system has been the development of the imperial CEO. The commanding general of an army must make critical decisions involving many lives and in some cases the fate of nations. These decisions must be made quickly and usually without adequate information. Commanders who do this successfully are recognized as special people. We award them great honor—sometimes we even elect them President of the United States. A CEO must make important decisions but with more time and lower stakes. The jobs are completely different, but we try to fit the CEOs into General Eisenhower's uniform.

Concurrent with the rise of the imperial CEO, the board continued to be a collegiate body, as it was with the owner-managers. The
term "collegiate" gives some dignity to an ego-stroking exercise for
the CEO. Certainly some harmony is necessary to have an effective
board, but harmony should not be the goal. Support of the CEO is
part of the directors' function, but uncritical support helps no one.

Fortunately, the system for picking "good old boy" directors is
not perfect, and a few mavericks slip through the fence. Otherwise,
many prominent CEOs would not have been kicked out. These actions have been a result not usually of the board but rather of one or
two strong-minded people whose desire for a good operation finally
exceeded their ties to the CEO and who convinced a majority of the
board to change CEOs.

Most CEOs, good and bad, rise through the organization's ranks
and are good managers in that they know how to get things done.
But the job of the CEO is completely different from that of a vice
president. A CEO's job is not to get things done but to decide what
to do, when to expand, how much and what kind of research to do,
and so forth. The CEO makes policy for others to execute. Most of
all, he or she must have good judgment in choosing subordinates
and the goals for the organization.

IBM got in trouble because they held to the objective of selling
large computers long after they were made obsolete by the development of small computers. The CEO of Westinghouse became unemployed because he concentrated on financial services without
having any background in that business.

Some historians claim to have traced the start of bloodshed of the
French Revolution to a particular incident. The beheading of CEOs
may have been started by the United Way incident. In February 1992
news stories disclosed that the national headquarters of the United
Way, an umbrella charitable organization that supervises hundreds
of local charities, had been badly run, so much so that it had become
a national scandal. Further, the board of the United Way consisted
of CEOs of major corporations and included the chairman of IBM

and the CEO of American Express—both of whom have since been pushed out of their jobs—and the CEO of Sears—who in 1993 was barely hanging on. The notion that some of these emperors of the corporate world had no clothes started to creep into the minds of large public-pension-fund managers, and they decided to do something about it.

Some of the prominent CEOs who lost their jobs were innocent, at least in the sense that most of the crimes had been committed by their predecessors. But the current CEO had to go, not because of what he did but because he was part of the system and was unlikely to change it. Such drastic action is a sign not of good corporate governance but rather that some board procrastinated much too long. What is needed is early director activity that leads to constructive guidance for the CEO long before he gets completely off track. In my time as a CEO I have been prevented from making serious errors by the counsel of my directors.

Good CEOs have a sense of their own fallibility and a capacity to work with their colleagues. A CEO must be able to get the support and guidance of his board, inspire his subordinates, and work well with bankers, large stockholders, customers, and suppliers. Good CEOs can make their organizations special places where people want to work and stockholders want to invest their money. Until recently, inept CEOs received raises and stock options until they retired with a handsome pension.

THE HOSTILE TAKEOVER

Poor corporate governance results in companies having a stock market value less than they are worth because they are known to be badly run. In earlier times people took over such companies either by buying control in the stock market or by engaging in a proxy fight. These takeovers aroused little interest beyond those affected.

In the early 1980s the same availability of credit that made my transactions possible also made more takeover transactions possible.

People got capital to buy the stock of undervalued companies at more than the market price but less than the value if the company had been well run. Had this been the whole story, nothing much would have happened except some stockholders would have received more for their stock than they ever expected and some poorly run companies would have been run better.

Until the hostile takeovers started, by law the board of directors of a business corporation had only one responsibility: to maximize the return to the stockholders. This simple mission became less simple when someone offered to buy all the stock of the corporation for more than the stock market value. There were several possible outcomes.

Where the management gained from the sale, a decision to sell the company for a price above market was easy, especially if the sale was to someone who planned to continue the operation with the same people in the same locations. Where the management controlled the board and had a larger stake in their jobs than in stock ownership, usually nothing happened, and the disappointed stockholders kept their stock and the management kept their jobs. In some such instances the buyer prevailed by bribing the management with employment contracts. Occasionally, buyers were successful despite the opposition of management.

Then, promoters of hostile takeovers did two things that slowed the process. First, they developed the two-tier takeover, which involved buying just enough stock to take control, leaving the stockholders who did not sell with an illiquid, or low-value, stock. Second, instead of running the takeover company better, a few promoters discovered that they could make more money breaking up the companies and selling the pieces, which meant shutting down plants and discharging employees. It does not help the unemployed people to say that some of the broken-up companies were conglomerates that needed to be broken up. Unfortunately, the people responsible for putting together these conglomerates fared well; only the innocent were hurt.

The threat to entrenched management aroused all our institutions to the protection of the status quo. Management had the money and power to influence the state legislatures, the SEC, the courts, and the local communities, while the stockholders were scattered and disorganized. As is often the case, the cure was worse than the disease. The courts that long had upheld the doctrine that a director's only obligation was to maximize the stockholders' return now found that directors of companies had obligations not only to the stockholders but also to the employees, the community, the suppliers, and the customers. In addition to the court's efforts to protect weak managements, companies changed their bylaws, and states passed legislation to make hostile takeovers more difficult. The SEC joined the effort to protect poor management by banning collaboration among unhappy stockholders.

Against such opposition the hostile takeover movement faded, but not without leaving some evidence of its passing. Some jobs have been lost and plants shut down, but the productivity of U.S. business showed a greater improvement in the 1980s than in any other decade. This cannot be credited entirely to the hostile takeover idea, but the spark that lit the fire in many companies was the concern that they might be next.

With the threat of a hostile takeover diminished, the capital markets were no longer a factor in corporate governance, and many companies slipped back into the old pattern. Again, it became obvious that some companies were poorly run and, if properly managed, could be worth more than their market value. With legal obstacles making a hostile takeover difficult, the stockholders remained as the principal source of discipline.

LBO CONTRIBUTION

The number of LBOs has declined, but not without leaving some marks. There are shut-down plants and people without jobs as a result of ill-conceived or poorly managed LBOs. At the same time many successful companies were once LBOs, and a general improvement can be seen in both the internal management and corporate governance of all businesses. Managers of LBOs, which often entail 90 percent debt and a heavy debt service requirement, have no room for error. The management of an LBO must be results-oriented, attentive to the use of capital, and watchful of cash flow. Most promoters of LBOs found this kind of manager by making them owners. The concept of employee ownership and involvement that originated with LBOs is spreading to the rest of business.

All my purchases were from willing sellers who had developed or acquired operations that no longer fit with their main business. Generally, these units were being operated as "cash cows." The owners were taking all the cash out of the business that they could, putting nothing back in, and planning to abandon the business when it was no longer a source of cash. The employees knew these operations had no future, but they were confident that their large employers, DuPont or Monsanto, would take care of them. Therefore, the drive for improvement was missing.

Our purchase of these businesses in LBOs converted dead-end operations into growing businesses that created jobs. These transactions made money for the promoters, repaid the bank debt with interest higher than usual, and gave a profit to the suppliers of subordinated debt. The pressure of debt forced the LBO companies to cut costs and be more productive.

CHAPTER THIRTEEN

THE
ECONOMY

IT SHOULD GROW FASTER

My INTEREST IN BUSINESSES HAS been replaced by a grandparent's need to make a better world for his grandchildren. In another time this need could have been satisfied by building a family business, developing a family farm, or immigrating to a new world. Today, the political decisions we make, especially the decisions that affect economic growth, will determine the kind of world our future generations will inherit. Since I do not have the personality or temperament to be active in politics and am uncomfortable with both political parties, I must find some other vehicle for shaping a better world. Therefore, I am supporting issues such as term limits for public office holders, a balanced budget amendment, the line item veto, and tax reform. Some of this support has been given directly, and some by supporting "think tanks" that have a free-market, limited-government philosophy, such as the Cato Institute, the National Center for Policy Analysis, and Citizens for a Sound Economy.

Our grandchildren will face a special problem. The Social Security system and Medicare will run out of funds before these children reach their peak earning years. They will not only have to support themselves, but they must also provide Social Security and health care for their parents as well as finance their own retirement. To do this, they must have a strong economy, one that provides good jobs for all the people. Without some major change in tax and regulatory policies these good jobs will not be there. Small differences in rate of growth make a big difference over twenty years. At a 2.5 percent growth rate, in twenty years the economy will grow 65 percent, and at a 3.5 percent rate, 101 percent. This makes a two-trillion-dollar-a-year difference, enough to solve many problems.

When the economy starts to grow at a rate of 2.5 percent or higher, the Federal Reserve Bank raises interest rates to discourage borrowing, and the growth slows. The Fed does not oppose growth; rather it recognizes that our ability to produce goods and services is increasing at 2.5 percent or less because of our limited savings and capital formation. An increase in money supply greater than the available goods and services causes inflation. To have greater growth, we must increase the capital invested in production of goods and services and use this capital more effectively.

Besides increasing growth, we must distribute the proceeds of growth more equitably. There are problems at both ends of the scale. At the upper end, weak boards of directors have pushed risk-free compensation of CEOs to heights their performance does not justify. At the low end of the scale, our poor educational system has left us with more unskilled people than unskilled jobs. The problem has been exacerbated by minimum-wage laws and union contracts that increase unskilled wages in relation to skilled wages.

Recently I went back to a chemical plant that I ran in the 1950s, a time when there were sixty unskilled workers, classified as "helpers" to skilled craftsmen—welders, machinists, and so on. These were black men straight from the cotton fields and farms of East Texas and Louisiana. Many of them sent children to college and to professional careers—their first step from poverty to the middle class. A typical work crew might consist of a welder and two helpers. Now all sixty helpers are gone. Because a series of wage negotiations with the unions gave the same pay increase to all classifications, the helpers' wages increased relative to the craftsmen's wages, so that it became cheaper and more productive to use two welders than to use a welder and two helpers. Unskilled labor was priced out of the market. Some of the helpers could be trained to be craftsmen; the others worked to retirement and were not replaced.

Economists agree that economic growth depends on finding new and better ways to do things, on technology, on investing the capital to exploit this technology, and on using capital and labor more efficiently. Of course, there must be skilled people to run these new businesses. If our schools can turn out people with the necessary basic education, industry can do the special training. The principal beneficiaries of increased growth will be low-income and unemployed people who will get the new and better jobs that are created by growth.

For there to be capital to invest, there must be savings to create capital. Such saving is in keeping with our Puritan heritage. But our saving rate is low, because our tax system discourages saving: We must put aside after-tax dollars and then pay taxes on any return. If the investment is in common stock, a double tax is imposed, first on the corporate profits and then on income to the stockholder. It is no surprise that many people have concluded that the future value of any savings is not worth the present sacrifice. The best prospect for a major increase in savings is in the privatization of Social Security, but this issue is too complicated to address here.

During most of my career I have been involved in improving and expanding large-scale manufacturing operations and continue to do so as chairman of Sterling Chemicals. I am a part-time venture capitalist as chairman of the Agennix and Lexicon Genetics corporations, both high-technology companies. These two activities illustrate two kinds of economic growth: doing better, or doing more of, the things that we are already doing and developing new and different products and services. Technology and the cost of capital affects each type of growth differently.

CONVENTIONAL GROWTH

The first kind of growth, which I will call conventional investments, is made generally in existing organizations and can include building more homes, de-bottlenecking and modernizing plants, and building new facilities to make current products. The risk in such investments is relatively low, and the required capital can come from conventional sources, such as corporate cash flow, bank or insurance company borrowing, and securities sales, both in the public market and privately.

Technology is important in this kind of growth but is not the driving force. Advances in information technology made possible major improvements in plant productivity and information distribution. Information technology, together with Dr. Deming's amazing discovery that most people do not need the amount of supervision they had been getting, led to reductions in operating costs.

All businesses of any size have a long list of conventional investments—far more than they can make with the capital available—but the return is modest. The number of investments that are made is very sensitive to the availability and cost of capital. Because of the relatively low return, small differences in the cost of capital (whether, e.g., it is 10 percent or 12 percent) make a big difference in the number of projects financed. Each time the Fed increases the cost of money in an attempt to reduce demand, they also raise the cost of capital and abort many investments in facilities that would increase supply. The short-term effect of the interest rate increase is to reduce demand, but with less new capacity being built, we are soon back at the same point. The reduced demand catches up with the limited supply, and another interest rate increase is necessary. Because most of the capital for conventional investments comes from internal sources, those who have money make more money. To spread the wealth, we need more entrepreneurial investments.

ENTREPRENEURIAL GROWTH

Growth from conventional investments often involves changes that reduce the ranks of the employed. From a broad perspective this change may be good, but the social cost in disrupted lives means that there is a limit to how much of such a good thing we can stand. We need more growth of the kind that creates jobs, which means more venture capital investments. We must develop and exploit new products, services, and processes. The first critical element here is technology, and the second is, of course, the availability and cost of capital; but venture capital projects require a different kind of investor than conventional investment projects. A third critical element is a person or group to put the technology and capital together and make the venture work: an entrepreneur.

THE ROLE OF VENTURE CAPITAL

If we are to have more growth of the kind that creates jobs, increases economic growth, and makes us feel good about ourselves and our prospects, we must have more venture capital investments. Some of this capital can come from institutions, but a larger portion must come from individuals. Many entrepreneurial projects are undertaken inside large corporations, especially in the electronics, computer, and biomedical industries. The capital comes from corporate cash flow, and an obvious requirement is that the basic business be profitable enough to support these high-risk investments.

A significant part of venture capital investing also takes place outside the corporate world, among individuals and small groups. These investments are high risk and must be financed by equity, some of which comes from institutions that have large sums to invest and are willing to risk some of it in high-risk, high-return investments through formal venture capital organizations. However, all of these institutional sources of risk capital fall short of the amount needed for dynamic growth. The balance must come from individuals.

A study would probably show that overall the venture capital business is a net loser, so why then should anyone make such an investment? Overall the lottery also is a net loser, but people still buy lottery tickets. They buy them because of the possibility of a big gain. People make venture capital investments for the same reason: not to double the treasury bond yield, but in the hope of getting back ten or more times their initial investment.

HIGH-INCOME INDIVIDUALS

For individuals to make this kind of investment, they must have money they can, or think they can, afford to lose and have the prospect of making a gain that justifies the risk. This requirement leads me to the unpopular task of defending high-income individuals against high income-tax rates and capital-gains taxes, which reduce the pool of capital available for venture capital investments. Just as the amount of risk capital available is affected by tax policy, so is the incentive to invest. Rewards from venture capital investments are reaped mainly as capital gains. Abolishing the capital gains tax, or at least indexing it for inflation, would provide a major incentive to make venture capital investments.

The problems of venture capital are the availability of capital and the return in relation to the risk involved. Tax rates on high-income individuals are lower now than they were eleven years ago, so there should be more risk capital available. However, before 1986 there was no limit on charging losses against income, and provisions of the tax code permitted expensing certain losses in small businesses as they occurred. In 1985, with a 50 percent income tax, venture capitalists were investing dollars worth fifty cents after taxes and expecting a return of a multiple of eighty cents after a 20 percent capital gains tax. They were more likely to invest than someone now investing one hundred cents today with none of the investment deductible and an expected return of a multiple of seventy-two cents after a 28 percent capital gains tax. Many of the economic limitations on both conventional and venture capital investments result from the Tax Act of 1986.

The amount of capital needed in conventional investments is determined largely by the cost and availability of capital from conventional sources. On the other hand, the amount of venture capital invested is determined by tax considerations. The tax rate on high-income individuals determines the amount of capital available, and the incentive to invest is determined by the amount left over after paying capital gains taxes.

Increased entrepreneurial investment is vital to the development of the kind of society we want. Essentially all the new jobs that are created will come from entrepreneurial investments. These will be good jobs because they will require new and different skills. There will be no place in these new businesses for the unskilled. Our educational system must turn out people with a basic education to be trained for these new businesses.

IMPEDIMENTS

To say that economic growth depends on technology, capital, and trained people is true, but it is not the whole truth. Two other factors that affect growth are the overburdening of our enterprises with excessive regulations and legal liabilities, and the worst possible tax system.

In addition to the time and money spent on regulatory matters, there are the opportunities lost or forgone because of concern for tort liabilities. For example, small airplane manufacturers moved out of this country because plane builders have been held liable for crashes of planes built more than twenty years ago. With the recent change in the liability law, some of these manufacturers have moved back.

The second problem is a tax system that seems deliberately designed to hinder economic activity:

- It is very complicated and costly to administer; estimates are that it costs taxpayers many tens of billions of dollars a year to comply.
- It is changed frequently, which introduces uncertainty in business decisions.
- It encourages the use of debt financing, thus increasing the risk of bankruptcy in a recession.
- It discourages the use of equity financing by the double taxation of dividends. Because of this extra tax, companies will sometimes retain cash that they do not need in the business rather than pay dividends. Most of the stupid acquisitions that have

been made by public companies are a result of there being excess cash in the till.

- It is an inefficient way to effect social change. There are cheaper ways to encourage home ownership than tax deductions.
- It supports more lobbyists in Washington than any other public policy issue.
- It is a "honey pot" for members of Congress who take donations from groups seeking special tax benefits.

The members of the House Ways and Means Committee are minor heroes in Washington because they have so much power to affect people's pocketbooks. They might be regarded as less than heroes if it were understood how many people are jobless because of their work.

There are three proposals out now to change the system.

- The proposal by Senators Sam Nunn and Pete Domenici only changes the present system by making savings deductible from income, which would increase capital formation, but leave all the deficiencies noted above.
- The flat tax proposal would create one rate, with a high personal and child exemption, and would tax all investment income at the source. This would be much more effective in capital formation than the Nunn-Domenici proposal, but it has political liabilities in that a revenue-neutral rate would penalize some middle-income people, and the idea of someone living off investment income without paying any taxes, even though their income is taxed at the source, is unpopular. The proponents of the flat tax are Dick Armey, Republican House leader, and the National Center for Policy Analysis in Dallas.
- Also proposed is a national consumption or sales tax high enough to replace both the corporate and personal income taxes. Theoretically, this option may be the best, but there is the problem that to be revenue-neutral, the rate would need to be about 20 percent. Add state and local sales taxes to this, and you rise to a rate above 25 percent. At this rate there is a great incentive to

cheat by using barter arrangements. The proponents of the
consumption tax are Bill Archer, chairman of the House Ways
and Means Committee; Leo Linbeck and Jack Trotter, who are
Houston businessmen; and the Cato Institute.

Another popular possibility that cannot be considered reform is
an across-the-board tax cut. A tax cut with a corresponding reduction in expenditures would help. A tax cut with no reduction in expenditures would push interest rates up and reduce growth.

The cost of capital is a major factor in economic growth. Economists regard this cost as a finite number like the interest rate, but the
truth is much more complicated. When I started doing LBOs and
reorganizing businesses in 1983, the prime rate was over 12 percent.
Today, it is about half that. It should be easier to make both routine
and venture capital investments now than it was eleven years ago,
but it is not. Why?

First, interest is only part of the cost of borrowing. There are
compensating balances and covenants in the loan agreements that
sometimes cost more than the saving in interest. Second, we thought
that business was regulated in the early 1980s, but now businesses
must raise additional capital to comply with a variety of new regulations, including asbestos removal (even though the removal process
is more dangerous than leaving the asbestos undisturbed); compliance with the uncertain requirements of the Super Fund Act (which
is the most confused and confusing legislation ever to come out of
Congress); compliance with the Toxic Substances Act (that defines
as a toxic substance phosphoric acid at about the same concentration
found in soft drinks); and compliance with changes in the Clean Air
and Clean Water Acts (the cost of which is much more than the
value of the benefits). Third, the largest cost of borrowing money
and one that is frequently overlooked is that it must be repaid. In
1983, with investment tax credits and accelerated depreciation, a loan
could be repaid with before-tax dollars. In 1994 it must be repaid
largely with after-tax dollars. The upshot is that all these burdens
made the total cost of capital higher in 1994 with a 6 percent prime
rate than it was in 1983 with a prime rate of 12 percent.

As burdensome as is the effect of taxes on new businesses, my lasting memory of the time I spent running small venture-capital operations is the many hours wasted on nonproductive activities. Whether it was getting a city building permit or trying to comprehend the latest interpretation of the wage and hour law, there seemed to be a conspiracy to make the process as burdensome and time consuming as possible.

We badly need Dr. Deming's ideas in government. The success of a new enterprise usually depends on the efforts of one or two people. The possibility of success is diminished by the amount of time these people must spend on the tax code, regulations from many government agencies, wage and hour regulations, and a long list of other regulations. This wasted time is a result of some legislative body, usually Congress, passing a poorly drafted bill designed to address a specific problem. Implementation of the law is given to a group of civil servants whose compensation depends on the size of the organization they manage. The original intent of the law is pushed beyond the limit, and the result is the removal of asbestos that would better be left in place and Super Fund sites that must be brought to a condition better than they were before Columbus landed. Congress is doing a poorer job in the oversight of agencies than the worst corporate board does.

In spite of all these impediments to growth and productivity, productivity improved in the 1980s. This state of affairs came about without any increase in savings and investment and without any improvement in the tax or regulatory climate. Part of the improvement resulted from better information technology that in turn allowed better management of the internal affairs of our businesses. Dr. Deming and the other management gurus also deserve some credit, as docs the threat of hostile takeovers.

What does all of this have to do with the quality of my grandchildren's lives? If by some magic I could leave them a rational tax system, a reasonable regulatory regime, and a fair tort system, it would do more for their well-being than all the money I might give them,

CHAPTER FOURTEEN

LOOKING BACK

T<small>HIS ACCOUNT BEGAN AS A MEMOIR</small> to my grandchildren to explain that books like *Barbarians at the Gate* did not tell the complete story of business in the 1980s. I could have written this as a case study, but the Harvard Business School had already done the case studies shown in the Appendix. The more I wrote, the more my motives became mixed, and writing became a way to purge myself of some of the ideas about business that I had developed over the years. I wanted to tell the thousands of corporate types that there is life outside of the corporate world. Young graduates should know that there are career paths off the beaten track and that losing or quitting a job is not always a disaster.

Nothing in my early years ever suggested that I would be an entrepreneur. In fact, nothing in my life ever suggested that I would make as much money as I have. My career has been a series of happy accidents. Had the price of cotton been twenty cents a pound in 1929 instead of six cents, I would have been a history professor. Only the unlikely exchange of a job for a fellowship to do graduate work kept me from becoming a professor of chemical engineering. But for World War II, I would have spent my career as a chemical engineer. Only the casual intervention of an unknown sergeant in Panama let me spend World War II as a soldier, not as one of the hundreds of engineers working on the atomic bomb. As a soldier the bravest thing I ever did was to give my first command to a company of regular-army soldiers in Panama. After the war the coincidence of my telling the president of the Freeport Sulphur Company that I was bored with my work just when he took a call from Jock Whitney, who needed someone for a special job in the Standard Perlite Company, led twenty years later to my being an entrepreneur (see Chapter 5).

There was part of Standard Perlite that I thought could be made into a viable business. My bosses did not agree. More to prove that I was correct than out of any desire to be an entrepreneur, I tried on my own to develop it into a successful business. I failed, but the failure left with me a need to prove that I could do something outside of the corporate world. Even so, I probably would not have left a good job at Conoco if I had not made a fair amount of money in the stock market, if my job at Conoco had not become less challenging, and if I had not disliked my boss there.

My first venture running small, troubled companies was no great success for reasons that I did not understand until later (see

The Louisiana Cains look back: Edward, Billie Jean, Frank, Ruth, Gordon, and Pola.

Chapter 6). Because these companies were so small, the people who worked in them were specialists too wrapped up in technical issues to be very helpful with solving the overall problems. Effectively, I worked alone. At Petro-Tex and at Conoco there were many problems, but there were also able people to help, and with their help, I could look like a genius. With no false modesty I must say that everything I have done has depended more on others than on me. If I have any advice to give a young person, it is to associate yourself with the brightest people you can. Some of it may rub off.

My decision to leave Conoco in 1970 meant giving up a high-paying job with a good company to take my chances in the outside world. Although it should have been a difficult decision, it was an easy one. Even after ten years on my own with no noticeable progress, I did not lose confidence that somehow I would make it. More important, my wife Mary never lost faith in me. Then in the early 1980s the stars aligned perfectly for me. Several big companies decided to sell parts of their enterprises that no longer fit in their main businesses. At the same time, for reasons I still do not understand, capital became readily available. Fortunately, I had also reached the point in my career where I had the skills to take advantage of the situation.

The result was the formation of Arcadian, Vista, Sterling Chemicals, Cain Chemical, Fiber Industries, and other companies discussed in Section II. Of these Arcadian and Sterling are still separate companies, while Vista, Cain, and Fibers have all been acquired by other companies and have for all practical purposes lost their separate identities.

In creating these companies, I made a lot of money. Over a hundred of my associates became millionaires; about five thousand employees made from three to five times their annual salary from profit sharing and ESOPs. And to bring me back to earth whenever I start feeling too noble, there is the memory of two lawsuits filed by some of these beneficiaries, lawsuits in which I was accused of venality and, worse, stupidity.

My interest in employee stock ownership and profit sharing does not spring from altruism but rather from the conviction that my chances for success are better if all my associates have a stake in the business. Nor does my interest in employee participation come from any social theory but rather from the conviction that the combined knowledge of all the people involved will give a better result than relying only on the skills of a few people at the top. I do not mean to imply that craftsmen are consulted about the corporate financing plan—everyone contributes where he or she has the knowledge, and we try to give everyone as much knowledge as possible.

Because I knew that my success depended on them, my associates have had a stake in all my LBOs, but this alone was not enough. An organizational structure had to be created in which their efforts could be effective. By the time of my first LBOs my ideas on organizations and management were fairly clear. I was convinced that most large U.S. businesses were overstaffed and overmanaged, that they were too concerned with procedure and not enough with the product and the customer, that they were too concerned with the process rather than the result. I remembered that I had been happiest and most productive when I worked for results-oriented bosses like Mr. Mc of Conoco.

Just when I was beginning to speculate on whether this looser, less-formal, top-level management structure might work at lower levels in the organization, Dr. Deming appeared. His quality program changed the way we think about getting people to work in an organization. Allocating credit is difficult, but Deming's techniques, the hostile takeover threat, and increased activity by public pension funds and large stockholders started changes in business that are still under way. These changes are making U.S. industry far more competitive than it would otherwise have been.

Without the development of the limited liability corporation we would never have been able to raise the amount of capital necessary for the industrial development of the past century. However, this has been accomplished at the price of a decline in owner control. As ownership of the corporations became more fragmented, the managers of corporations took control. Some of these managers have done excellent jobs, but others allowed greed and ego to take over and were excessively compensated for poor performance. Some of these poorly managed companies became the targets for hostile takeovers.

The critical books and news stories about hostile takeovers and LBOs were about a failure of corporate governance, about managers who failed to maximize the value of the assets entrusted to them while collecting high compensation for their efforts. The LBOs in which I have been involved did not fall into this category. We purchased parts of well-run corporations that had developed more lines of business than they had capital to exploit. Our LBOs converted these static parts of large corporations into growing businesses, and we did this without selling assets, laying off people, or reducing research and development. Some of these LBOs were sold, and some were taken public at prices that gave the stockholders a substantial reward. Two are still operating as public companies. The employees in all of them were stockholders and shared in the rewards, which is as it should be. The employees were responsible for the success.

My files have many letters from employees who paid off mortgages that they never expected to pay off and who sent children to college. The most touching letter is from a woman who wrote that she and her husband never expected to live in anything but a mobile home; now, with the money from the ESOP, they could buy a real home. I like to think that the success of these enterprises has encouraged other companies to use ESOPs and profit sharing to give their employees greater interest and involvement in the operation. I am most pleased that many of the managers of my LBOs have gone on to be successful entrepreneurs.

My companies were in the forefront of the movement to improve quality, increase employee participation in operations, and develop greater teamwork among employees—a movement leading to greater productivity and competitiveness by American industry. The 1980s saw more change in the corporate world in the United States than any other decade in history. Those of us in management finally started to accept what any good workman could have told us: The workers did not need the amount of supervision they were getting. The function of a manager has changed from directing the efforts of the people under him to being a coach, a goal-setter, an internal consultant.

This change has not been without some cost. Less supervision means fewer supervisors, as the announcement of layoffs of thousands of white-collar employees from General Motors over the past few years testifies. Sadly, this reduction happened at a time when the machine that usually would have produced jobs for these people stalled. Most new jobs are created by small and medium-sized entrepreneurial companies. This sector of our economy is bogged down by excess government regulation, a tax system that discourages new enterprise, and the difficulty of raising capital.

One of the results of being active for a long time is that people frequently ask you for advice. Whenever a young person planning to enter the business world asks for my advice, I always suggest that he or she get a job selling. The advice is the same whether the person plans to be an accountant, an investment banker, or whatever. Upon hearing this advice, some people will mention "marketing" as though it were an honorable calling and selling were something done only by untouchables. Others sometimes change the subject and bring the session to a close when I make it clear that by selling I mean getting someone to pay you money or to sign a purchase order.

Business starts with someone making a sale. There is a factory to produce the product because someone sold a source of capital on the idea of investing. There are people to operate the business because someone sold them on the idea of working there. Successful business means making one sale after another, and sales are made only by people who not only communicate but who also persuade others.

In reflective moments I realize how fortunate I am to have been born into a warm, intelligent family with a strong commitment to education; to have had a father who was a model of integrity and responsibility; and to have had my mother's place filled by my stepmother, Ruth, who was warm and practical. She brought order into our family's economic life. My first wife, Lucia, was a loving and an outgoing person, who turned a self-centered bachelor into a human being. Most of all I am grateful for Mary, who has made my life a joy. Some of these business deals would not have been done without her encouragement when some seller was being unreasonable.

Making a lot of money has made little difference in Mary's and my life. We live in the same high-rise condominium we lived in before. In the summer we go to the same prefabricated house in the mountains of North Carolina that I built in 1978 with borrowed money. It is still superbly decorated with the same old pieces of furniture that Mary found in consignment shops and at estate sales when we had very little money.

Because I want to stay active, and staying active in business requires travel, I bought a plane with my money, not with that of the stockholders of some corporation. I no longer have the strength or the will to cope with the missed connections and the long trek in the airport from one gate to another carrying a heavy briefcase and an overnight bag. The plane is an expensive indulgence, but it is better than retiring. I look at the expenses of the plane only once a year. The shock wears off in a few days, especially when I recall some of the difficult trips of the past.

The luxury we enjoy most is our farm, where we can hunt. Both Mary and I grew up with fathers who liked to shoot birds. Mine shot quail; hers shot ducks and geese. When we married, Mary agreed to learn to play golf if I would provide her with a place to hunt. I could not afford a hunting lease, and I certainly could not afford to buy a place, but at that time we fortunately had many friends who invited us hunting on their places.

Now we have a rice farm. In season it is especially attractive to ducks and geese, and big expanses of uncultivated land have been converted to cover for quail. Some birds get shot, but the number is only a small fraction of the total saved or raised by the food and shelter we provide for them. In fact, shooting is a minor part of the exercise.

Gordon Cain with Mary Hancock Cain, ca. 1990.

Duck hunting is not for everyone, but there is something exciting about getting up before daylight and sitting in the cold duck blind to watch the sky light up in the east. Just before the sun appears on the horizon, birds start moving from their resting ponds, where no shooting is permitted, to a place to feed. Sometimes our decoys entice them to land close to us.

Before the birds become visible in the dim light, our Labrador retriever somehow senses that they are on the way. He tenses, knowing through some faculty denied to humans that ducks or geese are coming; flights of seagulls or coots do not interest him at all. If you are lucky and skilled at arranging decoys in a particularly enticing pattern, the ducks circle in the predawn light to a point downwind from the decoys and then turn into the wind and aim for them. Just short of the decoys and about ten feet above the water, the ducks set their wings to land. Usually, the first time it happens in the morning, you are so bemused by the wonder of it that you forget to shoot.

Men are sometimes called lions or tigers. A more flattering model from the animal world would be a well-trained Labrador retriever. They are big and strong but gentle. Our Lab treats our grandson's new boxer puppy with all the gentleness of a mother. I wish I were as good at my job and as focused as he is. In the field he lies on his belly alongside the blind in the cold marsh, head flat to the ground, eyes following the birds as they circle. When birds are shot and he is sent to retrieve, his low position usually does not let him see where the birds fell. He rushes in the general direction, then stops and looks back for hand signals to send him to the right spot. When he returns, he is like a child who has learned a new trick and expects to be praised. He drops the birds on the ground in front of you and waits to be patted. If you are not alert, he shakes vigorously and sprays water all over you.

It is a chastening experience to look at your Lab after you have missed a shot. He will look up at you with eyes that show great sadness at your ineptness. Finally, to end your embarrassment, he will look away in search of other birds. I have learned not to look at him after I have missed a shot.

Embarrassment at missing a shot is a small matter compared with the repeated embarrassment of facing my inadequacy as a writer. The prompting of friends and the vanity that I had an interesting story to tell led to the expansion of a letter to my grandchildren into a full-fledged book. In explaining business in the 1980s I have described a few benign LBOs. Others have given more vivid accounts of LBOs that led to accusations of greed. It is easy to recite facts, to give an account of what happened that is intelligible to people of backgrounds similar to mine. My problem comes in trying to explain why and what it all means to people who think LBO means "linebacker, outside."

I have never undergone psychoanalysis, but writing a book like this must come close. It is a humbling experience, one that forces you to realize that a long series of transactions that appear to have been brilliantly conceived and expertly executed were a long series of fumbles that could at any point have gone awry. Fortunately, at each critical point luck or the intervention of colleagues, or in some cases an opponent, saved the day.

I am deeply grateful for having lived at a time when what one could do was limited only by skill and imagination. I am astonished at how much can be done with some luck and a lot of help from others. If I have any wish for my grandchildren, it is that they have the same opportunities I did.

Gordon Cain's grandchildren. From left to right: Alyson Aydam Weaver, Gordon Daniel Oehmig, and James Kyle Weaver.

Appendix

Harvard Business School   **9-492-021**
Rev. 10/22/92

Gordon Cain and
The Sterling Group (A)

Gordon Cain

8 Greenway Plaza East, Suite 702
Houston, TX 77046

December 18, 1989

Dear Professor Jensen:

...I have been a modest player in the LBO scene, having done over 25 LBOs in the past seven years. The most important have been in the chemical business and include:

Vista Chemical	formerly	Conoco Chemicals
Sterling Chemicals	"	Monsanto - Texas City
Cain Chemical	"	6.5 plants, various owners
Fiber Industries	"	Celanese
Arcadian Corporation	"	5 fertilizer companies
INDSPEC	"	Koppers Chemical
Pawnee	"	Privately owned

...We started with no capital and a commitment to put all the after-tax portion of our fee into the deals. This meant that we operated out of personal savings and, at least in the early stages, sold out at the first opportunity. We have been successful enough now that we invest substantially more than our fee in each deal.

Professor Michael C. Jensen and Research Associate Brian K. Barry prepared this case as the basis for class discussion rather than to illustrate either effective or ineffective handling of an administrative situation.

Copyright © 1991 by the President and Fellows of Harvard College. To order copies, call (617) 495-6117 or write the Publishing Division, Harvard Business School, Boston, MA 02163. No part of this publication may be reproduced, stored in a retrieval system, or transmitted in any form or by any means—electronic, mechanical, photocopying, recording, or otherwise—without the permission of the Harvard Business School.

The typical division of equity of one of our deals is 10% to 15% by an ESOP; 20% to 25% by the management; 20% to 25% by The Sterling Group; the agent bank for the senior credit will buy 10%; the investment bank that sells high-yield bonds will buy 10%; and the balance goes for employee stock options and warrants attached to preferred stock. All stock is sold at the same price, and we insist that the key managers dedicate a substantial part of their personal net worth to the purchase of stock. We prefer situations where we can bring outsiders into at least some of the key spots. We put in a profit-sharing plan that includes everyone.

As a result, we operate with one-fourth to one-third the overhead of the predecessor company and have much higher morale, commitment, and involvement. The key people have a greater stake as stockholders than they do as managers. As a result, there is no empire building and no tendency to protect the prerogatives of a particular department. The quality of the management is far superior to their peers in the industry.

The problems come with success. At some point the key people start to realize that their stake in the company is worth more money than they ever expected to have, and they start thinking about how they can cash in. This pressure for liquidity by the key people, most of whom went into debt to buy their stock, has been a major factor in deciding to take some companies public. There is also a small but appreciable fraction of the management who, once they have a large paper profit, become very conservative and want only to protect their new estate.

In a nonpublic company arrangement, we must develop a way to give the management stockholders some liquidity: first, to let the management get out of debt; second, to buy out the few people who make all the money they want and are no longer motivated by the prospect of making more; and third, to give the key people assurance that when they decide to retire they can reap the benefits of their success.

The first of these can be done informally by sales of stock to the company or the ESOP. The second and third involve many millions of dollars per person, and I do not yet have a satisfactory solution.

Sincerely,

Gordon Cain

Gordon Cain

Gordon Cain was a manager in the chemical industry for 35 years, primarily as vice president and chief operating officer of Conoco's chemical and plastics division. He left Conoco in 1970, at age 58, to become an entrepreneur. He then purchased a variety of businesses, specializing in petrochemicals. In 1982, he cofounded The Sterling Group, a private financial organization that identifies and arranges leveraged buyouts. *Business Week* featured Cain in a 1988 article (reproduced in **Exhibit 1**). **Exhibit 2** summarizes The Sterling Group's LBO transactions from 1983 to 1989.

Exhibit 1   "The Midas Touch of Gordon Cain," *Business Week*, May 16, 1988

Business Week has restricted the use of this exhibit.

Exhibit 2   Transactions by The Sterling Group, 1983-1989

Company	Description	Transaction Value ($ millions)
1983		
Balco International	Specialty building products	$ 3.6
1984		
AAC Holdings, Incorporated [1]	Nitrogen and phosphate fertilizer	86.5
Pawnee Industries [2]	Plastic sheet extruder; custom products	10.5
Vista Chemical Company	Surfactant chemicals and polyvinyl chloride	506.0
1985		
Steffen Dairy Foods	Dairy foods	6.0
Hawkeye Chemical Company [1]	Nitrogen fertilizer	37.5
A-1 Rental Car	Rental car franchise	7.0
1986		
Airtron, Incorporated	Heating and air-conditioning contractor	13.0
Knox Lumber Company	Lumber and hardware retailer	29.0
Sterling Chemicals Incorporated	Commodity chemicals	215.3
Pawnee Industries [2]	Plastic sheet extruder; custom products	32.5
Rives Smith Baldwin Carlberg	Advertising agency	NA
1987		
Cain Chemical Incorporated	Ethylene and ethylene derivatives	1,080.0
1988		
Sirena, Incorporated	Women's swimwear	20.0
Fiber Industries, Incorporated	Polyester textile fibers	253.0
Kranco, Incorporated	Overhead cranes	9.8
CJC Holdings, Incorporated	Commitment jewelry manufacturer	145.0
Texas Supermarkets, Incorporated	Grocery retailer	190.0
Impact Plastics [3]	Plastic sheet extruder	29.5
INDSPEC Chemical Corporation	Industrial specialty chemicals	204.0
1989		
Craft World International, Incorporated	Distributor of craft supplies	25.0
Arcadian Corporation	Nitrogen and phosphate fertilizer	545.0
	Total	$3,448.2

NA = Not available.

1. Folded into Arcadian Corporation in 1989.

2. Originally purchased from its founder and taken public; subsequently, taken private again by management and The Sterling Group.

3. Purchased as adviser to Pawnee Industries.

Source: The Sterling Group.

Sterling Chemicals Incorporated

In August 1986, Gordon Cain, The Sterling Group, and Virgil Waggoner, a self-employed consultant in the petrochemical industry, formed Sterling Chemicals Incorporated (SCI) to purchase Monsanto's Texas City plant in a $215 million LBO. SCI bought the plant with $6.8 million of equity. Texas City was a unionized plant that produced six commodity chemicals: styrene, acrylonitrile, acetic acid, lactic acid, plasticizers, and tertiary butylamine. The plant's operating earnings had been stagnant for several years, and total employment had fallen to 909 people, down from 1,636 in January 1982. After the LBO, the Texas City plant's performance improved dramatically: the company's annual gross profit increased 476% in the first two years.

The increase in SCI's value created pressure for liquidity among its management and nonmanagement employees, many of whom owned significant equity stakes in the company. Between April and September of 1988, SCI's equity holders, who had purchased their stock for $10 per share, received dividends of $237.50 per share—a total of $190 million. Together management and directors received dividend payments totaling $92.8 million during this period; the median nonmanagement employee received $28,500 through an employee stock ownership plan (ESOP). Yet SCI's management and nonmanagement employees wanted more liquidity so they could diversify their equity holdings, and SCI's board of directors wanted to help them acquire it. The board discussed three main options for achieving this: selling the company, taking it public, or releveraging it.

While examining SCI's alternatives, Cain recalled his experiences at Cain Chemical Incorporated, which he had sold to Occidental Petroleum less than five months earlier.

Background: Cain Chemical Incorporated

In July 1987, The Sterling Group formed Cain Chemical Incorporated (CCI) with the purchase of six-and-one-half intermediate petrochemical plants and related pipelines along the Texas Gulf Coast. CCI's three main products were ethylene (a colorless gas) and its two major downstream derivatives, ethylene glycol and high-density polyethylene (HDPE). Ethylene glycol is used in the production of polyester products and antifreeze; HDPE is used to produce a wide range of plastic products such as trash bags and containers for milk, laundry detergent, and motor oil.

Cain perceived significant profit opportunities in the ethylene industry. First, the industry had undergone a substantial tightening of capacity since the early 1980s, and little new capacity would come on-stream before 1990. Second, Cain believed that ethylene demand, which had been growing at 1% per year, would grow 2% or 3% per year because of declining oil prices.

Based on these expectations, Cain began seeking an acquisition in the ethylene industry. In Corpus Christi, he located an ethylene plant that was jointly owned by ICI, Solvay, and Union Pacific, but the banks would not finance a deal for a company with only one plant and one product. Cain located five-and-one-half additional plants scattered along the Texas Gulf Coast—three HDPE, one ethylene, one ethylene glycol, and a 50% interest in another ethylene glycol—and the banks agreed to finance the deal. Purchased in four separate transactions, the six-and-one-half plants and related pipelines cost $1.08 billion, which The Sterling Group financed with 88.2% debt. Panel A of **Exhibit 3** lists the plants that Cain acquired; Panel B summarizes CCI's capital structure and breakdown of equity holdings.

Exhibit 3   Summary of CCI's Acquisitions, Capital Structure, and
Breakdown of Equity Holdings

Panel A: Plants Acquired by CCI

Application of Funds	Number	Type of Plant	Location	Purchase Price ($ millions)
PHYSICAL ASSETS				
Seller				
Du Pont	3	HDPE	Matagorda, Orange, and Victoria	
	1	Ethylene	Chocolate Bayou	$ 507 †
ICI-Solvay-Union Pacific	1	Ethylene	Corpus Christi	303
ICI	1	Ethylene glycol	Bayport	95
PPG	0.5	Ethylene glycol	Beaumont	51
Total Plants Acquired	6.5	3 HDPE, 2 ethylene, 1.5 ethylene glycol		$ 956 ††
FEES AND EXPENSES				56
CASH AND SHORT-TERM INVESTMENTS				52
PREPAID INSURANCE AND OTHER ITEMS				16
TOTAL COST				$1,080

† Includes the South Texas Pipeline, a 280-mile feedstock and product pipeline system.
†† Includes the price of all assets and working capital items.

Source: Cain Chemical Incorporated, Prospectus, June 29, 1987.

Panel B: Capital Structure and Breakdown of Equity Holdings

	$ Millions	% of Total Funding	% of Total Equity (fully diluted)
DEBT			
Bank Term Loan—Secured	$ 578.0		
Bank Revolver	28.0		
Subordinated Debt	350.0		
Total Debt	$ 956.0	88.2%	
PREFERRED			
Class A—Subsidiary Preferred	15.0		
Class B—Convertible Preferred	85.0		
Total Preferred	$ 100.0	9.2%	
EQUITY			
Banks and Investment Banks †	11.2		40.0%
Management ††	8.7		31.1
The Sterling Group	4.6		16.4
ESOP	3.5		12.5
Total Equity (fully diluted)	$ 28.0	2.6%	100.0%
TOTAL FUNDING	$ 1,084.0	100.0%	100.0%

† Includes $2.4 million of common stock (at original issue price) acquired through conversion of warrants upon CCI's sale to Occidental Petroleum.

†† Includes $2.6 million of common stock (at original issue price) acquired through conversion of warrants upon CCI's sale to Occidental Petroleum.

Source: The Sterling Group.

Exhibit 4   Map of CCI Plants and Related Pipelines

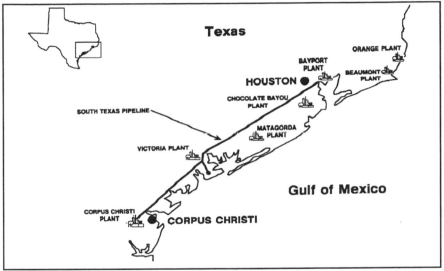

Source: Cain Chemical Incorporated, Prospectus, June 29, 1987.

   Exhibit 4 displays a map of the CCI plants, and **Exhibit 5** illustrates the integration of the plants and the distribution of their output. The plants were connected by the 280-mile South Texas pipeline, through which the Corpus Christi and Chocolate Bayou plants supplied ethylene to their five sister plants for conversion into ethylene derivatives. The Bayport and Beaumont plants produced ethylene glycol, and the Matagorda, Orange, and Victoria plants produced HDPE. Before the LBO, the Corpus Christi and Chocolate Bayou plants had a combined rated capacity of 2.4 billion pounds of ethylene per year. CCI planned to channel about two-thirds of this ethylene to the downstream plants, and to sell the remaining one-third on the spot market. CCI committed 43% of its pre-LBO ethylene glycol capacity, and 22% of its HDPE capacity, under long-term contracts.

   The CCI plants had been linked together since the early 1970s and were part of a large network of competing pipelines that spanned the Texas Gulf Coast. These pipelines connected hundreds of plants, with different owners, producing many different intermediate and final products. The Gulf Coast's commodity chemicals infrastructure, including the pipelines, service and maintenance apparatus, and human capital, had evolved over a 75-year period and gave the region a distinct competitive advantage over other parts of the world. Because of the extensive pipeline network and the homogeneous nature of commodity chemicals, each plant could choose from whom it received its raw materials and to whom it distributed its output. Output that did not go to other plants in the region was shipped out through the Gulf of Mexico.

Exhibit 5   Integration of CCI Plants and Rated Annual Capacity
(volumes in millions of pounds, prior to LBO)

Note: Rated capacity takes into account average expected downtime—for scheduled
maintenance—of about two weeks per year (scheduled maintenance takes place every
three years and lasts about six weeks).   Thus, for example, Corpus Christi's and
Chocolate Bayou's combined *weekly* rated capacity was 48 million pounds
(2,400 million pounds ÷ 50 weeks per year).

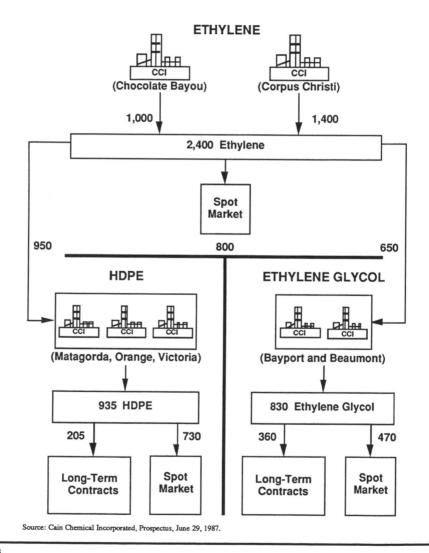

Source: Cain Chemical Incorporated, Prospectus, June 29, 1987.

When Cain bought the CCI plants, he did not expect to benefit much from technological improvements to their chemical processes: the previous owners had already taken such steps as increasing heat efficiency and optimizing output per unit of raw materials. Nor did he expect to gain from adapting production to changing input and output prices: each plant took in a predetermined input mix and put out a single product. But Cain believed CCI could increase throughput and lower unit costs by maintaining the equipment better and by monitoring the processes and making timely adjustments. He planned to accomplish this by improving employees' compensation, decentralizing decision-making, and installing a quality program.

Compensation

After the LBO, CCI gave all of its employees stakes in an ESOP that owned 12.5% of the company's equity. Cain and William McMinn, CCI's president and CEO, believed stock ownership was necessary to promote value-maximization, but they did not think the ESOP by itself was sufficient. They believed that because the ESOP had no immediate effect on employees' standards of living, and because there was no market for the company's stock, most employees did not perceive the link between changes in the company's value and changes in their own wealth. For this reason, Cain and McMinn believed it was necessary to supplement the stock ownership plan with more immediate payoffs.

The company instituted a profit-sharing plan for all employees, based on EBDIT (earnings before depreciation, interest, and taxes). CCI defined baseline EBDIT as the EBDIT projections it gave to the banks plus 20% of its cumulative capital expenditures from the time of the LBO. Ten percent of excess EBDIT—actual EBDIT above the baseline—went into the profit-sharing pool. CCI then divided this pool among all employees, with higher-paid people receiving larger bonuses. Of the company's seven plants, one (Beaumont) employed union labor and six employed nonunion labor. CCI did not distinguish between union and nonunion employees when installing the profit-sharing plan and ESOP. Employees received their profit-sharing checks at special quarterly meetings. McMinn described these meetings:

> Every quarter, I would go to each plant and review its performance with the employees. We would go over the results and discuss why they were what they were. We would always start by reviewing the plant's safety performance. When we were satisfied we had fully covered the safety aspects, we would go over the latest quarter's financials. We would discuss how the plant performed against the budget, and what its sales and EBDIT were. We would then review the factors that contributed to the improvements in EBDIT: pricing, volume, and costs. After we finished reviewing the financials, employees would ask questions about other matters. They were usually most concerned with how our competitors were doing: they wanted to know how we compared on costs. At the end of the meeting, I would hand out the checks.

> The special meetings were a critical factor in our success—you have to keep the employees fully informed about what's going on. All seven plants got the reports and the checks within one week after the quarter closed, not three months later. We did this by visiting one or two plants a day. Because they received their profit-sharing checks immediately after discussing the quarterly results, employees understood where the money was coming from.

Employees responded favorably to the meetings and the new bonus plan. McMinn described the reactions at CCI's Beaumont plant:

I explained to the employees that the bonuses were based on excess EBDIT. I told them I didn't know exactly what EBDIT was, "But let's call it everybody doing it together." After the first meeting we had a company party. The employees showed up with T-shirts that said "EBDIT" on the front and "EveryBody Doing It Together" on the back.

The ESOP and the profit-sharing plan together definitely made a big difference. Before, the top people would get all the money and the employees would get a pat on the rear and a doughnut. After the ESOP and the profit sharing were in place, they could say this company belonged to them.

David Burgess, vice president of CCI's ethylene business, described the employees' new attention to EBDIT:

EBDIT was a nice, simple goal—how much money did we make? Management said, "This is what we promised the banks, and if there's any left over we'll split it with you."

We didn't want to grow the company. We didn't want to operate in every part of the globe or invent new technologies. We weren't even that concerned with how much ethylene we produced. We were concerned with how much money we made.

It was a very simple goal. People knew what to do. If they didn't, then they went and found out. Keeping the plant running smoothly at high rates had a big effect on EBDIT, so employees would anticipate things that led to downtime. They were quicker to step in and take charge when things went wrong.

We eliminated a lot of waste, we were getting things done more quickly, and people were having a lot of fun. The night shift would go off duty and people would stick around to see how things were going.

Besides changing employees' compensation, CCI delegated more decision-making authority to plant managers and the employees below them. This gave employees more freedom to make minor adjustments to equipment and to respond more quickly to unforeseen changes at connected plants. CCI also implemented a new quality program, which Cain had found to be effective in several of his other LBOs. Tom Barker, manager of CCI's Victoria plant, commented on the company's new focus:

The employees could relate the pounds we produced per hour to the margins we were getting on our products. It was almost as if we had a taxi meter that tracked our output in dollars and pounds. The employees knew what EBDIT would be for the quarter, and they knew what their share was. If they found a way to get another one million pounds out of the plant, they knew that was $10 in their pockets; if they could shave one-tenth of a cent off our unit costs, they knew that was another $20.

On one occasion, we had a motor go out. Normally, we would send it out to a specialist to have fixed. One of our instrument mechanics, who had some prior experience in an electrical shop, recognized that this would leave us operating at half-rate for two days. So he sat out in the field that night, under the lights, and rebuilt the motor while another guy delivered him tools and parts.

This type of employee commitment showed up in all our day-to-day activities: finding cheaper raw materials, negotiating better terms with our vendors, rebuilding spare parts instead of junking them, keeping the unit on-stream, and trying to figure out "How can we get an extra 1,000 pounds per hour out of this plant?" The reason was that everyone saw they made a difference.

Ben Breeding, manager of the Bayport plant, commented:

Employees started finding ways to reduce costs. For example, it required a lot of personal attention to maintain the product purity in our distillation column. You could reduce the personal effort required if you operated the column with higher energy input. Our employees reduced costs by relying more on their own effort and attention, and less on energy input, to operate the column.

But it wasn't just financial performance that improved. The changes were across the board: plant reliability, employee morale, environmental performance, productivity, and safety performance. Once we became a private company, for instance, safety improved dramatically. The employees realized that there was no large corporation there to bail us out if anything happened to the plant, so they started treating it as if it was their livelihood. People were more vigilant and the plant didn't have to shut down as much. In the year after the LBO, there was a total of 1 hour and 38 minutes that we were not on-stream. Before, the best we could have held it to was a few days.

Performance

CCI's productivity and profitability improved dramatically during its first 10 months of operation. Annual EBDIT increased 254% as the company's gross profit margin rose from 22.6% to 30.3%. Quarterly payments from the profit-sharing plan in the first three quarters averaged $950, $2,030, and $5,000 per person. CCI spent $20 million on capital expenditures during this period, which it used to increase the capacity of its Matagorda plant and to perform scheduled maintenance on its Corpus Christi plant. **Exhibit 6** compares selected financial information for the combined plants in the periods before and after the acquisitions. Several factors contributed to CCI's turnaround.

The ethylene industry   CCI benefited from a substantial industrywide upswing shortly after its startup. Ethylene prices nearly doubled in the 10 months after the LBO—increasing more than raw materials costs—and CCI's gross profit-per-pound of ethylene increased from 7.74 cents to 15.13 cents. **Exhibit 7** tracks the price of ethylene before and after the company's formation.

Overhead   Cain bought only the plants of the acquired divisions. In his first deal, Vista Chemical, Cain had taken the plants' entire senior management team from the seller. CCI's senior management team was composed entirely of outsiders; of the five most senior managers, only two knew each other before the deal. Cain retained all employees at or below the plant-manager level, but did not take anybody from overhead departments such as finance, accounting, environment, or personnel. CCI kept its overhead departments small and transferred many of these functions to the line people. To encourage a lean staff, Cain prohibited allocating corporate overhead to the plants and made McMinn directly accountable for it. The previous owners had allocated a

314

492-021

Exhibit 6 Selected Financial Information for CCI Before and After the
LBO

(in $ millions)

	Pro Forma Year Ended 12/31/86	CCI [†] 10 Months Ended 5/02/88	% Change from Pro Forma
NET SALES	$ 821.0	$1,496.8	+ 82.3%
Cost of Goods Sold	635.2	1,043.0	+ 64.2
GROSS PROFIT	185.8	453.8	+ 144.2
Gross Margin (%)	22.6%	30.3%	
Overhead Costs	50.0	20.4	- 59.2
Other Costs	13.4	=	
EBDIT (before extraordinary items)	$ 122.4	$ 433.4	+ 254.1%
Profit-Sharing Payments	—	21.4	
[†] Annual equivalent.			

Source: The Sterling Group.

combined $50 million of annual overhead to the plants before the LBO; CCI slashed these costs
to $17 million per year.

Increased output The CCI plants had been running at rated capacity before the LBO, yet
afterward their combined throughput rate increased by 25%. This allowed CCI to take greater
advantage of the increase in product prices. McMinn gave an example of the effect that
decentralization and improved employee effort and morale had on CCI's output:

Exhibit 7 Monthly Ethylene Prices, 1986-1988

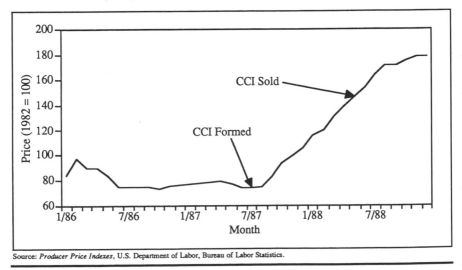

Source: *Producer Price Indexes*, U.S. Department of Labor, Bureau of Labor Statistics.

We do a turnaround at our Corpus Christi plant every three years. We take the whole plant apart, lay it out on the street, dust it off, make sure all the parts are clean as a whistle, and put it back together again. The standard time for this turnaround operation is six weeks, but we did it in four. This made a big difference for our profits. We found out later that the employees from our Chocolate Bayou plant, which is 150 miles away, drove to Corpus Christi on their days off, at their own expense, to help with the turnaround.

During the 10 months after the LBO Corpus Christi and Chocolate Bayou plants produced about 2.5 billion pounds of ethylene.

Selling CCI

In April 1988, Occidental Petroleum offered Cain $2.2 billion in cash for CCI. The proceeds of $1.2 billion to CCI's equity holders would be 43 times their original $28 million investment, and the company's 1,337 employees would keep their jobs.

Cain was hesitant to accept, even though selling CCI would yield $100 million on his $2.3 million personal investment. Cain explained why he was reluctant to sell:

My reluctance to accept the Occidental offer did not come from a belief that the price was too low. I was confident that the high price for ethylene would not last much longer and that if we were to sell at all, this was the right time. Rather, I was reluctant to sell because we had created an unusual organization with low overhead and a high level of commitment and involvement by all employees. It had been in operation less than a year, and I wanted to prove that what we had created was not a transient phenomenon.

Despite Cain's reluctance, it was difficult for him to refuse the Occidental offer. He knew CCI's management and nonmanagement employees wanted to liquidate some of their equity holdings. One executive, for example, who had originally invested $200,000 in the company, would receive $8.6 million if the deal went through. Each of CCI's employees would gain more than $100,000 from the ESOP, and 57 plant-level employees would become millionaires overnight. Selling the company would enable management and nonmanagement employees to reduce risk by diversifying their holdings, and would allow them access to cash for consumption. Cain described his difficulties with the decision.

By this time, I had enough money so that getting more would not change my lifestyle, and I had established more-than-adequate trust funds for the grandchildren. However, all the managers had gone into debt to buy stock. Their entire estates and their prospects for comfortable retirement rested on the company. Further, through the ESOP, each employee would get more than four times annual salary. This would pay off mortgages and send kids to college. I could not risk losing this to prove that my ideas on how to run a company were correct. If we had taken a vote, the outcome would have been 1,337 to 1.

Employee Response

In April 1988, CCI's board of directors agreed to sell the company to Occidental. Gary Rosenthal, senior vice president of administration, expressed his reaction to the sale:

At age 38, I thought it would be really nice to have the money, but there were other personal considerations. I was a lawyer previously and had gotten out of that profession to gain some business experience. My main hesitation was that, nine months into the deal, I had not yet fully established myself in a business capacity. But from an investment point of view I was totally undiversified. I had one major asset—Cain Chemical. It was only six months after the October 1987 stock market crash. The market had stabilized since then, but most of us were concerned about what could happen. We were confident about our business and enthusiastic about being its principal owner. But there was always the possibility that the often-predicted recession would begin, followed by the already-announced significant new capacity coming on-stream. No one ever got poor by selling too soon.

CCI's employees were excited and grateful about the increase in their fortunes. As a surprise to Cain, they raised funds among themselves to pay for a full-page ad in *The Wall Street Journal*, thanking Cain for "his vision of a company where each employee is part owner, and for the privilege of sharing in the creation and success of our company." **Exhibit 8** displays a framed copy of the ad, signed by all 1,337 employees, that hangs in Cain's Sterling Group office.

Several CCI employees also sent letters to Cain. Following are two samples:

Mr. Cain,

I thought I would write you a note to express my appreciation for the most rewarding 10 months of my working career. I want to thank you for being instrumental in making so many dreams come true . . . for myself, my family, and my friends and fellow employees. My youngest daughter, an honor student, will begin high school in the fall. Her dream of attending the University of Texas is now a reality.

You and the others who created Cain Chemical are certainly an audacious bunch and, I might add, unique among industry leaders in this country. I had always thought that I would like to own my own business. For the past 10 months, thanks to you, I have done just that. Your idea of allowing everyone to share in the profits has accomplished changes in attitudes and work habits that I have never before seen nor would have believed possible.

After the first bonus checks were handed out, and the initial shock and disbelief wore off, it was as though someone kicked on the afterburners. Chocolate Bayou became like a colony of army ants . . . very happy army ants. No item was too small or insignificant to critique in order to improve production or quality and to cut costs. Everything became important. What a thrill and joy to work in a place where everyone is doing their best and working toward the same goal! When our people tell others that they work for Cain Chemical, they do so with pride.

Seriously, Mr. Cain, it has been a profound pleasure to have participated in this once-in-a-lifetime (ad)venture, and I again want to thank you for your vision and the tenacity to carry it through. Someday, I'd like to meet you just to shake your hand.

— Maintenance Technician
Chocolate Bayou Plant

Dear Gordon:

Although we said it en masse in *The Wall Street Journal,* I wanted to personally thank you for the experience of being part of Cain Chemical. Not only have we achieved some financial results that are beyond belief, we've made an impact on the chemical industry and the business community at large that will be remembered for years to come.

In my life "BCC" (before Cain Chemical), in addition to fighting the battles at [the Corpus Christi plant], I had the opportunity to teach some evening Business Management courses at the University of Houston. . . . I am anxious to participate again this fall as a guest lecturer, on an occasional basis, in order to tell the "Cain Story." That story isn't in the fact that we individually made a considerable amount of money, but it is in the philosophy of pushing the decision-making process as low as possible in the organization; in the principle of every employee having a stake in the Company and, when the Company does well, everyone enjoying the benefits. It's a story that needs to be heard, and I hope to have the chance to tell it. . . .

— Purchasing Manager
Corpus Christi Plant

Exhibit 8 Ad in *The Wall Street Journal*—Placed and Paid for by CCI's Employees (May 5, 1988)

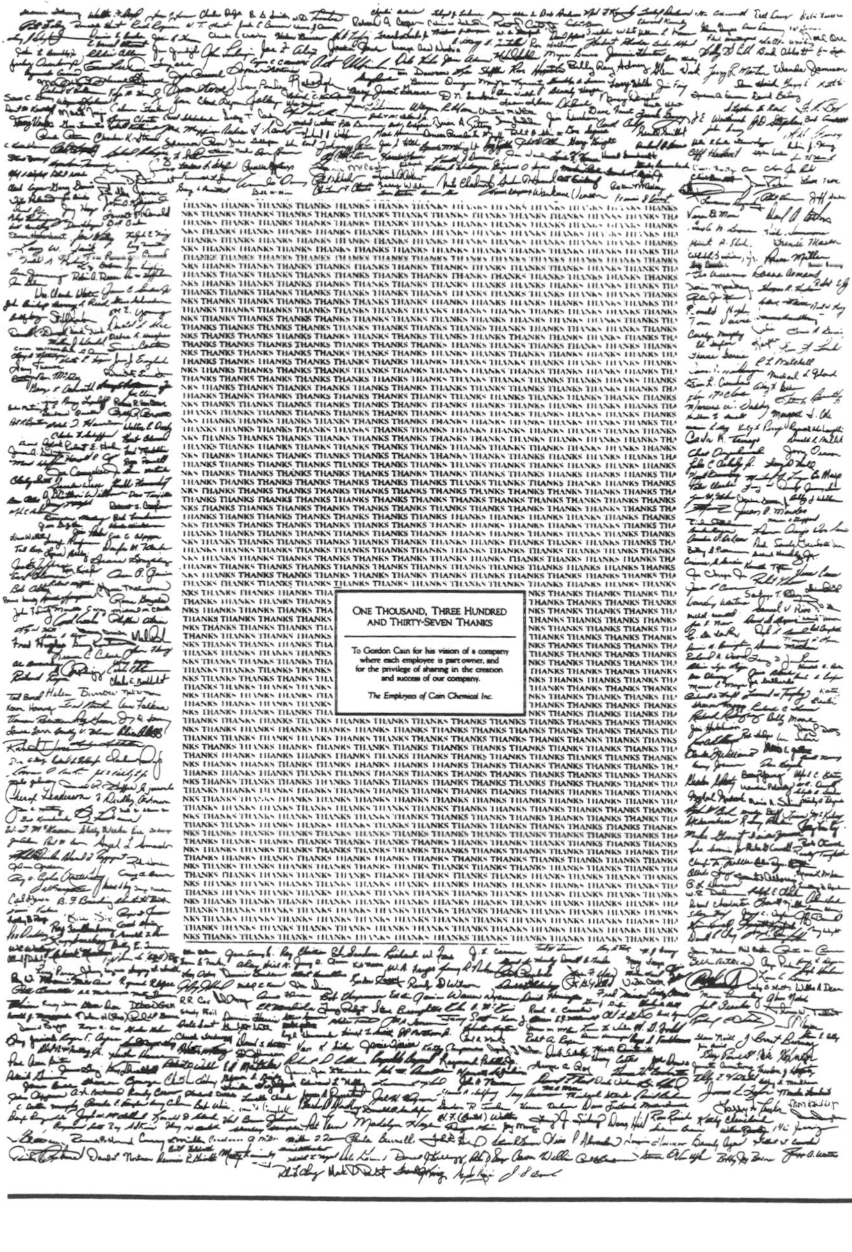

ONE THOUSAND, THREE HUNDRED AND THIRTY-SEVEN THANKS

To Gordon Cain for his vision of a company where each employee is part owner, and for the privilege of sharing in the creation and success of our company.

The Employees of Cain Chemical Inc.

Sterling Chemicals: Formation

Gordon Cain and Virgil Waggoner, who had been friends for 30 years, acquired Monsanto's Texas City plant in August 1986, 11 months before the Cain Chemical acquisition. The two friends had been pursuing the Texas City deal independently when, in November 1985, Cain asked Waggoner to join forces: Cain and The Sterling Group had already done nine LBOs, and Waggoner, who had worked at Texas City from 1950 to 1980, knew the plant, the people, and the business. They shook hands the next day, and put the deal together in six weeks. Monsanto accepted SCI's bid in January 1986, and in August 1986 SCI acquired the Texas City plant. **Exhibit 9** summarizes SCI's capital structure and the breakdown of equity holdings following the LBO. The Sterling Group financed the $215.3 million transaction with 93.1% debt.

The Texas City plant contains six separate processing units producing six different commodity chemicals. **Exhibit 10** gives the capacity of each unit and each unit's share of 1985 net sales. The six units are linked, through pipelines and railways, to several other plants, which either supply Texas City's raw materials or consume its finished products. After the LBO, Texas

Exhibit 9   SCI's Capital Structure and Breakdown of Equity Holdings

	$ Millions	% of Total Funding	% of Total Equity
DEBT			
Senior Debt	$ 80.5		
Subordinated Debt	120.0		
Total Debt	$ 200.5	93.1%	
PREFERRED			
Total Preferred[†]	$ 8.0	3.7%	
EQUITY			
Management			
Virgil Waggoner	0.8		11.8%
Gordon Cain	1.2		17.6
Others	1.8		26.5
Total Management Equity	3.8		55.9%
The Sterling Group	1.3		19.1
Employees (ESOP)	1.2		17.6
Institutional Investors	0.4		5.9
Outside Directors	0.1		1.5%
Total Equity[††]	$ 6.8	3.2%	100.0%
TOTAL FUNDING	$ 215.3	100.0%	100.0%

† Each share of preferred stock (80,000 shares total) was convertible into 1.5 shares of common stock.
†† Includes 500,000 shares of original common stock plus 180,000 shares of common stock acquired through conversion of warrants and incentive stock options. All 680,000 shares were purchased for $10 per share.

Source: Sterling Chemicals Incorporated.

Exhibit 10   Shares of Rated Capacity and 1985 Net Sales for Each of SCI's Six Products

Chemical	Rated Capacity (millions of pounds)	% of Total Rated Capacity	% of 1985 Net Sales
Styrene	1,500	54.5%	43.6%
Acrylonitrile	452	16.4	22.8
Acetic Acid	490	17.8	14.5
Plasticizers	282	10.3	15.0
Lactic Acid	17	0.6	2.2
Tertiary Butylamine	12	0.4	1.9
TOTAL	2,753	100.0%	100.0%

Source: Sterling Chemicals Incorporated.

City received much of its raw materials from, and distributed much of its output to, the same plants as it had under Monsanto's ownership. Monsanto itself continued to be one of Texas City's customers after the LBO.

As with most of his deals, Cain left the corporate overhead departments with the seller. After the acquisition, about half of SCI's new senior management team were outsiders: of the five most senior managers, two were insiders, two were outsiders that had left Monsanto years before, and one was an outsider from a local law firm.

Total employment increased slightly, from 909 people to 919, immediately after the LBO. The additional 10 people filled corporate functions—such as Treasury, Accounts Receivable, and Billing—that Monsanto had previously performed for the plant. Over the following two years SCI's total employment increased to 959 people, 21 of whom worked at the company's corporate headquarters.

Marketing Strategy

Before completing the deal, SCI entered into several conversion agreements—long-term contracts under which it dedicated much of its capacity to processing partners' raw materials—with large chemical companies such as Monsanto, BASF, Polysar, and British Petroleum. SCI designed each conversion agreement to align its incentives with its partner's, and each agreement had unique features. The first contract SCI signed was with British Petroleum (BP), and was crucial in getting the banks to finance the deal. BP was expanding its US operations and wanted to secure for itself a supply of acetic acid. The conversion agreement granted BP exclusive rights to SCI's entire output of acetic acid for the first 10 years after the LBO, plus two options to extend the agreement for consecutive 5-year periods. In exchange, BP contracted to reimburse SCI's costs based on a formula that included raw materials, plant overhead, taxes, and insurance. BP signed a promissory note guaranteeing SCI a minimum profit that was enough to cover all of the monthly installments on a $60 million bank loan. With this guarantee, the lead bank agreed to finance the deal: it provided a $60 million project loan plus an additional $60 million credit facility that included $40 million of excess financing to be used for operations. An investment bank then agreed to provide an additional $120 million of subordinated debt. Waggoner points out that SCI was the first petrochemical company to make extensive use of junk bonds.

After completing the conversion agreement with BP, SCI signed agreements with several other partners. Most of these contracts included cost-recovery formulas, with SCI keeping a portion of the difference between the finished products' market prices and the contracts' target costs. In some instances, the company and its customers agreed to collaborate to improve the Texas City plant's performance, and SCI incorporated these joint efforts into its conversion agreements. For example, the company entered an agreement in which one of its partners gave it raw materials and energy saving technology. The two parties shared the resulting savings. In another instance, a customer planned to pay the costs of increasing capacity in one of SCI's units and was concerned that it would not capture its full share of the gains if SCI did not renew the conversion agreement. SCI agreed that if it chose not to renew it would repay some of the costs.

SCI dedicated its entire output of acetic acid, plasticizers, and tertiary butylamine through conversion agreements, along with one-half of its styrene capacity and one-third of its acrylonitrile capacity. The conversion-agreement marketing strategy significantly reduced SCI's operating risk. Besides partially insulating the company from volatile output prices, it permitted SCI to operate with a small sales force, which significantly lowered overhead costs. The agreements also reduced the company's working capital by requiring its partners to supply their own raw materials.

Compensation

Management compensation was strongly tied to SCI's success. The company paid senior management salaries that were 40% to 60% of industry averages, and Cain anticipated that a large fraction of management's compensation would come from profit sharing and equity ownership. Cain encouraged all senior managers to purchase equity in the newly formed company. This was typical of Cain's deals: of all the managers in his LBOs only a handful of middle managers declined to purchase equity stakes. Many members of SCI's new management team had to take out personal loans to obtain the funds. Cain helped find cooperative banks, but the company did not guarantee the loans or subsidize the interest. Management purchased a combined 55.9% of SCI's total equity.

SCI formed an ESOP and used the proceeds of a $1.2 million bank loan to acquire 17.6% of the company's equity. SCI encouraged all employees to contribute to a savings and investment plan; for each participating employee, SCI made a matching contribution to the ESOP of 60 cents on the dollar. The ESOP used the money from the company's contribution to repay the bank loan, and credited an equivalent amount of SCI stock, based on a $10-per-share cost, to the participant's ESOP account. After the LBO, 92% of SCI's employees chose to participate in the ESOP.

ESOP participants who left the company were the only equity holders to whom the company had an obligation to repurchase stock. When they left, they could take out their equity in cash—based on the valuation of an outside, independent appraisal firm—or shares. All other stockholders were prohibited from selling their shares to third parties without first offering them, at the same price, to the ESOP, the company, and SCI's other stockholders.

The company instituted a profit-sharing plan for all employees. The plan was typical of Cain's LBOs, and used a formula based on EBDIT. A gradually decreasing marginal percentage of excess EBDIT[1] went into the profit-sharing pool, which SCI then divided among its employees. Higher-salaried employees received larger fractions of the pool. Like McMinn, Waggoner met with all employees as a group each quarter, reviewing the plant's progress on key performance measures and discussing the reasons for these results. Unlike McMinn, however,

---

[1] Baseline EBDIT equals the EBDIT projections SCI gave to the banks plus 20% of its cumulative capital expenditures from the time of the LBO. Excess EBDIT equals earnings above this baseline level.

Waggoner gave out the profit-sharing checks only once a year, at special annual meetings. He explained SCI's emphasis on EBDIT and why he believed annual bonuses were more effective:

> Our commitments to the banks are based on annual cash flow projections, and it would be inconsistent to reward employees based on anything else. Employees got educated about cash flow very quickly. We explained that net income after taxes wasn't an accurate measure for an entrepreneurial LBO company: EBDIT determines how much cash you have, and it can be used for many things. In addition, EBDIT was the only thing the banks were interested in. Because our commitments to the outside world were on an annual basis, we decided to calculate the profit-sharing payments annually as well. I explained this to employees by telling them the quarterly checks might be too small for the desired impact. It's a question of whether you want to give one check for $5,000 or four checks for $1,250 each. With one big check, the employee might save for the children's education or do something else important. But money is not the only motivator: one of the strongest motivators is a sense of ownership. When the employee says, "I own part of this company now," it makes a big difference.

Quality Program

About the time of the LBO, Ford Motor Company began encouraging its suppliers, including SCI, to emphasize quality control. SCI implemented a quality program about one year after its formation. There had been no previous quality problems with the plant's output, yet the program generated substantial benefits for the company. Waggoner described the program:

> Quality improvement works best when you start at the top and go right down through the organization. We sent our 18 senior managers to a four-day session on quality control and set up a review team to pursue "quality as a way of life." We said, "We believe in it, and we expect people to respond." Pretty soon, employees began to see that there really is something to this; there really is a better way, and commitment to continuous improvement is essential.

Cain discussed the program's impact:

> We started the program and found it was the most effective thing that had ever been done to change the culture of the organization. Previously, the plant was very status quo; the attitude was, "if it ain't broke, don't fix it." The combination of the quality program and the new compensation system turned all that around. We slashed the time it took to get invoices out from one week to one day after the shipment left the plant. Maintenance and repair tasks were performed better and were carried out in a more timely fashion. The maintenance improvements had a big impact because uptime and physical output of the plant are closely linked.

Performance

SCI's financial performance improved dramatically in the two years after the LBO. Gross profit doubled the year following the LBO, increasing from $61.7 million in Monsanto's 1985 pro-forma fiscal year to $134.2 million in SCI's 1987 fiscal year. In fiscal year 1988, gross profit nearly tripled again, to $355.6 million. SCI's capital expenditures were $13.2 million and

492-021

Exhibit 11   Selected Financial Information for SCI Before and After the LBO
(in $ millions)

> After the LBO, the company produced a substantial percentage of its
> output under conversion agreements, in which it processed customers' raw
> materials and returned finished products. Thus, although the company's
> reported Net Sales and Cost of Goods Sold are not directly comparable to
> those under Monsanto's ownership, Gross Profit is comparable.

	Owned by Monsanto (pro forma) †					Private †	
	1981	1982	1983	1984	1985	1987	1988
NET SALES	$859.5	$687.7	$666.5	$766.5	$649.1	$413.2	$699.0
Cost of Goods Sold	778.7	653.5	653.0	673.7	587.4	279.0	343.4
GROSS PROFIT	80.8	34.2	13.5	92.8	61.7	134.2	355.6
Gross Margin (%)	9.4%	5.0%	2.0%	12.1%	9.5%	32.5%	50.9%
SG&A ††	NA	NA	NA	NA	NA	4.7	7.5
EBDIT	NA	NA	NA	NA	NA	$122.8	$335.0
Profit-Sharing	NA	NA	NA	NA	NA	$6.7	$13.1

NA = Data not available for period 1981-1985.

† Fiscal year ended 12/31 for period 1981-1985; fiscal year ended 9/30 for period 1987-1988.

†† SG&A data were not available for the Texas City plant for the period it was operated by Monsanto. SCI
estimated that SG&A was between $20 million and $27 million before the LBO.

Source: Sterling Chemicals Incorporated.

$17.0 million, respectively, in 1987 and 1988. **Exhibit 11** contains selected financial
information for the years before and after the LBO.

Most of SCI's success was due to an increase in styrene prices, especially those for
styrene exports. Export premiums for styrene had ranged as high as 25 cents above the domestic
price in 1988—a 50% premium. Although SCI had already committed about 80% of its styrene
production through long-term contracts, it was able to take advantage of these premiums by
exporting the remaining 20% on the spot market. Styrene accounted for 55% of SCI's physical
production and 85% of its EBDIT in 1988.

SCI used its increased cash flow to retire its subordinated debt. In late 1987, it
repurchased on the open market 51% of its 13.5% bonds at a $4 million premium over face
value. Then in March 1988, after 20 months of continued success, SCI made a $69 million
tender offer to repurchase the remaining 49% of its outstanding bonds at a $10 million premium.[2]

Getting Liquidity

Eliminating its subordinated debt released SCI from bond restrictions that precluded
paying dividends, and it then began paying out some of its increased cash flow to investors. The
company paid a $100-per-share dividend in April—ten times shareholders' original investment.
SCI paid another $12.50-per-share dividend in July, followed by a $125-per-share dividend in

---

[2] As of June 1988, SCI had $52.7 million outstanding of its original $80.5 million of senior debt.

Exhibit 12   Median Dividend Payments to SCI Employees[†] in the ESOP
from April 1988 through September 1988

Date	Dividend per Share	Number of Shares	Payment to Median Employee
4/88	$100.00	120	$ 12,000
7/88	12.50	120	1,500
9/88	125.00	120	15,000
TOTAL PER EMPLOYEE	$237.50	120	$ 28,500
TOTAL (All 850 Participating Employees)	$237.50	120,000	$28,500,000

† The median SCI employee received 120 shares through the ESOP, initially worth $1,200.

Source: Sterling Chemicals Incorporated.

September. Holders of SCI's convertible preferred stock swapped their preferred shares for common shares to take advantage of the cash dividends.[3]

Exhibit 12 summarizes the median dividend payments to SCI employees between April and September of 1988. The median employee—who owned 120 shares of SCI stock (originally worth $1,200) and had an annual salary of $32,000—received $28,500 in dividends over six months. Total dividend payments to employees in the ESOP were $28.5 million, which the ESOP passed directly through to employees.

Exhibit 13 lists the dividends received by each of SCI's executive officers and directors over the six month period. As a group SCI's management and directors received dividend payments totaling $92.8 million.

Despite SCI's large dividend payments, its employees wanted more liquidity. The increase in SCI's value had created problems similar to those at CCI: management and nonmanagement had substantial wealth at risk in the company. Waggoner explained:

> There was a feeling among the employees that, while we remained a private company, they held paper that, even though it was lucrative paper, only had a theoretical value. We told them quarterly what their stock was worth, based on the appraiser's valuation. But they all felt, to one degree or another, that if they could pick up *The Wall Street Journal* and see what it was really worth, they would have greater security and comfort.

Cain commented:

> Once an LBO is successful and pays off most of its debt, the managers spend some of their time estimating its value as a public company and calculating the

---

[3] After the conversion, there were 800,000 shares of common stock outstanding: 120,000 shares issued to preferred holders plus 680,000 shares previously outstanding.

amount of their stake in it. At this point, the pressure to get some liquidity for these people, who have gone into debt to buy their stock, becomes overwhelming.

Also, many of our employees would be retiring at roughly the same time. During Monsanto's workforce reductions, its most senior employees had opted for early retirement, while its most junior employees had been laid off. The employees who remained were from the same age group, and would be retiring within the next 15 years. It wouldn't make sense for these people to continue holding a private equity interest in a company they no longer worked for, so we had to find a way to help them cash out.

Options for SCI

SCI's board of directors wanted to acquire more liquidity for its management and nonmanagement employees. Unlike CCI, there were no satisfactory offers to buy SCI, and although selling the company would provide shareholders with 100% liquidity, the board was reluctant to search actively for buyers. Doug Metten, SCI's chief financial officer explained:

> We were so closely held that if we shopped around it would adversely affect our employee motivation. We were very concerned about that because the employee family had a lot to do with our success.

If no buyers materialized, SCI had two other alternatives: going public and releveraging. An investment banking firm informed SCI that if it went public, its stock would be worth about $1,200 per share—$960 million total. Initially, equity holders would be able to sell about 20% of their shares. SCI's nonmanagement employees would have access to a total of about $30 million in cash, its management and directors about $100 million.

After an initial public offering, however, several factors would limit stockholders' ability to sell additional shares. First, the underwriters of any public offering would prohibit them from selling for 180 days afterward. Second, although SCI's nonmanagement employees would be able to sell their shares freely after a 180-day waiting period, members of its management, its board, and The Sterling Group would not. Rule 144 of the Securities Act of 1933 would prohibit each of these insiders from selling more shares, during any three-month period, than either the stock's average trading volume over the four weeks preceding a sale or, if greater, 1% of the firm's total outstanding shares. For example, if SCI's stock was not trading actively, Virgil Waggoner—who would own about 8% of SCI's common stock after going public—would only be able to liquidate one-eighth of his shares every three months. The public securities markets would also constrain SCI insiders from selling their shares too rapidly. Large sales of stock by management or The Sterling Group might cause the price of their remaining shares to drop.

SCI's other alternative was a leveraged recapitalization: it could releverage the company and pay out the cash to its investors in one large dividend. The amount of liquidity available under this scenario depended on how much the banks were willing to lend. A recapitalization would leave management with a larger equity stake than a public offering, in which it would sell some of its stake. The banks were wary, however, of lending money to a management team that was already wealthy. Several investment banks informed SCI that its shareholders could expect to take out the same amount of cash with this alternative as they could get initially with a public offering. The drawback was that there would be no public market for the company's stock, so equity holders would not be able to liquidate any shares after a restructuring.

The board continued to consider the releveraging option. Although it believed a public offering would, over time, provide equity holders with more liquidity, releveraging would allow SCI to remain a private company. Cain, in particular, favored releveraging for this reason. He explained why he placed such a high value on staying private:

> First, this is a cyclical business. Public companies in this business have to continually explain their performance to the security analysts. Because dealing with security analysts requires high-level people, the CEO and CFO use up a lot of time and energy that could be better spent elsewhere.

> Second, public companies have an obligation to pay dividends. If you're a no-growth company, it's awfully hard to justify holding on to money if you don't need it for expansion. We believed that as a private company we would continue paying it out to our equity holders, but we wanted more freedom to make that decision ourselves.

Yet although Cain personally favored a leveraged recapitalization, he was not sure it was the best route for SCI's employees and managers. He explained why:

> In a situation like this, there is a very strong bias against releveraging. When you have 95% debt and a low margin of safety, and you get out of it, you're reluctant to go back through the same thing again. I had enough money saved up that I could safely take on the debt again, but our employees had much less of a cushion.

Waggoner favored the greater liquidity that he believed a public offering would provide, but did not think SCI could get a fair price for its shares of stock:

> We were reluctant to go public because we thought the net present value of our future cash flows was worth more than we could get from an offering. But because of the desire for more liquidity and diversification, we continued to consider it.

When weighing its options, the board considered SCI's prospects for the coming fiscal year. It expected earnings to decline some from their 1988 levels, but still expected the company to perform well. Waggoner explained:

> Styrene prices had reached historic high levels in 1988 and there could be no assurance that the highly favorable market conditions would continue. We had told the banks, in 1986, that we expected $40 million to $45 million per year of EBDIT. But in 1988, we earned EBDIT of $335 million, which was just phenomenal. That was partly due to the 25-cent export premium, which was an unprecedented situation compared to what I've seen in the last 40 years. By the end of fiscal year 1988, the export premium had declined to about 10 to 12 cents, and we expected it to fall another 5 cents in 1989.

Goldman Sachs[4] estimated that, in the event of a modest industrywide recession, SCI's 1989 EBDIT would be $178 million.

In early-October 1988 the board had still not received a satisfactory offer for SCI, and it was still attempting to choose between going public and releveraging.

---

[4]   Goldman Sachs, December 1988.

492-021

Gordon Cain and the Sterling Group (A)

Exhibit 13   Total Dividends Received by SCI's Executive Officers and Directors, April to September, 1988 and 1988 Annual Cash Compensation

Name, Position, and Background	Number of Shares Owned	Dividends Received ($ Millions)	Annual Cash Compensation †
Gordon A. Cain — Chairman, Director (Age 76) Mr. Cain is Chairman of the Board of The Sterling Group. Prior to organizing The Sterling Group, Mr. Cain was involved in the purchase of a variety of businesses and provided consulting services to these and other companies.	122,345	$ 29.1	$100,000
Virgil Waggoner — President, CEO, Director (Age 60) Mr. Waggoner was President of El Paso Products Company, a commodity chemicals company, from 1980 to 1983 and was a self-employed industry consultant from 1983 to 1986. From 1950 to 1980 he was employed by Monsanto, last serving as Group Vice President and Managing Director of Monsanto's Plastics and Resins Company.	80,875	19.2	$809,050
Gene L. Tromblee — Vice President - Operations (Age 54) Mr. Tromblee was employed by Monsanto from 1963 to 1986. He became plant manager at the Monsanto Texas City facility in 1979.	21,000	5.0	$429,220
Robert W. Roten — Vice President - Commercial (Age 54) Mr. Roten was President of Materials Exchange, Incorporated, a Houston-based petrochemical and plastics marketing firm, from 1983 to 1986. He spent the first 25 years of his career with Monsanto, and served as Vice President - Sales and Marketing for El Paso Products Company from 1981 to 1983.	18,500	4.4	$434,430
Douglas W. Metten — Vice President - Finance (Age 46) Mr. Metten was employed by Monsanto from 1966 to 1986. From 1977 to 1986 he served as Superintendent of Accounting and Control at the Monsanto Texas City facility.	13,000	3.1	$356,380
J. David Heaney — Vice President - Administration, Secretary (Age 40) Mr. Heaney was a member of the law firm of Bracewell & Patterson, in Houston, Texas, from 1980 until 1986.	12,000	2.9	$345,960
Ben L. Roberts — Treasurer, Assistant Secretary (Age 43) Mr. Roberts, for more than five years prior to 1986, was employed by Roy M. Huffington, Incorporated—a private, international oil and gas company with headquarters in Houston, Texas—most recently as Vice President - Financial Administration of the Indonesian Joint Venture Division.	8,000	1.9	NA

Source: Sterling Chemicals Incorporated.

Exhibit 13 (continued)

Name, Position, and Background	Number of Shares Owned	Dividends Received ($ Millions)	Annual Cash Compensation †
William A. McMinn — Director (Age 58)	2,500	0.6	$19,000
Mr. McMinn was Corporate Vice President and Manager of the industrial chemical group of FMC Corporation, a manufacturer of machinery and chemical products, from 1975 through 1985, when he retired. He became President and Chief Executive Officer of Cain Chemical in 1987, and served in that capacity until its sale in May 1988. He is currently associated with The Sterling Group.			
W. Fred Massey — Director (Age 71)	2,500	0.6	$19,000
Mr. Massey was a tax partner of Peat, Marwick, Mitchell & Company prior to 1975. He was Chief Financial Officer of Bass Brothers Enterprises, Incorporated of Fort Worth, Texas from 1975 to 1982 and a consultant to that corporation from 1982 until his retirement in 1986.			
James J. Kerley — Director (Age 65)	2,500	0.6	$19,000
Mr. Kerley has been a financial consultant since his retirement in January 1986. From 1981 through 1985 he was Vice Chairman of the Board of Directors and Chief Financial Officer of Emerson Electric Company, an electrical and electrical manufacturing company. For eleven years prior, he was Chief Financial Officer of Monsanto.			
James W. Glanville — Director (Age 65)	2,500	0.6	$19,000
Mr. Glanville has been general partner of Lazard Freres & Company since 1978, and is the Vice President of Financial Affairs for Rice University. He is director of Halliburton Company and International Minerals & Chemical Corporation.			
Gilbert M.A. Portal — Director (Age 58)	0	0.0	$19,000
Mr. Portal has been President of Elf Aquitaine Petroleum U.S., Incorporated, an oil and gas exploration and production company, and Senior Vice President of Elf Aquitaine, Incorporated since 1982.			
TOTAL (All Management and Directors as a Group)	390,787	$ 92.8	NA

NA = Not available.

† Directors who are not executive officers of the company are paid an annual fee of $16,000 and an attendance fee of $600 per meeting (the Board of Directors meets about five times a year). Mr. Cain receives an annual fee of $100,000 for his services as the company's Chairman.

Source: Sterling Chemicals Incorporated.

Harvard Business School

9-492-022
Rev. 10/22/92

Gordon Cain and
The Sterling Group (B)

In October 1988, Sterling Chemicals' board of directors approved a public stock offering. SCI first executed a 75-for-1 stock split. It then offered 12.65 million shares—21% of its common stock—to the public at $16 per share. Shareholders were not required to sell. Those that elected to participate sold their shares pro rata based on the percentage required to deliver the 12.65 million shares.

After the offering the median employee—who originally held 120 shares of SCI stock in the ESOP worth $10 per share—had $28,500 in dividends from the previous six months, plus an ESOP account with $30,400 in cash and 7,100 shares worth $113,600 (at the offering price). Unlike the cash dividends, employees were not allowed to withdraw from the ESOP account their cash proceeds from the offering. Employees can withdraw their equity in either cash or shares as they leave the company.

Exhibit 1 lists, for each of SCI's executive officers and directors, the number of shares sold, cash received, and shares remaining after the initial public offering (IPO). Management and directors as a group received $107.3 million in cash from the IPO and retained ownership of 37.7% of the company's total outstanding shares.

SCI added only one person at corporate headquarters, to manage investor relations, in the two years after going public, bringing the total to 22 people.

Post-IPO Performance

SCI's performance slipped considerably in the year after going public, primarily due to a fall in styrene profit margins. Styrene export premiums, which had been extraordinarily high in

Professor Michael C. Jensen and Research Associate Brian K. Barry prepared this case as the basis for class discussion rather than to illustrate either effective or ineffective handling of an administrative situation.

Reprinted by permission of Harvard Business School.

1988, fell to zero in 1989. This situation was exacerbated by two of SCI's competitors, who were planning new capacity to come on-line two or three years later and were trying to win long-term customers by reducing domestic prices. The industrywide slump depressed SCI's profits: gross profit was $185.7 million in fiscal year 1989. Although this was triple the plant's 1985 gross profit—the last year before the LBO—it was down 47.8% from 1988. By the end of fiscal year 1989, SCI's stock price had fallen 45%, to $8.75 per share. **Exhibit 2** tracks SCI's stock price, as listed on the New York Stock Exchange, from the IPO to June 30, 1991. **Exhibit 3** compares selected financial information for SCI before and after the IPO. Virgil Waggoner— SCI's chief executive officer—discussed his disappointment with the company's 1989 performance:

> When we did the public offering, we told the buyers that prices had reached historic high levels in 1988 and that there could be no assurance that the highly favorable market conditions would continue. But we didn't realize how fast, and to what extent, they would fall. Styrene prices dropped, and the export premium vanished. By mid-1989, we were exporting at domestic prices.

Burdens of Public Ownership

Two years later, SCI's directors and officers reflected on the decision to go public:

Gordon Cain—Chairman:

> The choice between an IPO and releveraging was a close one. We chose an IPO on the incorrect assumption that it would give management and The Sterling Group greater liquidity. We underestimated the extent to which we, as major stockholders, would feel constrained from selling stock after the IPO, especially if the stock price went down. Partly out of embarrassment about the performance of the stock, and partly because of the possible adverse effect of sales by senior management, the principal stockholders have not sold any stock since the IPO.

Doug Metten—Chief Financial Officer:

> Originally, we believed that if we went public we would have access to additional liquidity in the secondary market. As it turns out, that isn't true: we're so closely held that liquidity is practically non-existent.

> There's also the question of what our stock is worth. We're basically a single-product company—styrene—and the stock market discounts us for it. It's clear why they do that—our business would be less risky if we were more diversified— but we think they discount us too much.

Gordon Cain:

> In hindsight, I believe we could have had the same liquidity that we have now through restructuring, without the constraints of public ownership. Had we known that, we might have chosen to releverage—we would be better off as a private company. But because we thought we could get more liquidity by going public, and because our employees were reluctant to go through a high-leverage situation again, we went ahead with the IPO.

Exhibit 1 Shares Sold in Public Offering by SCI's Directors and Officers [†]

Name	Position	Shares Sold (Millions)	Shares Remaining Millions	Shares Remaining % of Shares Outstanding	Cash Received ($ Millions)
Gordon A. Cain	Chairman	2.101	7.075	11.8%	$ 33.6
Virgil Waggoner	President, CEO, Director	1.389	4.677	7.8	22.2
Gene L. Tromblee	V.P. Operations	0.361	1.214	2.0	5.8
Robert W. Roten	V.P. Commercial	0.318	1.070	1.8	5.1
Douglas W. Metten	V.P. Finance, CFO	0.223	0.752	1.3	3.6
J. David Heaney	V.P. Administration, Secretary	0.206	0.694	1.2	3.3
Ben L. Roberts	Treasurer, Assistant Secretary	0.137	0.463	0.8	2.2
William A. McMinn	Director	0.043	0.145	0.2	0.7
W. Fred Massey	Director	0.043	0.145	0.2	0.7
James J. Kerley	Director	0.043	0.145	0.2	0.7
James W. Glanville	Director	0	0.188	0.3	0
Gilbert M.A. Portal	Director	0	0	0.0	0
TOTAL (All Management and Directors)		6.709	22.600	37.7%	$107.3

[†] In October 1988—before the public offering—the company executed a 75-for-1 stock split. The total
number of shares outstanding increased from 800,000 to 60,000,000.

Source: Sterling Chemicals Incorporated.

Exhibit 2 SCI's Stock Price, October 13, 1988 to June 30, 1991

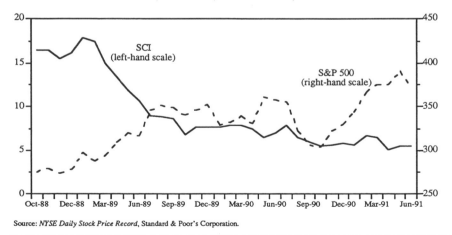

Source: *NYSE Daily Stock Price Record*, Standard & Poor's Corporation.

492-022

Exhibit 3   Selected Financial Information for SCI Before and After Going Public
(in $ millions)

> After the LBO, the company produced a substantial percentage of its output under conversion agreements, in which it processed customers' raw materials and returned finished products. Thus, although the company's reported Net Sales and Cost of Goods Sold are not directly comparable to those under Monsanto's ownership, Gross Profit is comparable.

	Monsanto[†]	Private[†]		Public[†]		
	1985	1987	1988	1989	1990	1991[††]
NET SALES	$649.1	$413.2	$699.0	$580.8	$506.0	$542.7
Cost of Goods Sold	587.4	279.0	343.4	395.1	$399.6	472.4
GROSS PROFIT	61.7	134.2	355.6	185.7	$106.4	70.3
Gross Margin (%)	9.5%	32.5%	50.9%	32.0%	21.0%	13.0%
SG&A	NA	4.7	7.5	8.5	10.6	7.2
Profit Sharing	NA	6.7	13.1	7.9	5.0	2.5
EBDIT	NA	$122.8	$335.0	$169.3	$ 90.8	$ 60.6

NA = Data not available for 1985.

† Fiscal year ended 12/31 in 1985; Fiscal year ended 9/30 for period 1987-1991.

†† Figures for 1991 are unaudited.

Source: Sterling Chemicals Incorporated.

INDEX